Cognitive Behavioural Coaching Techniques For Dummies

C000194124

Being a CB Coach

A few of the main things you need to do and be as a CB coach, in the form of a handy mnemonic:

- **C**hange-catalyst
- **O**bjectives-focused
- **A**sks thought-provoking questions
- **C**hallenges NATS and norms
- **H**elps change limiting beliefs and habits
- **I**mpartial sounding board and expertise
- **N**avigate the process to client's goals
- **G**ive confidential support

Controlling your Thoughts

Thoughts shape our emotions, behaviours, decisions and actions. So take control of your thoughts and don't let them be in control of you:

- Challenge them
- Stop them
- Change them
- Balance them
- Meditate and relax with them
- Focus them in the now
- Make pictures with them
- Tune into your senses with them
- Concentrate on goals with them
- Get creative and problem-solve with them

The Main Characteristics of Good CB Coaching

- Solutions focused
- Time limited
- Psycho-educative
- Client involvement in homework
- Here and now and future-oriented
- Empowering the client to become own coach
- Developing psychological resilience to life's challenges
- Awareness of how to manage thinking, moods and emotions

Knowing the Dangers of Negative Thoughts

Warning: misuse of your brain can damage your health! Negative or stressful thoughts can:

- Reduce your immune system
- Limit your behaviours and actions
- Cause anxiety where there may be no need for it
- Can make things seem worse than they are
- Cause conflict

For Dummies: Bestselling Book Series for Beginners

Cognitive Behavioural Coaching Techniques For Dummies®

Cheat Sheet

Your Thinking Toolkit

Be sure to practise the following every day:

- ✔ Notice and acknowledge emotions
- ✔ Analyse what the thoughts and expectations are that drive your feelings
- ✔ Categorise the thoughts and become aware of negative thinking habits
- ✔ Recognise the gap between the event and the response – the moment of choice
- ✔ Identify the positive outcome: what would success look like?
- ✔ Question whether the thought is rational or helpful
- ✔ Understand the power to change the experience through thought, behaviour and action
- ✔ Choose to adopt a more constructive thought and approach to achieve objectives
- ✔ Experiment with new ways of thinking and behaving
- ✔ Adopt positive body language and energy
- ✔ Act as if the situation is going well – even if it isn't
- ✔ Keep observing, reviewing and learning

For Dummies: Bestselling Book Series for Beginners

Cognitive Behavioural Coaching Techniques

FOR

DUMMIES®

Cognitive Behavioural Coaching Techniques

FOR DUMMIES®

by Helen Whitten

A John Wiley and Sons, Ltd, Publication

Cognitive Behavioural Coaching Techniques For Dummies®

Published by
John Wiley & Sons, Ltd
The Atrium
Southern Gate
Chichester
West Sussex
PO19 8SQ
England

E-mail (for orders and customer service enquires): cs-books@wiley.co.uk

Visit our Home Page on www.wiley.com

For general information on our other products and services, please contact our Customer Care Department within the U.S. at 800-762-2974, outside the U.S. at 317-572-3993, or fax 317-572-4002.

For technical support, please visit www.wiley.com/techsupport.

Wiley also publishes its books in a variety of electronic formats. Some content that appears in print may not be available in electronic books.

British Library Cataloguing in Publication Data: A catalogue record for this book is available from the British Library

ISBN: 978-0-470-71379-2

Printed and bound in Great Britain by TJ International Ltd., Padstow, Cornwall.

10 9 8 7 6 5 4 3 2 1

WILEY

About the Author

Helen Whitten is an experienced and accredited coach, facilitator, mediator, trainer and writer. She applies Cognitive Behavioural Coaching (CBC) methodology to personal and professional development, enabling individuals to develop confidence, break through old patterns of behaviour and achieve greater potential in their lives and in their careers.

Helen's career began in publishing and historical research. In mid-life she retrained and decided to work with people. She set up her company Positiveworks Ltd, London, in 1993. By applying CBC models and strategies to help launch herself in her new career, she became convinced of the power of CBC to enhance confidence and performance. She has since coached and trained individuals and teams in major organisations throughout the world.

Helen's philosophy is that positive people deliver positive results for themselves and those around them. She believes that people have the potential to enhance every aspect of their life, happiness and performance when given the right tools and techniques. Her aim is therefore to share her methods and learning with as many people as possible.

Author's Acknowledgements

I would like to thank my sons Rupert and Oli for their constant encouragement and support over the years. They are a continuous source of delight and wisdom – and new perspectives to challenge my thinking.

To my mentors Gladeana McMahon and Professor Stephen Palmer who always provide me with both knowledge and support.

My clients from whom I continue to learn so much.

For the team at John Wiley, for their editorial comments, encouragement and support in bringing this book to publication.

To my niece Antonia Fernand, who is also a coach, for her excellent editorial comments and professional assistance.

Publisher's Acknowledgments

We're proud of this book; please send us your comments through our Dummies online registration form located at www.dummies.com/register/.

Some of the people who helped bring this book to market include the following:

Acquisitions, Editorial, and Media Development

Project Editor: Simon Bell

Content Editor: Jo Theedom

Commissioning Editor: Samantha Spickernell

Publishing Assistant: Jennifer Prytherch

Copy Editor: Kim Vernon

Technical Editor: Gladeana McMahon

Publisher: Jason Dunne

Executive Project Editor: Daniel Mersey

Cover Photos: © Simon Holdcroft / Alamy

Cartoons: Ed McLachlan

Composition Services

Project Coordinator: Lynsey Stanford

Layout and Graphics: Carl Byers, Reuben W. Davis, Nikki Gately

Proofreader: Laura Albert

Indexer: Becky Hornyak

Contents at a Glance

Table of Contents

Introduction

. . . .

Cognitive behavioural coaching, or CBC, brings together the practice of coaching with the concepts and methods underlying cognitive behavioural psychology. In a nutshell, cognitive behavioural psychology works on the premise that how you think impacts on how you feel – and that how you feel impacts on your behaviour and the actions you take. For example, if you think 'I'm not sure that I can do this', you may feel uncertain of your abilities and competence. This uncertainty is likely to make you hesitant and the end result may be procrastination.

Coaching is a process that supports a client in achieving their life and work goals and in being the person they want to be. A cognitive behavioural (CB) coach provides an environment and process that facilitates this end, focusing on how the client's current thoughts and approaches may limit the achievement of goals. Through using CBC models and questions, the client develops new ways of thinking and behaving that are more aligned to their objectives.

You may have heard of cognitive behavioural therapy and wonder how CBC differs. Put simply, CBC is solutions-focused and not remedial. In the past 20 years, psychologists have moved on from treating people with specific problems such as 'neurosis', 'psychosis', or 'paranoia' and applied psychology in everyday life to help people make the most of themselves and their lives. CBC has evolved as a method to enable anyone, at any stage of their life, to develop thinking patterns and behaviours that support their goals.

In this book I aim to provide a background to CBC and to introduce you to techniques that you can apply as a coach, in your own coaching sessions. Alternatively, you may be a manager wishing to coach your team, or someone who is interested in self-coaching. I have applied all the methods in this book, with clients or in my own life. I hope that you find the experience as informative and helpful as I have.

About This Book

I have worked in the CBC field for many years and am continuously delighted by how CBC can enhance a person's life. CBC opens doors to perceptions and provides insights about yourself, others, and the world. CBC shows you how your thoughts may trip you up. Providing the key to those doors and helping a person move forward is some of the most fulfilling work a CB coach does.

Training in CBC showed me personally how I limited myself in so many ways through thinking habits that were negative, critical, or full of self-doubt. The important thing I discovered, and have shared with many clients, is how often our thoughts have no basis in reality. In this book I provide models and methods that check whether your client's thoughts are rational or supposition.

CBC aims ultimately for the client to become their own coach. As a CB coach, you share your knowledge and techniques so that your client can continue their journey alone, challenging themselves and devising strategies for success. This process is an empowering one. I hope that you enjoy reading this book and discovering how you can apply these concepts for yourself.

Conventions Used in This Book

To help you to gain the most from this book and be able to pick up information as quickly and effectively as you can, I use certain conventions:

- ✔ I refer to a cognitive behavioural coach as a CB coach.
- ✔ I refer to the person being coached as the 'client', whether they are in a formal coaching session or a member of staff being coached by their manager.
- ✔ The case studies are taken from specific experiences of CBC but are not a direct representation of any one particular client.
- ✔ Arbitrarily, I have decided to use the term 'him' in even-numbered chapters and 'her' in odd-numbered chapters to demonstrate that coaching is inevitably inclusive of both genders.
- ✔ I used italics to indicate key concepts.

Foolish Assumptions

I assume, though I may be wrong, that some of the following applies to you:

- ✔ You are a coach or a manager who wants to get more out of the people with whom you work.
- ✔ You've heard something about CBC and want to know what all the fuss is about.
- ✔ You want handy tools and techniques to apply in coaching sessions.

✔ You are a curious and sensitive person with an interest in the potential of human beings.

✔ You realise that CBC can help people achieve their goals and that you are interested in applying it.

✔ You know that these techniques can also be applied for self-coaching.

How This Book Is Organised

This book is designed for you to be able to dip in and out and pick up tips and techniques as speedily as you need. You don't have to read it cover to cover. You may have a specific issue with a client and want ideas about how to manage it. Alternatively you may be seeking background information on coaching and cognitive behavioural methodology. Just pick the chapter that looks most relevant to you – but don't let that stop you reading it from start to finish if that is what you prefer.

I have divided the book into five parts, as follows:

Part 1: Introducing Cognitive Behavioural Coaching

In this part I introduce the fundamental principles of CBC and show you how different patterns of thinking impact on a person's behaviours and decisions in life. I introduce specific models of thinking – 'thinking errors' – that show that not all thoughts are rational or helpful. I demonstrate how CBC has developed over centuries, originating in Stoic philosophy and applied today as a way of thinking and a way of life. I also introduce the aims, scope, and boundaries of CBC, explore what being a CB coach involves, and show the importance of your client's participation and their responsibility for their own continuous development.

Part 11: The CBC Process

In this part I take you on a coaching journey from undertaking a coaching assignment to the final session. I explain the importance of agreeing terms, expectations and responsibilities and how to develop trust and collaboration between you and your client. I consider the importance of listening and working at your client's pace, how to be sensitive to specific 'tell-tale' words that illustrate limiting beliefs and how to apply the CBC questioning process to unlock new approaches. I show that no one can be a 'perfect' coach and that you, like everyone else, are fallible and need supervision and support.

Part III: The CBC Toolkit in Work and Life

In this part I introduce specific aspects of coaching that you may encounter as you go through the CBC process, including enabling a person to understand and manage themselves and to develop confidence so as to be able to develop their ability to broaden their goals and perspectives. I cover the all-important area of relating to others, and managing and respecting their own needs alongside respecting the needs of others. I offer hints about helping your client develop choices for work and life within the long-term context of their whole life, and I show that CBC is a lifetime's journey that your client can continue on their own, as their own coach.

Part IV: Applying CBC in Organisations

In this part I focus specifically on workplace issues and introduce some of the topics that clients are likely to raise in such sessions. I explore career transitions such as promotion, redundancy and retirement, and cover how to help clients to maintain peak performance under pressure of targets and workload. I also cover managing other people, including issues such as conflict, influencing, motivation, and building effective and creative teams.

Part V: The Part of Tens

In this section I give lots of quick reference hints and tips. These include ways to help people develop a positive focus and imagery exercises to develop confidence. I provide gentle reminders to you, as the coach, to remember that both you and your client are human and fallible. We all screw up occasionally because everybody does so I include tips about self-acceptance and continuous development.

Appendix

Here you find an ABCDE form that you can apply as a CB coach, as well as a list of useful organisations and websites that provide further information about CBC.

Icons Used in This Book

I use the following icons in this book so that you can quickly identify which areas of the book are relevant to your needs.

This icon highlights practical advice for applying the techniques of CBC.

This icon indicates a client story or experience that illustrates a specific issue that has arisen within a session and that you may also encounter.

This icon indicates an area that you may need to consider carefully within sessions.

CBC touches on many broad and deep areas of life and work and this icon signals that you may want to reflect on this information further between sessions.

This icon emphasises important points to remember during CBC sessions

Background detail on CBC which enhances your understanding of the subject. Not essential, but useful.

Where to Go from Here

I suggest you take a look through the table of contents and then flick through the whole book to get a feel of the topics covered and familiarise yourself with the layout. In this way you may spot sections that jump out at you and look interesting. You may want to bookmark those pages that appear to be most relevant to you.

The main thing is that you feel in control of this book: this book is not in control of you! You can pick it up and use it exactly as you want to. You can mark areas that you want to remember, scribble in it, highlight tips, and turn down pages. Most of all, relax, stay curious, and enjoy the process.

Part I
Introducing Cognitive Behavioural Coaching

"Now for a start, we have to get rid of your negative patterns of thought about the world."

In this part . . .

This part introduces the basics of CBC, and shows you how different patterns of thinking impact on your behaviour and the decisions you make. In it I introduce specific models of thinking and show that not all thoughts are rational or helpful.

I also introduce the aims, scope, and boundaries of CBC, explore what being a CB coach involves, and show how important it is that your client participates and takes responsibility for their own continuous development.

Chapter 1

The Principles behind CBC

Some fundamental principles and concepts underpin the practice of CBC. These principles developed from cognitive behavioural therapy (CBT), whose founders were Aaron Beck and Albert Ellis.

The keystone principle of CBC derives from Epictetus, who was a Greek Stoic philosopher. Stoic philosophy promoted theories of mind that encouraged the development of logic and self-control as a way of living life wisely. Epictetus lived in the first century AD and stated that 'people are disturbed not by the things that happen, but by the views which they take of those things' – that is, your own thoughts and opinions shape your feelings about and reactions to an event. By accepting this principle, the individual takes personal responsibility for her own reaction to a situation, whether she is stuck in traffic or made redundant, on the understanding that another person may have a different viewpoint and therefore a different reaction. This attitude opens up new perspectives and approaches to everyday events. The client learns to become an observer of her own thoughts and can assess whether those thoughts help her to achieve her life and work goals.

As the client investigates her thoughts, she may discover that the mind leads her astray occasionally, and therefore she exaggerates difficulties, fears situations that may never happen, or assumes that someone has a bad opinion of her although she has no concrete evidence of the fact. The CBC process applies what is known as Socratic dialogue, which is a form of philosophical enquiry that originated from the Greek philosopher Socrates. In Socratic dialogue, the questioner explores the implications of the opinions and statements of the other person, in order to stimulate rational thinking and insight. Applied in CBC, this form of questioning is designed to reveal the reality of a situation rather than a 'twisted' version of it. The aim is to develop thoughts that are both realistic and in perspective. The process encourages the individual to develop more self-enhancing and supportive ways of viewing the world so as to manage life's challenges. The questioning aims to help a person analyse her thoughts and, should she in some way not come up to her own standard or expectations, to accept herself as a fallible human being.

In this chapter, I explain some of the theories and concepts underlying CBC, and introduce models that you can apply to the situations that your clients bring to coaching sessions.

Investigating the Evolution of CBC

CBC evolved from cognitive behavioural therapy, or CBT. In addition, sports, acting, and singing coaching have all influenced CBC, as have theories of motivation and goalsetting. The focus of CBT is on treating people with disorders. In CBC, we shift the focus to helping people develop and achieve their goals. This transition has been influenced by interest in personal growth and by the focus of organisations on learning and development as a means to productivity. My own definition of CBC is 'an alliance of cooperation between client and coach. The coach supports the client in developing and achieving the specific goals and objectives identified by the client at the outset. The focus in CBC is developing constructive thoughts and behaviours to support action towards the identified goals.'

Unlike therapy, coaching focuses on the present and the future. Coaching applies problem-solving methods to enhance happiness, performance, and the achievement of personal objectives. CBC focuses specifically on analysing the thoughts and behaviours the client applies to a challenge, and checks whether the client's approach supports or limits her efforts. As thoughts and behaviours are a part of every human endeavour, CBC can therefore be applied to address any situation your client brings to her coaching sessions, such as:

- ✔ Enhancing performance at work
- ✔ Developing confidence
- ✔ Taking action to achieve specific goals
- ✔ Gaining perspective
- ✔ Developing thoughts and behaviours to develop skills
- ✔ Managing situations more effectively

Psychology's been around a long time

People have practised psychology, or the investigation of the human mind, for centuries. The earliest recorded psychology works date back to around 600 BCE and philosophers such as Anaximanda, Pythagoras, Socrates, Plato, and Aristotle. It was also discussed in the ancient cultures of Egypt, China, and India. Originally, psychology was regarded as an area of philosophy. In the 19th century, psychology became a formal area of study in its own right.

Moving from CBT to CBC

The founders of CBT, Aaron Beck and Albert Ellis, identified that we all have a constant chatter going on in our heads. They termed this chatter *internal dialogue*. Study of this dialogue lies at the heart of both CBT and CBC.

Beck and Ellis's research in the 1960s and 1970s demonstrated that some internal dialogue is muddled and contradictory. Perhaps you've noticed this fact yourself. Imagine today is the first day of a new year. Last night you made a resolution to get fit. You lie in bed thinking 'I really ought to go to the gym,' while another voice (but the same brain) argues 'But it's so lovely and warm here in bed. . . .' The voice that 'wins' impacts on your behaviour and actions. Our thoughts are at the heart of the decisions we make about our lives and the actions we take. The key to CBC is to think about thinking.

A report by the London School of Economics, published in June 2006, commented that CBT, being a fixed course of task-oriented sessions rather than an open-ended programme that can extend over years rather than months, makes it attractive. The UK Government has pledged £170 million to train new CBT therapists so that the NHS can offer this form of therapy to around 1 million more people in due course. Rhena Branch, a psychologist who practises CBT at the Priory, believes CBT is more empowering than certain other forms of therapy: 'CBT doesn't just provide someone with an hour of introspection which is then forgotten until the next session. There is much more interaction, and the aim is to give someone the tools to be able to function as her own therapist in the future.' The effectiveness of CBT as a remedial intervention provides credibility to CBC as a development process, because CBC adapts the techniques to help clients move forward and achieve their work and life goals.

Beck and Ellis identified that many people have thoughts, or cognitions, that are unhelpful to their goals. When a person changes the way she thinks, the way she feels also changes. Beck and Ellis applied their CBT methodologies in counselling and therapeutic sessions for remedial purposes. They used a psycho-educational model in which they shared models and methods with their clients, who can then apply the techniques themselves.

> ## Sandra's workload
>
> Sandra came to coaching sessions feeling thoroughly demotivated. Her company had restructured and made several of her colleagues redundant. Sandra missed her friends. She also had an increasing workload to compensate for her colleagues' absence. She struggled to get through her emails every day and fell behind in finishing her projects. Much of her conversation was in the past and focused on how things had been rather than on solutions. She said things like 'It wasn't fair that they were made redundant,' 'This should never have happened,' and 'Things were so much better when they were here.' During the sessions, she began to accept what she could not change and instead focused on what she could do about her current situation in order to make it more manageable and enjoyable in the future.

The development of positive psychology

Until recently, psychology focused on repairing mental illness using a disease model of human functioning. Now the focus is on how to apply psychology to build on existing strengths in order to help people live happier and more productive lives. Dr Martin Seligman, a psychologist working at the University of Pennsylvania, termed this approach *positive psychology*. He applied cognitive behavioural methodology to develop resilience, hope, and optimism in clients, and was instrumental in creating a positive psychology unit at Harvard University. David Burns' book *Feeling Good,* which popularised CBT in the 1980s, also influenced therapists and coaches to apply psychology to people who were not necessarily suffering from disorders but wanted to experience personal growth. Psychologists Professor Stephen Palmer and Gladeana McMahon (who have also been change-makers in my own professional life), Windy Dryden, Michael Neenan, and Nick Edgerton have all been leaders in this evolution, lecturing, practising and writing on the application of CBC as a solutions-focused practice. This book represents what I have learnt from these founders, and reflects my own interpretation and experience of applying CBC methods with clients since 1993.

Focusing on Solutions

CBC focuses on the future, on solving problems, and on developing solutions to your client's challenges. Because of its speed and efficacy, many people use CBC in the workplace to enhance their performance by challenging limiting beliefs and behaviours and enabling them to move forward into situations they may not have dared to enter before.

CBC uses a time-limited three-stage process to help your client achieve her goals:

1. **Current situation:** What's happening?
2. **Goal-setting:** What do you want to happen?
3. **Strategies and action:** What do you need to do to achieve your goals?

CBC has a psycho-educative aspect: you share knowledge, models, and methods with your client, so eventually she becomes her own coach. In order to integrate new discoveries and habits, you give your client assignments to practise between sessions – homework, if you like. This home practice reinforces your client's new thoughts and behaviours and helps her take responsibility for her own change rather than relying on what takes place within the coaching session.

Thinking about Thinking

Thinking about thinking is an underlying principle of CBC. By considering the way she thinks, your client becomes an impartial observer of her own thoughts. Eventually, your client notices the impact of her thoughts. She learns to reflect on how her thoughts, beliefs, and expectations influence her feelings and in turn impact her behaviour, the decisions she makes, and the actions she takes. She also becomes aware of how her physiological responses differ depending on whether she thinks positively or negatively.

People behave differently according to their emotional mood. By using the principles of CBC, you client becomes a watcher or controller who mentally stands back from the situation and considers how her thoughts and feelings shape her actions and behaviours. For example, if your client is hassled by everyday concerns, she may question whether the events warrant the amount of emotional energy that she generates, or whether she exaggerates her problems. I give an example of how cognitions influence behaviours in Table 1-1.

Table 1-1	How Cognitions Influence Behaviours
Cognition	*Behaviour*
I can't stand this.	Procrastination, giving up
I can't manage this.	Undermining ability to finish the job
I bet he thinks I'm unattractive.	Doesn't ask him out on a date

As a CB coach, you provide practical models and processes to enable your client to develop an internal dialogue of constructive thoughts and pragmatic approaches that support the achievement of her goals. Practising CBC is like learning another language. And just like learning another language, CBC can be hard work and needs daily repetition to achieve change.

Putting thoughts into perspective

CBC works on the principle that people develop twisted views of themselves, others, and situations as they go through life. CBC investigates whether a client's thoughts are based on evidence or are outdated or out of perspective.

As a CB coach, you help your client review how she approaches a situation. Your focus is to investigate your client's thoughts; in doing so, you help your client become aware of her views and how those views impact on her emotions and behaviours.

Although your client may be aware of some of the thoughts going on in her head, many of her thoughts are unconscious and go unnoticed. That is where you come in – helping your client to stop and to reflect on her thinking habits, including:

- **Developing healthy emotions to motivate actions:** Check whether feelings are appropriate to the situation at hand.

- **Developing perspective and reality**: Challenge where your client is catastrophising or maximising problems, or imagining outcomes for which no evidence exists in reality.

- **Identifying negative automatic thoughts**: Negative thoughts block or limit your client's actions.

- **Observing thinking errors:** Check twisted ways of thinking about herself, others, and the situation, which may be making the situation seem worse than it is.

- **Shifting thinking patterns:** This shift stimulates emotional and behavioural change.

Your main aim as a CB coach is to help your client develop the mental and emotional strategies to achieve her identified goals. Ask your client whether her thoughts are:

- **Rational**: Is there a law of the universe that says that she must think this way in this situation?

- **Empirical**: Must everyone respond in the way she is, or would other people respond differently?

- **Helpful**: Is her way of thinking and approaching the situation actually helping her to manage it successfully? If not, how else might she think?

CBC questioning methods

CBC is a process of questioning based on Socratic dialogue, which I mentioned at the beginning of this chapter. The questions are designed to help the client analyse her thoughts and opinions so as to clarify whether her approach is supporting her to achieve her goals. The premise is that the client is the best person to make her own decisions. A CB coach does not tell her client what to think or do. The client has the answers, provided she is asked the right questions – you provide those questions to take her from the position she is currently in towards the thoughts and actions that help her reach her goals.

The CBC process is collaborative rather than confrontational, but it may be challenging because Socratic questions aim to provoke insights that help the client move forward. This process encourages your client to look at the evidence for her unhelpful or limiting belief and to see where she holds back.

You help your client to become her own coach by sharing the questioning techniques with her. For example, if your client feels overburdened by her workload but feels unable to say no to her boss, you may ask her Socratic questions that open up options for her:

- ✔ Where is it written that you must. . . ?
- ✔ Who says that you must. . . ?
- ✔ Does it follow that. . . ?
- ✔ What is the evidence that. . . ?
- ✔ Is this belief logical?
- ✔ Where is the evidence for your belief about this?
- ✔ Might you be exaggerating the importance of this problem?
- ✔ Are you concentrating on the negatives and ignoring the positives?
- ✔ Are you taking things too personally?
- ✔ What's the worst that can happen?
- ✔ How important will this problem be in six months?
- ✔ Just because this situation has happened once, how does it follow that it must happen again?
- ✔ How might others approach this situation?
- ✔ How does failing (your exams, for example) make you a complete failure?
- ✔ Are you worrying about how you think things should be, rather than dealing with the situation as it is?
- ✔ Is your belief helping you achieve your goals?
- ✔ How else can you think about this situation?
- ✔ If you thought differently, how would that impact your outcome?

By answering these questions, your client reviews her approach and checks whether this approach is rational and helpful. You can then help her to develop more constructive self-talk and approaches based on evidence and reality. The ABCDE model developed by Albert Ellis provides a structure to identify and dispute old beliefs and exchange them, where relevant:

- ✔ **A**ctivating event
- ✔ **B**elief or expectation
- ✔ **C**onsequence – emotion or behaviour
- ✔ **D**isputing the belief or expectation (B)
- ✔ **E**xchanging thoughts to be more rational and constructive

For more on the ABCDE model, check out Chapter 2.

Understanding the mind–body connection

In CBC, we apply what we know about neuroscience. Until the fairly recent advent of magnetic resonance imaging (MRI), scientists could only research the brains of dead people. Through MRI scans, we can see the brain in action, which gives us far more information about how the brain functions. We can now watch how a thought leads not only to a feeling but also to a physiological change in the body. Scientists recognise that how we think can impact many aspects of our body, including:

- ✔ Immune system
- ✔ Blood flow
- ✔ Heart rate
- ✔ Breathing function

 Stressful thoughts lead to the release of cortisol, adrenaline, and noradrenaline in your body, suppressing the immune system. When you're fearful, your body becomes more rigid, you get butterflies in your stomach, and your hands sweat. Enthusiastic or supportive thoughts, on the other hand, cause the release of beta endorphins and human growth hormone, which make you feel physically lighter and full of energy. You can trick your brain into releasing immune-boosting endorphins by focusing your mind on a pleasant scene that relaxes your body.

Just as our thinking impacts our physiology, so our physiology impacts our thinking. When we are stressed, the brain is starved of blood and oxygen. You can show your client techniques to manage these physiological changes and enable her to develop thoughts that maintain her body's *homeostasis,* or equilibrium. Such techniques include the following:

- ✔ Breathing exercises to regulate oxygen and carbon dioxide levels
- ✔ Exercise such as walking and running
- ✔ Physical movement to relax the body, such as t'ai chi and yoga
- ✔ Meditation and progressive relaxation

See Chapters 13 and 21 for more information on keeping healthy and balanced.

CBC is based on your client's thoughts and views. Because the brain impacts every area of the body, CBC is a *holistic* approach to self-development, which means that it does not just address the mind but addresses the life, work, and health of your client. As she takes more control of her thoughts and viewpoints, she begins to manage her emotions and physiology. As she feels more balanced, this balance can have far-reaching benefits on her health, creativity, and relationships.

Accepting Our Common Humanity

One of the principles of CBC is that humans are unique and marvellous, and also make mistakes. We make, therefore, a thinking error if we expect ourselves or others to be perfect. Acceptance of human fallibility is a theme that runs through all CBC models. Accepting fallibility is not to accept failure. You can show your client that she can continue to develop herself and her performance by seeking excellence and not perfection.

Many people get into the habit of blaming themselves and others for not coming up to their own constructed standards of behaviour. When people condemn and label others as stupid or heartless, they're generally doing so from the point of view of their own needs and expectations, and frequently from the evidence of one or two specific occasions. Thus the statement can be an exaggeration. Although the person may have acted stupidly in one situation, it does not make her stupid in all situations.

Words such as should, must, and ought to denote personal rules of behaviour that your client has constructed about herself, others, and situations in general. You need to help your client to view behaviours objectively and learn to respect herself enough to be able to respect others even when they don't agree with her approach.

Here are a few examples of thoughts your client may have:

- ✔ 'I should have been able to get through all those emails last night' demonstrates that the client did not come up to her own standards. This thought can reduce confidence and self-esteem.

- ✔ 'He should have called me to tell me he was going to be late' demonstrates that the client has expectations of how other people should behave, even though she may not know whether the person had a phone on her. This expectation can lead to anger and relationship problems.

- ✔ 'I ought to have visited my mother this weekend' demonstrates that the client had beliefs about how she should treat her mother. This kind of belief can lead to guilt.

To develop more balanced viewpoints, you can challenge these statements with questions such as:

- ✔ Do all your colleagues get through their emails every day?

- ✔ Has there ever been a time when you couldn't call someone to tell her you were late?

- ✔ Is there a law that says you have to visit your mother every weekend?

Eventually, the client comes to see that every person struggles in her own way to make a success of her life, and that people have different methods of approaching situations. Like your client, other people try to do their best, even if that best does not match your client's view of best.

Developing self-acceptance

Self-acceptance is fundamental to self-esteem and self-confidence. Many clients are hard on themselves, criticising themselves for mistakes, and not appreciating their good points. You may need to explain that self-acceptance *does not* mean any of the following:

- ✔ Giving up on self-improvement
- ✔ Saying 'this is the way I am; live with it'
- ✔ Not learning from mistakes
- ✔ Not analysing what you can do differently

Self-acceptance *does* mean the following:

- ✔ Accepting that you're human and that all humans have strengths and weaknesses
- ✔ Recognising that making a mistake does not mean that you're stupid or a failure, just that you happen to have made one mistake
- ✔ Recognising that you have your quirks and can be sensitive to their impact on others
- ✔ Taking responsibility for yourself and working on behaviours that you wish to adapt
- ✔ Understanding that you won't be loved and approved of by everyone – and nor will anyone else
- ✔ You can focus on your strengths and put your weaknesses in context

I cover many techniques that help you to develop your client's self-acceptance in Chapter 9.

Seeking excellence and not perfection

A principle of CBC is human fallibility. This signifies that CBC regards perfectionism as unattainable. It would be nice, of course, if life were the way we wanted it to be and if all our expectations were met – but that's in our dreams. And that's the problem. We inevitably want things to go our way and turn out the way we want them to, but it simply isn't a rational or realistic belief to expect this perfect outcome all the time. However, this belief causes a great deal of stress.

Ask your client to analyse her expectations of herself, others, and the world. You may unearth thoughts such as:

- ✔ 'I should be more efficient.'
- ✔ 'Others ought to treat me with more consideration.'
- ✔ 'Life should be easier than it is.'

The underlying assumption here is that a perfect standard exists, which has to be reached. Your job is to show your client that this standard is constructed in her own head and is generally not a scientific law of the universe.

Perfectionism is irrational: your perfect may not be the same as your colleague's. It also inspires a fear of failure, and this fear can lead to paralysis. Perfectionists can be driven, spending hours over a task that can be done to an excellent standard in less time. This kind of behaviour can play havoc with deadlines and have a knock-on effect on those with whom you are working, because it can lead to delay, especially when someone can't start her piece of work until the previous person has finished.

Excellence is a rational and achievable goal. You're endeavouring to do the best you can. This belief tends to remove fear and inspire an enthusiastic state rather than a fearful one.

In Table 1-2, I demonstrate some of the differences between perfectionism and the pursuit of excellence.

Table 1-2	Differences Between Perfectionism and the Pursuit of Excellence
Perfectionism	*Pursuit of Excellence*
You're driven by fear of failure.	You're motivated by enthusiasm.
You work out of a sense of duty.	You enjoy the challenge of new tasks.
You're nervous of change and taking risks.	You enjoy taking calculated risks and finding new ways of working.
None of your accomplishments are ever quite good enough.	You achieve a sense of satisfaction from your efforts even if they haven't worked out perfectly.
You judge others by your own perfectionist view, so no one else is ever quite good enough either.	You accept that others are doing the best they can and can develop.
Your self-esteem depends on external achievements at work.	You feel you have intrinsic value in yourself, outside your external achievements.
You seek to impress people with your knowledge.	You feel accepted without trying to impress people all the time.
If you don't achieve an important goal, you feel like a failure.	You realise that everyone makes mistakes occasionally, and, while you don't seek to fail, you accept that you can learn from experience.
You feel you must be strong and not share vulnerabilities.	You can be vulnerable and share doubts and feelings with others.
You expect others to work in your way.	You allow others to work in their own way.
You miss deadlines because you're still striving to get it just right.	You know when a piece of work is good enough.

These are very different ways of operating. The perfectionist will never be happy with her efforts. This results in low self-esteem and a fear-based approach to life and work. Enabling people to realise that it is more realistic to seek excellence enables them to free up their creativity and enjoy the process of working.

Chapter 2

The Basics of CBC

In This Chapter

▶ Introducing the ABCDE process from thoughts to feelings

▶ Spotting thinking errors

▶ Explaining how CBC helps clients break through outdated beliefs

*I*n this chapter, I introduce some of the theories and models of CBC and demonstrate examples of how they can be applied within your coaching sessions.

Your specific focus, as a CB coach, is to help your clients identify the thoughts, beliefs, and expectations that shape their responses to the situations they face in life and at work. You provide CB models that investigate your clients' current approaches and give them step strategies to achieve their goals.

In this chapter, I include methods and examples of how you can help your clients to overcome limiting thoughts and behaviours, enabling them to manage their challenges more effectively in future.

Starting in the Mind

CBC is all about thinking and the way we respond to the world. We all have thousands of thoughts each day. Your brain constantly fires electrochemical messages from one neuron, or brain cell, to another. Each neuron connects with thousands of its neighbours. The areas that join up are the axons, which conduct signals away from the cell, and the dendrites, which receive incoming information. Where each axon meets a dendrite there is a gap; this is called a synapse. Neurotransmitters send the current of information across this gap. Millions of neurons must fire in unison to produce even the most simple thought.

Over time, patterns of thought strengthen these connections, developing *neural pathways*. The more often you repeat a thought, the more the pathway becomes hard-wired in your brain. This hard-wiring is what enables you to develop the complex process of driving a car and then, once you've mastered it, to be able to drive several miles without thinking about it. The process has become automated. This process is how your brain develops.

The same process happens with your thoughts. Those thoughts you have frequently become automatic and unconscious. Since the day he was born, your client has built up perspectives of himself, other people, and the world. For example, if he has believed since childhood 'I am bad at maths' then the moment he sees a mathematical sum, his mind is likely to switch into the 'I'm no good at maths' state. He probably won't even be conscious of this thought because he's had it so often. The thought has become a *negative automatic thought*. It is described as automatic because he has had the thought so often that the brain has learnt to hard-wire that thinking process in his brain – each time he sees a number, it automatically fires the 'I'm bad at maths' thought.

The trouble is that, conscious or unconscious, a thought such as 'I am bad at . . .' or 'I'm no good at . . .' tends to lead to anxiety. Anxiety undermines your ability to think clearly, and so the thought can become a self-fulfilling prophecy. Negative thoughts ultimately diminish self-esteem. The inability to carry out one task leads people occasionally to lose perspective and consider themselves incapable of carrying out all tasks.

As a CB coach, you help your clients to:

- ✔ Become aware of their thoughts
- ✔ Consider whether the thought helps them manage the situation
- ✔ Consider whether the thought is in perspective
- ✔ Develop a balanced view so as to be able to manage the situation in future

For example, you may help your client to see whether he can think of a more useful way of approaching maths, such as 'I may not be brilliant at maths, but I am good at other things and I can work through the problem step by step.'

Your clients bring many topics to your coaching sessions. As a CB coach, you explore the inner working of your client's mind. You help your client tune in to the conversations in his head. In CBC, we call the endless stream of thoughts that occur in our brains every day *internal dialogue*.

TECHNICAL STUFF

The brain's plasticity

As neuroscience develops, we are able to see the brain in action using magnetic resonance imaging (MRI) scans. Neuroscientists now understand that the brain's nature of *plasticity* literally means that it has the potential to change and develop at will through our lifetimes. Plasticity is the lifelong ability of the brain to reorganise neural pathways based on new experiences, thoughts and learning. Pathways that are no longer used are pruned, while new learning and experience develops new pathways, literally changing the structure of an individual's brain's wiring as he chooses to focus on something new. We are not totally stuck in our physiology but can make choices. We can become who we want to be. We can develop skills and ways of thinking that support us in our endeavours instead of incapacitate us. This is an exciting development, and you're a part of a generation that will learn more about your brain as this research expands.

As your client becomes aware of the habitual thoughts that have built up over his lifetime, he can create new pathways of thinking that are more relevant, more rational, and more empowering. You can explain how thoughts themselves are only as important as the meaning that a person gives them. The 'I'm no good at maths' thought can make one person feel inadequate but another person think 'So what? I can't be good at everything.'

Understanding the process from thoughts to feelings to behaviours

The moment you have a thought, you also experience a feeling. For example, if your client is a salesperson who thinks 'I hate making cold calls,' he may feel anxious every time he phones a new client. Alternatively, if your client thinks 'This cold call can win me commission,' he may feel quite excited and enthusiastic about making the call. Your client's thought has an immediate impact on his emotional state.

As a CB coach, you help your client to become aware of his thinking. This is like shining a torch into his brain so that he can identify those automatic thoughts that he may not notice. You can then question whether these thoughts are rational and helpful, or irrational and limiting. You do this within the specific situations that your client brings into the coaching session, so the process always focuses on your client and the challenges and goals he faces.

John's meeting

John came to his coaching session and set a goal to speak up at the next team meeting. He had previously sat there allowing his colleagues to do the talking. Although he had ideas and suggestions to contribute, he held back and did not share them. As a result, his boss had given him feedback that he was not being sufficiently proactive. John was losing confidence and was frustrated that he felt inhibited in these situations.

During the coaching session, we explored the nature of the thoughts he was having during these meetings. Here are a few examples:

> 'Someone has probably already thought of that solution.'

> 'I may look stupid.'

> 'I don't like talking up in front of my boss.'

> 'I don't always agree with what my boss is saying, but I don't like conflict.'

> 'What if I say something and no-one hears me?'

As John became aware of his thoughts he realised they were self-defeating and gave him feelings of inadequacy and fear. He saw that his fear stopped him speaking up and that this behaviour could seriously impact the future of his career. He saw a real benefit in changing his behaviour.

In order to achieve his goal of speaking up at the next meeting, John worked through ways of challenging his limiting beliefs with some of the following questions:

'What evidence do you have that someone has already thought of that solution?'

'What is so awful about looking stupid? Have other people looked stupid occasionally and survived?'

'What leads you to believe that disagreeing with your boss would be so awful?'

'What can you do to ensure that you're heard?'

John managed to see that much of his thinking was based on supposition rather than evidence. He realised that fear was driving his behaviour and holding him back. He set himself a manageable goal to say one thing at the next meeting and to ensure that he projected his voice more forcefully so that everyone heard him. In order to do this, he identified the following thoughts that would help him to feel calm and confident in the meeting:

> 'I am knowledgeable and have valuable ideas to share with others.'

> 'It is fine to provide a solution, whether or not others have thought of this before.'

> 'If someone thinks my idea is stupid, it does not mean that I am stupid.'

In this way, John set rational and practical goals to provide him with supportive techniques to achieve his objective of speaking up at the next meeting.

A useful starting point is to ask your client to keep a *thinking log* (Table 2-1). A thinking log is a model that helps your client track his thought processes within the situations he encounters. The thinking log enables him to become more aware of his thought patterns and to identify how those thoughts make him feel.

Table 2-1	Thinking log	
Situation	*Thought*	*Feeling*

The thinking log also provides you with a helpful exercise to work on in subsequent coaching sessions as you help your client review whether his thoughts are supporting his goals or holding him back. You can ask questions such as:

- ✔ 'How did this thought make you feel?'
- ✔ 'How did that feeling influence your behaviour?'
- ✔ 'In what ways may this thought be limiting your actions?'
- ✔ 'What may be a more helpful way of thinking?'

Gradually, your client comes to understand how his thoughts influence his feelings and behaviours. You work to show him that he can consider alternative ways to approach situations. As your client sees that by changing his thoughts he can change his experiences, he develops a greater sense of control. The thinking log provides a focus to integrate this thought-changing process into your client's life.

Thinking backwards: From action to thought process

One of the core models of CBC is known as the ABCDE model (see Figure 2-1) originally developed by Dr Albert Ellis, President of the Albert Ellis Institute for Rational Emotive Behaviour Therapy. This model can be used to enable your client to track and analyse the process of his response from the outcome he desired back to his initial thought or expectation of the situation. It is also a model with which to develop more constructive thoughts in future by adding the E for Exchanging the thought and approach.

A = the Activating event or situation your client faces.

B = the Belief, thought or expectation your client has of the situation.

C = the Consequential emotion and behaviour resulting from B (your client's thought).

D = Disputing the belief, questioning whether the client's thinking is rational and helping him achieve his desired goal (in A).

E = Exchanging the thought for another thought that is constructive and supportive of the goal.

The ABCDE Model

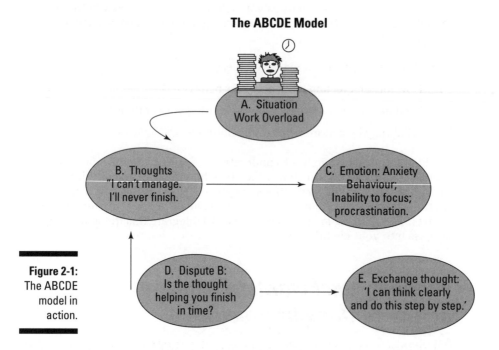

Figure 2-1:
The ABCDE
model in
action.

The ABCDE model helps you and your client work through his challenges and goals in a systematic way. You help your client to unpack his thoughts within a specified situation that he has experienced and identify how these thoughts have influenced his emotions, behaviours, and actions. Here is an example of the process you could follow:

A = The activating situation. For example, your client Derek says he had a situation where he felt pressurised by work overload.

B = The belief, thought or expectation of the situation. You ask Derek to identify a thought he had at the time. Derek replies 'I'll never finish this in time.'

C = The consequential emotion and behaviour resulting from B (the thought). You ask Derek how the thought 'I'll never finish this on time' had an impact on his feelings or behaviours. Derek says the thought made him anxious and unable to focus properly. This led him to procrastinate and not think clearly about his priorities.

D = Disputing the belief. You question whether Derek's thought 'I'll never finish this on time' was rational and helped him achieve his desired goal (in A). You ask Derek whether the thought helped him get through his work effectively within the allocated period. Derek sees that his thinking is irrational and unhelpful as he has no evidence to show that he could not finish on time, and the thought made him panic and think less effectively.

E = Exchanging the thought for another that is more constructive and supportive of the goal. You ask Derek what thought may be more helpful the next time he feels under pressure of a workload deadline. Derek replies that the thought 'I can think clearly and do this step by step' would help him stay calm and focused and be more likely to help him complete the work on time.

After you show your clients how to use the ABCDE model, they can apply it in everyday situations they face. The model provides a system to question a client's current approach and develop constructive thoughts to stimulate positive feelings and behaviours, enabling him to achieve his goals and objectives.

The ABCDE working log, which I show in Table 2-2, can be a useful home-practice exercise. Ask your client to record at least three different situations that occur between two coaching sessions, so that you can explore how the model works in action in his life. Going through the log together provides useful review and discussion of your client's thoughts and approaches in the next session, so that you can help him integrate new habits of thinking into his daily life.

Table 2-2		ABCDE working log		
A. Situation	**B. Belief and Thought**	**C. Consequence**	**D. Dispute your thinking**	**E: Exchange**
		Emotion:	Was it helping you achieve your goal?	What would be a more helpful thought if you face this situation again?
		Behaviour		

Reviewing thoughts and expectations: Yours or your parents'?

Many of your client's thinking habits have built up over his lifetime. Some of these thoughts likely reflect beliefs that are actually not your client's own. We pick up our attitudes and approaches to life from our parents and other adults who are influential in our lives when we are young. You may need to help your client review his beliefs and check whether he has unconsciously obtained his approach to a situation from a parent or teacher. We call this belief a *learned belief.*

For example, many people in senior management feel inadequate if they don't have a university degree. This thought often comes from the 'if . . . then . . .' process, where a teacher or parent expressed the opinion: '*If* you don't have a university degree *then* you won't reach the top of your career.' As a CB coach, you help your client review whether this belief, which derived from one or two people's opinions, is the truth. You can help your client challenge his perspective by asking him to identify other people who have reached the top of their careers without degrees.

Underlying our actions is a set of beliefs and values. The five-level reviewing beliefs model, which we show in Figure 2-2, is a way to review and revise beliefs and expectations.

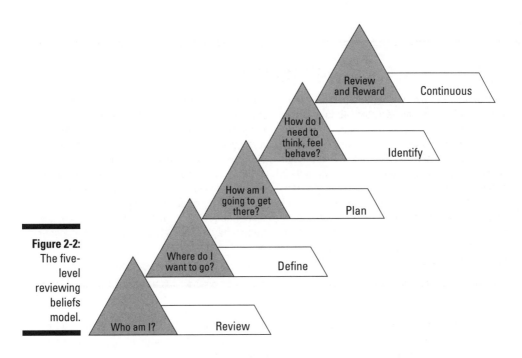

Figure 2-2:
The five-
level
reviewing
beliefs
model.

When your client takes action from a decision, he operates at five different levels:

1. **Beliefs and values**

2. **Thoughts and expectations**

3. **Emotions**

4. **Behaviours**

5. **Actions**

Learned expectations

An example of a learned belief is a fear of dogs. In a family where a parent is nervous of dogs, the child tends to pick up the message that dogs are scary things. This belief leads the child to expect that dogs could be dangerous, and he may be nervous of stroking them. In another family with a dog as a pet, the child learns that dogs are nice gentle companions, and this belief leads the child to expect that most dogs are friendly and can be stroked.

Cooking the ham

An example of how our behaviour can derive from that of our parents is a story about a family who were cooking a joint of ham. A woman was struggling to cut the bone off the end of the ham, as she had done since she first started cooking. Her husband noticed this and asked 'Why do you always cut the end off the ham bone?' The woman looked puzzled and said 'Well, because my mother did.' 'Why did she do that? It doesn't seem necessary,' said the man. 'I'll call her and find out,' his wife replied. When the woman called her mother, she was given the same answer. 'Well, I always did it because *my* mother used to do this,' the woman's mother laughed. 'Tell you what, I'll give her a call and find out what made her do this.' So the woman's mother called Grandma, who replied 'Well in those days, my oven was too small to fit the whole ham bone!' This was not the case for her daughter or grand-daughter, whose ovens were adequately large to fit the whole ham and bone. They had simply followed the behaviour without questioning.

The decisions and actions that a client has taken through his lifetime will often have been influenced by his underlying beliefs, values, and security needs, even though these influences may be unconscious. Your role is to help your client become conscious of how these different levels operate within his life, so that he has more conscious options to respond to situations.

Consider the following example:

A coaching client, Dina, wants to change job roles. She needs to decide between a senior management post and a sideways move to a different location. Dina wants you, the CB coach, to help her make her decision and plan a positive strategy to achieve her goal:

1. **Beliefs and values:** You help Dina identify what values and beliefs drive her forward or hold her back. For example, Dina's father became wealthy and successful through workaholic behaviours, and made statements such as 'If you work really hard, then you will become a wealthy senior manager like me, able to afford a large house and big car.' You question whether the values of hard work, money, large house, and senior management reflect Dina's values now that she is an adult in her own right. If they do, that's fine. If not, Dina can update her belief.

You're there not to judge your client in any way, but to help your client build decisions based on his own set of beliefs and values, not those of someone else.

2. **Thoughts and expectations:** You explore the thoughts and expectations Dina has about her career, and check whether these thoughts help her develop her potential or are old, limiting, habitual patterns of thinking that need to be upgraded. For example, you challenge the thought 'I ought to go for the senior management job because it gives me more money' by questioning how that supports her values. Your aim is to help Dina make an objective and empowered decision.

3. **Emotions:** You help Dina develop thoughts that create an emotional state to enable her to manage the job selection process. This may include overcoming old fears and anxieties in order to develop a more confident emotional state. For instance, Dina may choose to think 'I can feel confident in choosing to apply for the sideways move, because I would find it really interesting to work in that location even if it isn't as well paid.'

4. **Behaviours:** You help Dina review her old ways of behaving and consider whether she needs to change any aspects of her behaviour in order to adopt behaviours suitable to her own values and the role she needs to play in the new job. For example, if she is unassertive, you can help her develop assertive behaviours reflective of what will be expected of her in the new job.

5. **Actions:** You help Dina to decide which post she wants to go for and what actions she needs to take in order to be offered the job – for example, writing an accurate and impressive CV, presenting herself professionally, articulating her strengths at interview, and managing her father's opinion that she should be taking the senior post.

Adopting the thoughts and approaches of our parents without scrutinising whether the approach is actually reflective of our own beliefs and relevant to our lives today is easy. Traditional family celebrations often give excellent examples of how individuals grow to believe that *their* way of doing things is the normal and right way, even if the family next door celebrates the same festival in a completely different way. Try investigating this with your client.

At the level of thoughts and expectations people adopt three main types of demand or expectation about:

- ✔ Self – how we want ourselves to be
- ✔ Others – how we want others to be
- ✔ Situations – how we want the world to be

In the sections below, I give examples of these basic demands and expectations:

About self

Common expectations of oneself, include the following:

- ✔ That you must be approved of by everyone
- ✔ That you should be thoroughly competent and achieve important things in order to consider yourself worthwhile

For example, the underlying expectations 'I must do well and be approved of, and if I'm not then it's awful' and 'If I do not do well then I am not a worthy person' can lead to stress, anxiety, shame, and guilt when you do not meet your own expectations.

In coaching sessions, you can help your client review his thoughts and consider what other thoughts and expectations may be more rational. Try asking what thoughts would help him to pursue excellence rather than perfection and accept himself as a fallible human being.

For example, your client may develop the thought 'It is best to do well, but if I make the occasional mistake I am not a failure or a bad human being.'

About others

Here are examples of expectations that your client may have of other people:

- ✔ That other people should treat me the way I want them to
- ✔ That I should be dependent on others and need someone stronger than myself on whom to rely
- ✔ That I should become upset over other people's problems
- ✔ That a right, precise, and perfect solution to human problems exists and nothing else is good enough

For example, the underlying expectation 'People must treat me well and fairly, and those who do not deserve to be punished' can lead to anger, aggressive behaviour, and even violence. Such an expectation may cause relationship problems when other people do not come up to the required standards.

You can help your client realise that all human beings are fallible. You can ask him what thoughts may help him to respect others even if they do not behave in exactly the way he wants them to, provided the behaviour is within the law.

For example, your client may choose to think 'I would rather x behaved in this way, but can cope with it if he doesn't. I can respect his freedom to behave the way he wants, and I can also express my needs in an assertive but not aggressive manner.'

About situations

Lots of people have expectations about specific situations and about life in general. Here are a couple of examples:

- ✔ That life should treat me fairly and be the way I want it to be
- ✔ That I am a victim of circumstance and of other people's decisions

For example, the expectations 'Life conditions must be the way I want them to be, and if they're not, it's unfair' and 'I can't stand it when things don't go well, and feel sorry for myself because I feel I have no control' can lead to self-pity and the idea that the person is a victim. It can also lead to unhealthy comfort habits such as over-eating, procrastination, or even to addictive behaviours such as alcoholism, because of a general feeling of helplessness.

You can help your client consider how to accept that life is not always fair and has its ups and downs. You can also help your client to see that although it may be difficult for him when things do not go the way he expects, he does have certain things within his control.

For example, your client may choose to think 'Occasionally life presents problems and can be tough, but I can practice being flexible and manage it when this happens.'

In CBC sessions, you have the opportunity to:

- ✔ Help your client review his expectations of himself, other people, and the situations he faces
- ✔ Check whether demands are indeed his own demands or those of a parent or influential other
- ✔ Develop new expectations that are rational, helpful, and appropriate to the situations he now experiences

Tackling Thinking Errors

As a CB coach, you need to attune your ear to *thinking errors* – specific ways in which people develop errors in their perceptions, leading to irrational views and lack of perspective. Thinking errors can lead to unhealthy emotions that limit constructive behaviour.

You may find that your client does not recognise that his thinking or interpretation of a situation is not based on evidence and is therefore faulty. Your client may be so acclimatised to his way of thinking that it seems normal and realistic to him – even if the thinking isn't normal and realistic. This situation is where you, as a CB coach, can give your client the ability to challenge his own perspectives, providing him with more choices and options.

Recognising where your mind deceives you

Even the most logical person has very illogical thoughts sometimes. In CBC, we call these illogical thoughts *thinking errors, twisted thinking,* or *faulty thinking*. One of the key tasks you can perform in coaching sessions is to listen and point out where your client distorts his thinking.

In CBC, we give these distortions rather technical names. Below I give the formal title for each distortion and then offer an example so you can understand what the distortion is.

All or nothing thinking

'It's completely useless': All experiences are impeccable or terrible, and the individuals often classifies themselves in the most negative way. This is also known as *black-and-white thinking,* where the person misses the fact that thought can also be many shades of grey.

A good example of this is a manager who receives a report from his direct report and decides that it's completely useless, without realising that this statement is subjective, reflecting his opinion rather than a logical truth. The manager's boss then reads the report and says 'It's pretty well written,' which illustrates that other people may view things in a different way.

Arbitrary inference

'They're planning something against me': Specific inference about a situation or person without evidence to support the conclusion. This is someone who jumps to conclusions, particularly with a focus on the negative. This distortion comes in two specific types:

✔ **Mind reading:** 'I know she doesn't like me' – making assumptions and suppositions about another person's behaviour, without necessarily having any evidence for these assumptions.

For example, three colleagues work in the same office. When two colleagues go out for lunch together and do not invite the third person, that person assumes that they don't like him, even though there may be another reason for them not inviting him.

> ✔ **Fortune telling:** 'He's going to dump me' – imagining a particular out-
> come from an event or situation, when in fact many different potential
> outcomes exist.
>
> An example of this thought pattern is someone who says 'I know you're
> going to make me redundant in the restructure' even though he has no
> evidence of this plan and may be worrying for no good reason.

Blaming

'It's all his fault!': Whatever happens is always the fault of another person,
so that the individual feels victimised and does not take responsibility for his
part of the problem.

For example, three members of a team make a sales presentation to a client
that does not result in a sale. Although there were many factors that caused
this result, one team member blames another for the failure.

Catastrophising

'It's simply awful and I can't stand it!': Making more of a situation than you
have evidence for.

For example, your email system has been down and you haven't received
confirmation of a purchase from a client. You get in a panic and assume that
if you can't access the email system immediately, the deal will fall through,
even though no evidence exists to suggest this would happen.

Emotional reasoning

'I feel so miserable that I am sure that this meeting won't go well': When a
person comes to a conclusion because of his feelings rather than because of
facts.

For example, someone has been expecting his new date to phone him the
night after their first evening out. When he doesn't receive a phone call, he
feels miserable and decides that the person couldn't have liked him. So when
he does get a call, he behaves in a defensive manner and, despite wanting the
relationship to continue, is cold and unfriendly.

Labelling

'I'm totally stupid': When a person brands himself or others with a label as a
result of one instance.

For example, a person who fails a specific examination as part of a professional qualification labels himself as 'totally stupid' even though he has passed other modules and knows that colleagues have also found this module particularly tough. Or he labels a colleague 'unhelpful' because she once refused to support him because of other commitments.

Low frustration tolerance

'I've had enough of this': When someone gets impatient with a situation or just can't be bothered to finish a task, even though he knows that it is to his benefit that he does so.

For example, someone who has to complete his tax assessment form by a particular date keeps postponing the task because he can't bear all the detailed work required to go through his expenses. The result can be that he ends up paying a fine for late completion.

Magnification

'This is the worst thing that could possibly have happened': Grossly magnifying the importance of an event or aspect of an event or experience.

For example, a member of staff is given an appraisal by his boss. The boss gives mainly positive feedback but comments on the person's need to develop better numeracy skills. The staff member then goes away, telling colleagues 'This is awful: my boss says I am innumerate.'

Minimisation

'It's not much, it's not really a problem': Distorting the significance or playing down the importance of an event.

For example, someone who has severe difficulties at home, with a sick partner, says 'It's no problem. I'm fine.'

Overgeneralisation

'This will never work': Drawing a general rule or conclusion as a result of one or two isolated experiences or events. This conclusion is then applied across the board to many similar and sometimes dissimilar circumstances.

For example, a company allows two managers to job share. When the relationship does not function well, the company assumes that job shares don't work.

Personalisation

'I must have done something wrong': Where a person takes personal responsibility for a failure or event despite there being others involved, or extenuating circumstances.

For example, a staff member who has a good relationship with his boss notices that she is not as talkative with him as usual and assumes that 'I must have done something wrong,' whereas the reality of the situation may be that the boss has something else on her mind.

Selective abstraction

'No-one appreciated my efforts': Concentrating on a detail taken out of context from an event or experience, while ignoring other factors of the event. This thought pattern frequently occurs when someone hears only the negative comment and does not hear the positive comments.

For example, a trainer running a training course gets nine out of ten people giving him an 80 per cent evaluation, but one of the delegates gave him 50 per cent. The trainer goes away feeling that he is a failure, because he ignores the positives and just focuses on the one negative.

Shoulds, musts, oughts

'I must get this promotion'/'He should be able to get this right'/'She ought to know that I need that information now': Demanding that events and people, including themselves, come up to a certain set of standards or rules that the individual has randomly set.

Examples of this include 'I feel guilty because I should have been able to complete this project by the deadline,' or 'I must get top marks in my study module otherwise others will think I am stupid,' or 'I complete this project this way so others ought to do it the same way as I do.'

Over time, you're likely to come across examples of all these styles of distorted thinking – and you may like to keep track of your own too, as we are all susceptible! The more you become attuned to thinking errors, the more you listen out for them, and you are then able to help your clients develop more realistic, balanced, and evidence-based thinking patterns.

Gaining perspective to develop emotional intelligence

You can help your client to regain perspective in many ways. In doing so, you help your client to achieve emotional equilibrium. CBC is about teasing out balanced viewpoints and approaches that more truly reflect the context in which your client operates. You help your client take the wool from his eyes and see the situation anew. Instead of regarding a situation in black-and-white terms of 'everything is awful' or 'everything is wonderful', your client gradually sees that most, if not all, situations exist in many shades of grey. The key is to provide your client with the ability to review his own thought processes and develop new ways of approaching situations that enable him to feel more empowered and emotionally balanced.

Emotional intelligence does not ignore the validity of emotional responses, nor does it persuade you to think in unrealistic positive-thinking terms. Emotions are strong survival mechanisms and alert you to the possibility of you being in danger. Being upset or angry can prompt you to act appropriately in an emergency. But when the thought is twisted or disproportionate, you end up with an emotion that is neither useful nor relevant.

As a CB coach, you set up your client with the models and skills he needs to feel and honour his emotions and to develop an emotional state that accurately reflects his situation. Your client can then begin to manage his emotions more effectively in future.

You can apply the ABCDE model (which I describe in the section 'Thinking backwards: From action to thought process') to help your client plan for future events. If he usually *catastrophises* his challenges, for example by describing his situation in an exaggeratedly negative way that emphasises his inability to cope, you can provide him with questions and a process to help him gain a more balanced, constructive approach in future.

First, start by explaining to your client that you plan to challenge his approach in three main ways. You will:

- ✔ Decide whether his approach is **rational and logical** in the context of the situation and evidence: 'Just because you would prefer the situation to be like this does it logically follow that it must be?'

- ✔ Investigate whether he has any **empirical evidence** for his perspective: 'What is the evidence for this viewpoint? Would everyone approach the situation in the way you do?'

- ✔ Analyse whether his approach is **helpful** within the context of the objective of the situation: 'Does this way of thinking support you in taking action to achieve your objective?'

Second, ask one or several of the following questions to help your client develop a perspective:

- ✔ What is the evidence for your assuming that the event will go badly?

- ✔ What aspects of the event are likely to go well?

- ✔ Who is there to support you?

- ✔ What has gone well in the past in similar situations?

> ✔ How might someone else approach this situation?
>
> ✔ What is the worst that could happen?
>
> ✔ If that did happen, how important would it be in a year's time?
>
> ✔ What is your ideal outcome for the event?
>
> ✔ What strategies can you put into place to plan for this successful outcome?
>
> ✔ What emotional state would you like to be in?
>
> ✔ What thoughts support your ability to feel in this state?

You can then suggest that your client completes this plan within the ABC context. In the following example, the client has to attend a difficult client meeting:

A = Activating event – a successful meeting.

B = Thought or belief that would be helpful – 'I can do my best, and if the meeting doesn't go perfectly then I can still manage to be professional.'

C = Emotional state – confidence to support calm professional behaviour.

Changing your cognitive approach changes your emotional experience of a situation. It enables you to feel more in control of your emotional state. It also helps you to identify which emotions are healthy and natural and which are the result of twisted thinking. Grief, concern, or sadness in relation to a specific event may be perfectly natural and healthy. Anxiety, blame, or guilt may well be the result of twisted expectations of yourself, others, or the situation. This situation can lead to unhealthy or unhelpful emotions such as over-anxiety or aggression if things don't conform to your demands. Developing rational thoughts that are in perspective can also help you to acknowledge and manage the emotions of other people by spotting when you or they are adopting irrational viewpoints.

Sally's pay rise

Sally was a marketing executive. She had worked hard over the past year and had achieved the majority of her targets. However, there had been one major account where the client had been unhappy with her approach. Despite the fact that her other clients were satisfied with her work, Sally focused on the client who complained. As her annual salary review approached, Sally catastrophised about the event and predicted (fortune-telling) that her boss would give her a hard time and not award her a salary increase. Sally was highly anxious. Her emotions affected her breathing and voice and she feared that she would be over-emotional during the pay review.

Sally and her CB coach went through the ABCDE model to explore whether she had developed thinking errors and investigate how these errors may be influencing her emotional state.

(continued)

(continued)

Sally's ABCDE log:

A = Pay review meeting with her boss following client complaint.

B = Her beliefs and thoughts about the meeting:

'This complaint shows that I am no good at my job.' (dichotomous thinking)

'Everyone will see that I have made this big mistake.' (selective abstraction)

'I am really incompetent.' (labelling)

'I am dreading the meeting with my boss, because I think she will tell me off for this complaint.' (fortune-telling)

'I feel really nervous about the meeting and I fear that I shall shake and not be able to remember all the things I want to say to her.' (emotional reasoning)

'I'll never get a pay rise now.' (overgeneralisation)

C = Sally was anxious and stressed. These feelings affected her ability to concentrate and present herself confidently.

D = Disputing whether her thinking was:

Rational? Was there a law to say that she had to think this way? 'No.'

Empirical evidence? Would everyone think in this way about this situation? 'No – my colleague John would just shrug it off and tell the boss how brilliantly he had met his targets.'

Helpful? Was her thinking helping her to manage the meeting? 'No.'

Sally decided that her approach needed to change.

E = Sally exchanged her old thoughts for new constructive thoughts:

'Everyone makes mistakes from time to time.'

'Although this one client has complained, all my other clients are happy with my performance.'

Sally then used the ABC process to plan how she would manage the meeting:

A = 'My goal is a successful meeting where I put my points across and receive positive feedback.'

B = Useful thoughts to support assertive behaviours:

'I can explain the circumstances of the situation to demonstrate why I took the approach I did.'

'I have achieved the majority of my targets and excelled in other areas.'

'I can listen to what my boss says and put my point of view.'

C = The emotional consequence of having these thoughts is:

'I can stay calm and confident even if the meeting does not go perfectly.'

Identifying Choices and Options

Losing perspective results in a narrow and limited viewpoint – rather like wearing blinkers. Lack of perspective limits the available choices. By helping your client see the context of his approach to situations, you open up many new avenues. Old patterns of thought and emotional response can hold back your client from taking new steps in his life. Your client benefits from analysing whether his perspective truly reflects his own viewpoint or whether he uses an adopted approach based on, perhaps, parental influence, a teacher's comment, or a cultural norm.

For example, I have met several people who were told by a teacher at an early age 'You can't sing' and have never sung again, even though they'd love to have a go. Through CBC, you can help your client understand that the comment 'You can't sing' represents just one person's opinion at a particular time in the client's life. Just because one person says that you can't sing, does not make it the truth or the only way of approaching the situation.

When your client sees that his approach has no basis in the evidence available today, he may open his mind to more possibilities and see that, logically, nothing can stop him from singing.

As a CB coach, you provide the framework for your client to open new doors of thought and action, thus expanding the choices and options available to him.

Evaluating what drives you

As I mentioned in 'Reviewing thoughts and expectations: Yours or your parents'?', many people act upon unconscious needs that drive their behaviour. When your client describes his reactions and approaches to situations, you can help him understand what propelled him to make some of his decisions. Common drivers are:

- ✔ **Ambition:** The need for success in whatever way you perceive success

- ✔ **Competition:** An inability to share success with others

- ✔ **(Need for) control:** Perhaps because you once trusted someone who proved untrustworthy and unconsciously decided to take control for yourself

- ✔ **Fear of failure:** Perhaps because you failed once, or because your parents were unforgiving of failure

- ✔ **(Need for) harmony and approval:** Making decisions based on a fear of conflict, disapproval, and the desire to keep things harmonious

- ✔ **Jealousy:** This feeling could go back to sibling rivalry or a recent experience where you hated someone else to do well or be rewarded

- ✔ **Perfectionism:** The need to get everything perfect, generally from a perception that you must get everything right, not realising that this need is optional behaviour rather than a factor of personality or a life requirement (refer to Chapter 1)

> ✓ **(Need to) prove oneself:** The need to show someone your worth
>
> ✓ **(Need for) security:** Financial security, job security; the need for things to be certain and sure
>
> ✓ **(Need for) variety and stimulation:** Constantly taking risks and changing your life around in order to avoid low frustration tolerance

You can help your client understand what has been driving him, by exploring the major decisions he has made in his life and investigating the thoughts, beliefs and expectations of himself, others, and the situations he has experienced. You often find that the major decisions in your client's life have been based on specific drivers.

As your client identifies his drivers, he can analyse whether these drivers help him and are relevant to his life today. If the drivers are not relevant, your client can develop alternative ways of approaching situations and goals. In your coaching sessions, you can broaden your client's viewpoint and open up new perspectives by asking questions such as:

> ✓ If you couldn't fail, how else might you think about this situation?
>
> ✓ If money wasn't an issue, what choices would you have?
>
> ✓ If security wasn't a requirement, what else could you do?
>
> ✓ If you weren't competitive, how many different options can you see in this situation?
>
> ✓ If you didn't need approval, what could you do differently?
>
> ✓ What could you discover from your colleagues' success instead of being jealous of them?

You may find that your client is amazed by how he has driven himself or limited his options in the past as a result of his unconscious automatic thoughts and drives. Enabling your client to move from an unconscious need towards a conscious decision can be one of the most liberating ways you can help him take control and move forward towards his goals. As you help your client review thinking errors and see clearly, he can come to understand that he has many more options and choices than he ever thought before.

Updating your viewpoint and discovering new choices

Realising that he has many more avenues open to him than he had previously considered can be quite overwhelming for your client. You need to be compassionate and understanding if your client feels frustrated that he had not seen these new choices before. Try to focus on the benefit of exploring the options your client has now, so that he can make good decisions in future.

Once you've explored many options, you naturally have to help your client narrow down his choices and move forward with a strategy and plan of action to achieve his goals. A *cost–benefit analysis,* which is a model developed by David Burns in *The Feeling Good Handbook* (see Table 2-3 for an example), is an effective method to examine the pros and cons of a situation. By exploring positives and negatives, your client accrues more structured information with which to make his decision.

You can use cost–benefit analysis to reflect upon the pros and cons of a variety of situations:

- ✔ Actions
- ✔ Behaviours
- ✔ Emotions
- ✔ Impact on others
- ✔ Plans

Table 2-3	Cost–benefit analysis
Cost	*Benefit*
It is more expensive to move	There will be more space in new building
Lots of organisation required	More room for files and resources with large storeroom in new building
No room for new staff currently	Plenty of room for new staff in new office space
Familiarity with location and local resources in old office	More central to the railway and shopping in new location
Cosy and friendly in old office	More professional in new building
I feel nervous about the risk of moving	I feel excited about being able to expand my business

Allow your client time to consider his options so that he can review the benefits of no action against the costs of change. You can explore each aspect of cost and benefit so that your client records and then unpicks his thoughts and feelings about each cost and benefit to discover the new choices that he has available.

You and your client may find that using a scoring system is helpful. For example, you may give –15 points for feeling nervous, +30 points for feeling excited, –60 points for too busy with moving to focus on clients, and +65 points for looking more professional. Analysing the costs and benefits leads your client to decisions as to how he will manage the situation, for example by delegating tasks and weighing short-term costs against long-term gains.

Andrei

Andrei was at a crossroads in his career. He had come to London for a short-term contract and was trying to decide whether to stay with his current employer or move back to Russia. When he explored the major decisions he had taken in his life up to that point, he realised that he had been driven by low boredom threshold. He could see that he had jumped from one job to the next, from one potential entrepreneurial idea to the next, because he was fearful of getting bored. He had recently married, and his wife was expecting their first child, so he needed to review whether this behaviour was helping him make a good career choice.

In his coaching sessions, he became aware that his decisions had been driven by this need for constant change. As he acknowledged this need, he also came to see that he was free to make conscious choices that were not necessarily driven by low boredom threshold. He could choose to manage his decisions in a different way. This decision management gave him a greater sense of control.

Eventually, he came to a balance – a long-term contract within a London consultancy firm that allowed him to have variety in the area of projects and clients.

Providing your client with new vistas is like taking him from the basement car park, where he just sees concrete walls around him, up to the roof terrace, where he sees a whole new panorama. Your client appreciates that his own mind built those concrete walls and that he has the power to change his thoughts, break through old perspectives, and develop new ways of thinking. It can be an exciting moment.

Chapter 3

Agreeing the Aims and Scope of CBC

In This Chapter

▶ Understanding what CBC is and isn't

▶ Setting up a coaching programme

▶ Understanding how the client feels

▶ Establishing boundaries and referrals

▶ Preparing for the first session

Different people have different ideas about what CBC is. You need to be as clear as you can about what you offer your clients. CB coaches apply their techniques in many different situations. You can adapt the techniques that I describe in this book to meet the diverse demands of a variety of clients. Many CB coaches specialise in a specific area such as *life coaching*, which focuses on a client's personal life, *executive coaching*, which focuses on a client's profession, or *performance coaching*, which seeks specifically to improve a client's competencies to increase performance in a particular area. You need to decide whether to specialise in one aspect of coaching or whether you want to cover a range of general coaching programmes. Before you start to work with a client, you need to outline what she can expect, agree on how you plan to work together, and explain how you can apply CBC to meet her needs and goals.

In this chapter, I consider some of the questions that your client may ask at the outset of her coaching programme. I also offer practical tips to help you and your client agree the scope and terms and conditions of coaching.

Every client-coaching programme is unique. The principles included in this chapter are general, so you need to adapt them to the specific circumstances in which you're operating. Planning and preparation of administrative practicalities in advance pays dividends in helping you concentrate fully on your client's needs during the coaching session itself.

Defining CBC

Your client may or may not have heard of CBC before, so make sure that you take time at the outset to explain how CBC works. CBC is a relatively new term for a form of coaching that has existed for a couple of decades. You can read more detailed information about how CBC evolved from cognitive behavioural therapy in Chapter 1.

Seeing what CBC is

CBC is a time-limited, goal-focused, problem-solving approach to achieving your client's objectives. Your client may ask how CBC differs from therapy or counselling. To answer this question, explain that the focus of CBC is forward-looking and explores your client's past history only where that history is directly relevant to your client's objectives. CBC is client-led, which means that your client is in charge of the agenda and what you discuss in coaching sessions.

You provide the process to help your client move forward in herself, her life, and her work. You work on the assumption that your client has the answers to her own problems – you ask questions aimed at revealing these solutions. You do not provide your client with advice.

You and your client work as an alliance, developing a strategy of action to achieve her goals. As a CB coach, you provide your client with models to help her develop the necessary mental and emotional approach she needs to achieve her goals.

You're a catalyst for change – but your client may be uncomfortable with change. Prepare your client by explaining that your role is to challenge limiting beliefs or behaviours that may block her progress. Emphasise that when you challenge your client, you do so for her own benefit: you are on her side.

The specific focus on the client's thinking patterns and behaviours differentiates CBC from other forms of coaching. The underlying principle of CBC is that the client's *views* of situations and goals, rather than the situations themselves, are key. As a CB coach, you ask permission to explore how your clients' everyday thoughts impact on their behaviours and endeavours. You then work with your client to develop thoughts and behaviours to manage more effectively the everyday ups and downs of life and work.

Definitions of coaching

It is good to compare some different definitions of coaching. My own definition is:

'CBC is an alliance of cooperation between client and coach. The coach supports the client in developing and achieving the specific goals and objectives identified by the client at the outset. The focus in CBC is developing constructive thoughts and behaviours to support action towards the identified goals.'

Other definitions talk of facilitating performance, assisting clients determine and achieve their goals, or facilitating the enhancement of work performance.

You may want to create your own definition of CBC in a way that specifically describes your personal CBC approach.

This example illustrates the importance of personal viewpoints and perspectives. Rashid and Marie work for the same bank. During a restructure, they're both made redundant. Rashid is delighted at being made redundant and thinks 'This is a great opportunity for me to review my career and possibly think about doing something different.' He doesn't take the event personally and doesn't lose confidence or self-esteem. Meanwhile Marie is devastated and thinks 'What's wrong with me? This is a disaster. I'm obviously no good and no other employer will want me now.' She takes the redundancy personally and feels crushed. Same situation – different response.

As a CB coach you facilitate change by enabling your client to address her perspective of the specific situation she faces. You provide models and methods to help your client develop thoughts, emotions, and behaviours that support her in reaching her goals.

Your client needs to realise that she is going to be doing most of the hard work, and that the real change happens outside the coaching room. CBC is self-directed. At the end of a session, you set tasks for your client to try at home. These tasks allow your client to practise and integrate new ways of approaching situations between sessions. You then review her progress together in the next session.

Realising what CBC isn't

Your client needs to understand the differences between CBC and other forms of coaching and therapy. Some clients believe that your job is to correct or fix a problem or disorder rather than develop their ability to achieve their specified goals. By explaining the differences between CBC and other coaching and therapies, you avoid any confusion in what your client may expect from you.

CBC differs from all the following:

- ✓ **Behaviourism:** An approach to psychology that emphasises observable, measurable behaviours.
- ✓ **Consultancy:** Bringing knowledge, processes, and systems to an organisation that lacks the time, resources, or expertise to carry out the function itself. Consultants act as advisors.
- ✓ **Counselling:** Exploring a difficulty the client is having, distress she may be experiencing, or perhaps her dissatisfaction with life or loss of a sense of direction and purpose.
- ✓ **Mentoring:** When someone shares her own experience in a specific business or field with those who have less experience. Mentoring includes sharing personal stories of what worked and didn't work, talking over pitfalls and successes, discussing development, and giving advice.
- ✓ **Neuro-linguistic programming (NLP):** Study of human excellence based on neuro (the mind) linguistic (language) programming (habitual patterns of behaviour). NLP seeks to transform habits into models of successful behaviour.
- ✓ **Positive thinking:** Focused on developing positive thoughts about everything, even if they're not based in reality.
- ✓ **Psychiatry:** Concerned with diagnosing mental illness and prescribing drugs to treat it.
- ✓ **Psychoanalysis:** A form of psychotherapy, originally developed by Sigmund Freud, that is intended to help patients become aware of long-repressed feelings and issues by using such techniques as free association and the interpretation of dreams. The process usually involves frequent sessions over a long period.
- ✓ **Psychotherapy:** A set of techniques used to treat mental health and emotional problems and some psychiatric disorders.

As coaches, we are not here to knock other fields. Each of the approaches that I mention in the list above is useful in the right context. We deal with unique individuals on a daily basis, and no one-size-fits-all solution exists.

Identifying Aims, Objectives, and Benefits

Before you start coaching a new client, an initial meeting with the client gives you the opportunity to explain your approach, identify your client's objectives, and agree the way you want to work together.

At this meeting, you and your client can ensure that you have a 'fit'. This fit signifies a compatibility to work together towards an agreed and common aim. It does not mean that you and your client have to be alike or be best buddies, but you do both need to feel that you can collaborate in the joint venture of achieving your client's goals.

The meeting is an opportunity to:

✔ Eye one another up

✔ Develop rapport

✔ Explain the remit and theoretical background to CBC

✔ Check whether you're able to provide the relevant approach for your client's needs

✔ Ensure that you feel comfortable enough with one another to work together

✔ Agree the general scope of the coaching programme

✔ Agree objectives, expectations, and likely timescale

✔ Explain and agree the client's commitment to completing tasks between sessions

✔ Agree venue, fees, and frequency and length of sessions

✔ Sign an agreement about how you will work together (see the section 'Analysing aims and scope')

✔ Arrange the next meeting

Mutual understanding at this early stage is important and helps to build trust between you and your client. Your client probably wants reassurance that you're qualified to work with her, so be prepared to share information about the following things:

✔ Your professional training

✔ Your qualifications

✔ Your membership of professional bodies

✔ Any arrangements that you have to be supervised and supported by a qualified coach

✔ Your code of values, ethics, and practice

✔ Your previous coaching and related experience and references

Considering confidentiality

Make sure that you are clear on the boundaries of confidentiality. Generally, whatever happens within a coaching session is totally confidential between coach and client.

If you work within an organisation, the HR department or senior manager may agree with the client that certain themes and progress may be shared. This sharing should always be agreed in a three-way meeting so that everyone understands the scope of the arrangement.

If you're a manager coaching a member of staff, clarifying the remit of topics and confidentiality is particularly important. You need to gain your client's trust by being specific that topics discussed in coaching sessions go no further than the meeting room. You also need to reassure your client with regard to how her coaching development may or may not impact on her appraisal and performance review.

Coaching and confidentiality

ABC Ltd set up a coaching programme for its senior management. Several coaches from one coaching organisation were involved. The coaches, the prospective coaching clients, and the HR representative held a meeting. The HR representative shared the organisation's objectives to develop a coaching culture within senior management. The coaching programme was designed both to develop each manager personally and professionally and to introduce managers to the principles and methods of coaching so that they could start to coach their direct reports. It was agreed that all personal information would be kept private, but that the coaches would share and discuss general themes that came out of the sessions to support HR in developing a coaching culture.

Analysing aims and scope

CBC functions within boundaries of agreed objectives, but the specific aims of each coaching programme differ from client to client. You may work with any of the following:

- An individual in a life-coaching situation
- An individual who wants coaching regarding her career performance and direction
- An organisation that has specific members of staff who it has identified would benefit from executive or leadership coaching
- A team that has identified a need to enhance teamworking and performance

Your clients may be individuals seeking personal coaching or may come from within an organisation. A client could be a chairperson or a newly recruited graduate. As a CB coach, you need to recognise your own professional offering and decide whether you feel competent to work at all levels of an organisation or whether your own expertise and experience is more suited to a specific area or type of client.

In your initial meeting, you work towards signing a contract together, outlining the following:

- **Scope of the sessions:** What are your client's specific goals? By narrowing down these goals, you ensure that neither of you takes on more than you can chew. Ask your client which goal is the most important to her, and start with that one.
- **Topics your client wishes to investigate:** Within the goals, there may be specific issues that your client wants to address, such as assertiveness or stress management – though be prepared for these topics to broaden during the coaching process.
- **Timescale:** When does your client want to achieve her goal? How much time does she have available for coaching sessions?
- **Budget:** Be clear about your fees, so that you tailor the coaching programme to fit your client's budget.

Working within an organisation presents additional specific issues. The coaching programme may well have been suggested by any one of the following people within the business:

- A representative from the HR department
- The managing director

> ✔ A line manager
>
> ✔ The individual herself who has been allocated a specific budget

If an organisation is funding the coaching programme, it will probably have certain expectations of how the programme benefits both the organisation and the individual. Therefore, in your set-up meeting with the organisation, you need to clarify expectations about the objectives of the individual and the organisation, measurement, confidentiality, and review.

Bashing out the benefits of coaching

You may use part of your initial meeting to identify the benefits your client is likely to receive as a result of the coaching sessions. Think of this part of the session as the 'What's in it for me?' factor. Identifying the benefits of CBC helps your client understand the purpose of coaching and engages her motivation and cooperation.

Consider some of the following benefits:

- ✔ **A sounding board** – you listen to them

- ✔ **An objective viewpoint** – you've no agenda and can give an objective view

- ✔ **Non-directive** – you're not there to advise them, just to provide a process for their development

- ✔ **Non-judgemental and safe environment for discussion** – you're not there to judge them, so you provide a safe environment to talk about their problems and goals

- ✔ **Professional expertise and support** – you offer professional expertise in supporting them to achieve their goals

- ✔ **Willing and supporting their success** – you're there to support them through change

- ✔ **Catalyst for change** – you provide a process for change

- ✔ **Challenging limiting beliefs, norms and habits** – you point out where they may be having negative thoughts or limiting behaviours

- ✔ **Providing models, questions and processes to help you achieve your goals** – you provide the CBC methodology and framework for their development

- ✔ **New ways of thinking and behaving** – you suggest thinking models that change the way they approach situations

- ✔ **Relevant case stories of success** – you've worked with other clients and can share observations of what works and what doesn't work

Measuring outcomes

At the start of the programme, you agree measurable outcomes with your client so that you can both evaluate whether you achieve her objectives. You and your client take mutual responsibility for reaching the agreed goals, but your client does much of the work outside the coaching sessions.

If you work within an organisation, you may need to use a formal measurement process such as a *360-degree feedback assessment* before and after the programme. The 360 is a commonly used form of appraisal in which the individual receives feedback from all those with whom she works or interacts, including subordinates, supervisors, colleagues, peers, and sometimes also internal or external customers., You may, alternatively, choose to seek informal feedback from your client's boss and colleagues before and after the coaching programme, or you may suggest that your client completes tailored questionnaires that measure her confidence, performance, and competence on specified issues before and after the programme.

Introduce a discussion about timescale. By what date does your client expect to see results? Are there identifiable step-changes that represent milestones of progress towards her goals? At what stages of the coaching programme do you and your client want to stop and review progress and give feedback?

Making goals specific, timely, and measurable enables you, your client, and your client's organisation (where applicable) to track change and build on successes.

Consider a client who would like the courage to give her direct report feedback. An example of a non-specific goal is 'improving communication with my direct report'. An example of a specific, timed goal is 'Giving constructive feedback to my direct report that she needs to improve her IT skills. I shall do this at our next appraisal meeting on 10 August.'

Talking about terms and conditions

Before you begin a CBC programme, you and your client need to agree on a few practicalities, which I list in the sections below.

Frequency and length of sessions

Agree how often you will work together and for what length of time in each session. Coaches vary in their approach, so you need to decide how you prefer to work and which approach best suits your client's needs and commitments. For instance, you need to decide between you whether you:

- ✔ Contract for an annual term
- ✔ Work on an hourly or two-hourly basis

✔ Sign up for a coaching programme of three to six sessions with a review mid-term

✔ Sign up for a 12-session programme

✔ Meet face to face

✔ Work via phone and email

✔ See one another once a week, once a fortnight, once a month, or on an ad-hoc basis

You may also agree a combination of these. What is important is that you're both clear as to what works best for you within the context of your client's lifestyle and goals.

Venue and fees

Consider where to hold your coaching sessions: on your client's site, in your own offices, or at a hotel or conference centre? If the latter, who is to pay?

Charges need to be discussed and negotiated. Coaches charge a variety of fees, depending on the type of coaching. For example, coaches charge different scales depending on whether the coaching is corporate or individual, private or public sector, and depending on geographical location. Professional coaching bodies (I list a few at the back of this book) can offer helpful advice on charging. You need to decide whether you're going to charge:

✔ An all-inclusive fee for a certain number of sessions

✔ An hourly rate as and when the sessions occur

✔ A fee that includes email and phone access – if so, how much and how many

✔ VAT: charging VAT is normal within the business arena and a requirement if you're VAT registered, but obviously adds a considerable amount for an individual client who is paying for CBC herself

✔ Travel expenses, costs, and charges for materials or venue hire

You also need to decide:

✔ Do you expect payment within 30 days? Do you charge for a cancellation less than 48 hours beforehand? Do you charge for postponement of a session?

✔ Admin – who issues the invoices and how are they to be paid?

When you've agreed all the above practicalities, you are ready to sign a contract with your client or your client's organisation, detailing the specific arrangements and terms that you've agreed. In Figure 3-1, I show an example of a coaching agreement.

SAMPLE COACHING AGREEMENT:

Coach Name: *Sue Jones*

Client Name:.........*Joe Brown*..............................Address...*London*............................

Tel: Home:...........................Work............................Mobile...........................email............................

Name of assistant to contact: *Sue*...........................Date of birth...........................

Main Objectives for Coaching:

1. *To communicate more assertively with senior managers*

2. *To be less stressed and manage my work-life balance more effectively*............................

Agreed Measurement of Success: by the end of the Coaching Programme:

To have shared my ideas and solutions more frequently at senior management meetings

To be feeling more relaxed and to have gone to the gym in my lunchtimes at lease twice a week...

Terms: Coaching is an 'alliance' of cooperation between client and coach. The coach supports the client in developing the specific goals and objectives identified by the client at the outset. All recommendations made in any form are made in good faith and on the information available at the time.

Number of Sessions Agreed: 6 x 2 hour sessions at a fee of £750.00 plus VAT, inclusive of travel and materials

Feedback and Review: Review with line manager after Session 3 and at the end of the programme

Payment is due upon completion of a coaching session or as per proposal agreement. Cheques should be made payable to 'A Coach Ltd.'. A cancellation fee is due if a session is cancelled less than 48 hours in advance of an appointment.

Sue Jones of A Coach Ltd follows the best professional practice in protecting the confidentiality of client information.

I understand and accept these terms

Client.................................... Coach.................................... Date:...................

Figure 3-1: Sample coaching agreement.

Home tasks and rewards

As well as the practicalities of terms and conditions of your coaching agreement, you can discuss the behavioural aspects of the coaching programme so that you agree expectations of one another.

One feature of your agreement is home tasks – tasks to be completed between sessions. These are an integral feature of CBC. Give your client tasks to work on at home or in the workplace, because home tasks are key to integrating change into her life and work situations. At the end of each coaching session, agree the format of the tasks and then choose tasks most relevant to the client's goals.

Here are examples of tasks to give your client to practise at home:

- Addressing a relationship issue
- Managing time and prioritisation more effectively
- Being assertive in a specific context
- Keeping a record of negative or faulty thinking patterns
- Maintaining a journal tracking emotional experiences
- Lifestyle changes such as nutrition and exercise
- Reading a relevant book or listening to a CD or DVD
- Making wise choices, for example in management of emails
- Attempting a task that previously caused anxiety

Identifiable home objectives give you and your client discussion and development points for each session. Home tasks also give you the opportunity to introduce your client to the concept of rewarding herself not only for good results but also for having a go at change – even if the efforts do not achieve precisely the result she seeks.

Reward is a powerful motivator and a key tool, because it encourages your client to stop and reflect on what does and doesn't work. In today's fast-paced world, many people move straight from one project or goal to the next without taking breathing space for reward, refreshment, or reflection – they may then make exactly the same mistakes over and over again.

For a reward system to work for your client, the reward must be meaningful to her. Everyone is different, and what motivates one client may not motivate another. Here are examples of rewards that your client may find useful:

- Taking time out
- Going to the gym or swimming pool
- Meeting a friend for a long lunch
- Going to the pub at the end of the day
- Buying a specific, significant item
- Praising herself
- Leaving work early

If you work within an organisation, you can discuss with the sponsor how the organisation can support your client in her change. Praise and recognition from a boss or colleague identifies noticeable improvements and encourages the individual to persevere, even when the tasks are difficult.

Julie's reward

Julie had been working extremely hard on a year-end project. It had involved her working 12- to 14-hour days for over a month in order to file accounting records for the auditors. Her coaching sessions had helped her to manage her stress and make sure that she took time each day to exercise. When she filed the accounts with the auditors, she promised herself a day off and an aromatherapy massage to reward herself.

Your aim is to build a continuous journey together for the period of the CBC programme. Your client is responsible for taking action towards her own objectives, and you're responsible for your professional conduct and providing the CBC process. You may also agree to provide a written record of key points raised in the coaching session.

Changing behaviour can be really difficult. The brain is designed to build habits of thought and behaviour. For example, the first time you do something, you may feel awkward and difficult. When you first use a new computer or piece of software, you may stumble about looking for the correct keys and functions. Over time, when you use the computer or program, your fingers find their way around without you really thinking about it at all. Your client goes through a similar process during the coaching programme.

Developing new ways of thinking and behaving is like acquiring a new language, and takes hard work and practice. Agreeing practicalities, scope, and expectations of one another at the outset enables you to focus your energy on supporting your client through this change.

Knowing Your Limits

In your coaching sessions, you may occasionally identify an issue beyond your own experience or expertise. Knowing your own limits and not feeling that you show a weakness if refer your client on to another coach or therapist is an essential part of CBC. Be willing to accept when your approach is no longer appropriate. Have a list of names and numbers of other coaches, therapists, counsellors, and psychiatrists to offer your client, as well as written information to help your client understand her options. This preparation enables you to manage your client's needs as seamlessly as possible. I give contact details for some of the relevant professional bodies at the end of this book.

Checking the boundaries: When to refer on

If you feel that your client requires more specialist help or therapy, you must be clear about your own boundaries. Whatever your own agenda, the client always comes first. I have known cases where a coach has gone beyond her remit and promised more than she can deliver. This false promise can be damaging for the client who expects to be cured of a problem and then isn't. The experience is not great for the client's wallet either.

Always be clear about what you can and can't offer.

Some clients may need a different approach, such as psychotherapy, but not wish to be seen to need it. The process of coaching can occasionally reveal an issue that the client has not recognised previously. This can enable her to face up to specific psychological or emotional distress and decide to take remedial action.

If you realise early on that your client has specific needs or problems that you can't address, raise the issue straight away and see what your client says. Here are a few situations where this problem may occur:

- ✔ The client expects you to have senior management or specific sector experience.
- ✔ You have a personality mismatch.
- ✔ You feel unable to provide the style of coaching that your client requires.
- ✔ You sense that the client has deeper emotional or psychological problems.
- ✔ The client demonstrates a specific condition that you do not feel qualified to manage such as Asperger's syndrome, which is a mild form of autism resulting in limited empathy, or obsessive compulsive disorder, which is characterised by excessive orderliness and rules.
- ✔ The client mentions a recurring behavioural pattern that you feel unable to address, such as a pattern of abusive relationships.
- ✔ You sense that the client may be experiencing depression or burnout, for example, where the client presents with exhaustion, a sense of hopelessness and fatigue, or frequently bursts into tears.

If you feel out of your depth or that your client requires specific attention, you must address the situation carefully and sensitively. You may refer your client to another coach who has more relevant business-specific experience or simply more coaching experience than you. Don't give the impression that you're brushing the client off. Explain your reasons carefully – and remember that coaching is a collaborative process. For example, you may say: 'I sense that there are some issues here that I may not be qualified to deal with. How would you feel if I were to give you the name of someone who is qualified and may help you better in this field?'

You can also discuss the situation at your supervision session, because coaching supervision provides a professional support system through which you can get advice and tips on how to manage this type of situation if it arises. See Chapter 4 for more information on supervision.

Trying CBC yourself

One way of understanding your limits is to have CBC sessions and be the client for a change. If you've not yet undertaken some form of training or coaching, I suggest you do so. In this book, I offer you valuable information and techniques, but experiencing coaching for yourself is the best way to understand the benefit of it.

It is advisable to receive formal training before working with clients. This provides you with several benefits:

- Immersion in the fundamental theories and principles of CBC

- Practise in the CBC process

- Experience of the hurdles and rewards of coaching

- Training and feedback on your progress

- Clarification of the boundaries between counselling, coaching, education, and directive advice, so that you can recognise where you are on the spectrum

- Practise in the language of CBC and applying it in role-play or real-time situations

You also find many benefits to being coached yourself:

- You understand what it feels like to be the client.

- You experience the language of CBC and review your own thinking errors.

- You experience the demands of doing home tasks between sessions, and the self-discipline this activity requires on the part of the client.

- You become more self-aware and empowered through being a part of the development process.

'Walking your talk' is a key aspect of building your clients' trust. The more you practise CBC yourself by observing your own thinking patterns and applying the models yourself, as well as with clients, the more integrity and authority you convey to your clients.

Salma

Salma had been promoted to a management post. She was the main breadwinner in her family. Just after her promotion, her 7-year-old daughter was diagnosed with leukaemia and was in and out of hospital. Although her husband managed their home and children, Salma was inevitably distressed by the situation. She wanted to be at home with her daughter, but was pulled in both directions because she felt she needed to show appreciation for her new role and demonstrate her capability as a manager. Her organisation was going through a period of change, and her team were demotivated. Her HR department arranged for her to have coaching, and her coach was working with her to align the team and develop a strategy to achieve targets in the following financial year.

Salma became exhausted from juggling so many pressures, but felt guilty that she was letting everyone down and not really doing any task or role properly. She would burst into tears in meetings and realised that she had come to the end of her tether. She mentioned this to her coach, who arranged a meeting with her and the HR representative. It was agreed that Salma needed time out and also that she would be referred on to a specialist stress counsellor to help her through this difficult period of her life. The coach was able to refer her on to a coach specifically qualified in stress and burnout.

Preparing for CBC Sessions

Before holding a coaching session, prepare yourself, the venue, and any resources such as handouts that demonstrate CBC models and theory. Having a clear mind for the session is important, so make sure that you've thought of as much as possible before the client arrives.

Considering the basics

For starters, consider the following points before each session:

- The client's history, needs, and goals
- Information on the client's work sector
- Likely processes, models, questions, and exercises for the session
- Relevant case studies
- Paper and pens

Being prepared frees you up to focus on your client's issues and needs without worrying about practicalities. Importantly, however, although you may identify a likely process, relevant questions, or exercises to introduce during the session, don't get bogged down in feeling that you have to stick to them. Being flexible and adapting to what your client brings up during the session are important aspects of CBC.

Allow yourself time before the session to prepare mentally and emotionally. A few minutes' quiet time before the session allow you to gather your thoughts and energy and let go of any worries or preoccupations. For this reason, I recommend leaving 30 minutes or so between one client's session and the next.

Getting the venue ready

Where possible, provide a venue that is comfortable, welcoming, and confidential. As CBC includes written exercises and discussion of specific models, a table and chairs are useful so that you can discuss exercises, review your client's journals and tasks, and show the client illustrations and diagrams to help her understand relevant concepts and theory.

Here are a few things you may want to consider in setting up the CBC environment:

- ✔ You may want to have your professional certificates on view to demonstrate your qualifications.

- ✔ Plants and natural daylight help maintain energy.

- ✔ When you're coaching an individual within her organisational environment, confidentiality and privacy are essential ingredients to the building up of trust. Finding a room on a different floor from your client's desk can help – also making sure that the room does not have a glass door or partition through which you can be seen by colleagues.

- ✔ Prepare the contract, questionnaires, handouts, and exercises in advance. It can be useful to have books on hand because these provide excellent back-up to integrate progress, as do related CDs and DVDs. You can also find excellent journals and articles that cover a range of relevant topics. These resources are sometimes referred to as bibliocoaching.

- ✔ Consider your own image – the clothes you wear make a difference. If you're going into a professional environment, your appearance is important to your impression of gravitas and authority. In other circumstances, you may wish to dress more like the client in order to make her feel at ease. Each situation is different, so give it thought up front.

Setting up support systems and resources

Clarify with your client how much support she can expect from you between sessions. Are you willing to be available to her for emails and phone calls, and, if so, on what basis? Agree expectations with regard to access so that you have no misunderstandings.

Anne's first coaching session

Anne recently qualified as a CB coach and decided to run coaching sessions from her home. She had two toddlers, so she arranged for her mother to come to look after them in the kitchen while she saw her clients in the sitting room. However, she found this situation disturbing both for herself and her client. She could not help wondering whether her children were happy, and she realised that her client was distracted by her children's voices and the sound of them playing. In future sessions, she asked her mother to look after the children in her own home, and later took steps to find a room in a conference centre, where she runs her coaching sessions in more peaceful surroundings.

Consider how to manage your administrative backup. How will you provide:

- ✔ A telephone answering system or voicemail
- ✔ Email
- ✔ Website information
- ✔ Administrative, PA, or secretarial resources
- ✔ Invoicing and accounting records
- ✔ VAT and tax records for your own business

Have back-up in case you're sick or on holiday. A coach needs rest and relaxation – so try to work out how to achieve time out as well as take care of your clients' needs.

Arranging supervision is important both to your wellbeing and your professionalism. Talking to another person provides space for you to discuss your clients' cases in confidentiality, either with a trained supervisor or you can make an arrangement with a peer to provide supervision to one another.

As a coach, you put other people's needs before your own, so creating boundaries of access is important.

Many individual coaches set up virtual networks, which provide both emotional backup for the coach, and a practical coaching resource for the client so that she has a point of contact if the coach is away or busy. A network can also provide you with a source of helpful ideas and support, which can be invaluable.

Chapter 4

Assessing the Attributes of the CB Coach

In This Chapter

▶ Checking your own agenda as a CB coach

▶ Picking out personal qualities and attributes that help the coaching process

▶ Developing your own unique coaching style

*E*very coach, including you, is unique. The personal energy and philosophy you bring to coaching are essential ingredients in the success that occurs in the relationship between you and your client.

CBC is client-led. Your part as a coach is to provide the process and coaching skills to enable your client to achieve his goals. Certain competencies and attributes support this process. Self-knowledge is a fundamental aspect of being a good coach, enabling you to check when you may be stepping into the area of stating your own opinion rather than allowing your client to develop his own opinion. Self-knowledge also enables you to continuously self-reflect so as to develop, adapt, and build your skill.

In this chapter, I cover information designed to help you consider and develop your own personal approach to CBC. Although you work within a professional framework, fostering your unique style is also important, because this style is the added ingredient that develops a successful client–coach relationship.

Considering Starting Points

Certain specific competencies influence your ability as a CB coach. In this section, I divide these competencies into three main areas:

✔ **You as a coach:**

- Your own professional knowledge and behaviour

- Your ability to continually review, acquire, and develop your coaching skills

✔ **Your approach to your client:**

- Your positive regard for and empathy with your client

- Your ability to foster and facilitate your client's growth and personal responsibility

✔ **The way you manage the coach–client partnership:**

- Your ability to develop rapport and effective communication

- Your use of an equality-driven, non-judgemental approach that is consistent with legislation, regulation, and relevant professional frameworks

Beginning with you

Understanding yourself helps the process. Reviewing and evaluating your own thoughts, emotions, behaviours, and methods enables you to continually assess your own coaching style and identify further areas of personal and professional development. You also become aware of when your own needs may impact on those of your client. CBC focuses on your client's agenda, not your own.

Here are some key ways in which you can apply your own self-knowledge to enable you to become a better coach:

✔ **Be non-judgemental.** Be open to the fact that your client may well have different views to yourself. You're there to help your clients, not judge them.

✔ **Check your own emotional responses to topics raised.** Sometimes a client will raise an issue or situation that reminds you of a personal experience or memory or touches you emotionally in some way. Acknowledge this situation and, where possible, do not let it impact on your professional conduct. If it becomes a problem, talk to your supervisor or mentor, or raise it honestly with your client.

✔ **Define a set of personal values and ethics.** Ethical issues can come up during coaching programmes, possibly because of something your client tells you, or because you're pulled in two directions. Take time to consider how values and ethics may impact on your relationship with your client.

✔ **Distance your own agenda from your client's goals.** Inevitably, the success or length of a coaching programme has an impact on your life, reputation, and probably your pocket! Stand back from your own needs and make sure that your actions reflect the needs of your client.

✔ **Know your own communication style.** Are you a slow reflective communicator or a speedy extrovert? Are you someone who is happier with facts than feelings? Can you be a patient listener or do you prefer to do the talking? Analysing your own style allows you to reflect on how to build rapport with someone who is different to you.

✔ **Know why you're a coach.** Something pulled you into coaching. Was it because you want to help people, to make money, or because you find it intellectually stimulating? Whatever your purpose, you're likely to be at your best and most motivated when you remind yourself why coaching is important to you.

Knowing your own values, goals, and communication style enables you to be alert to any temptation to impose your own needs and views on your client.

Remembering codes of conduct

The various coaching organisations issue codes of professional ethics encompassing specific behaviours expected within the coaching relationship. These include the following behaviours:

✔ Being diversity-inclusive

✔ Not becoming sexually involved with your client

✔ Being clear about confidentiality

✔ Honouring agreements

✔ Not misleading the client or making false claims

✔ Referring the client on where appropriate

✔ Avoiding conflicts of interest

✔ Treating your client with dignity

Following such a code of conduct lies at the foundation of any good coaching relationship. By being clear about your behaviour and boundaries at the outset, you help to prevent any confusion or misunderstanding as your client progresses through his coaching programme.

Try writing out a personal philosophy that underlies your approach to coaching. This writing-out helps you to give shape to your thoughts, values, and beliefs about coaching. I give an example in Figure 4-1.

As a CB coach I provide a process by which my client can better achieve their personal goals and potential. Goals and discussion topics are always set by my client. I am trained to be non-judegemental and help my client to develop their own solutions. I don't give them advice as I believe they have the best answers to their own problems. I provide a process and a set of questions that are designed to help them access those answers.

I facilitate my client to make choices and decisions that may take them beyond what they would have decided or achieved on their own. The intention is always for my client's best interests and to achieve the goals identified by them.

Through my experience and expertise I seek to observe and share patterns and models of thoughts, human behaviour and communication whereby my client is better able to understand the part they play within any personal or work challenges they are experiencing. Through questions that may be sensitively challenging, I enable my client to see more options that might be available to them. I may share case studies, theories, metaphors and stories to illustrate a point and help my client to understand its relevance to their own situation.

Figure 4-1:
Sample
coaching
philosophy.

As a CB coach I aim to help my client break out of their limiting belief systems and develop new ways of thinking, feeling and behaving that support their ability to meet their goals. My aim is my client's aim and my approach is therefore client-driven.

Working through your prejudices

We all carry baggage – that is, prejudices, opinions, judgements, and beliefs – but the coaching environment is not the place to share your views on life or politics. The coaching relationship with your client needs to be non-judge-mental. That means the following sorts of thought are not appropriate within the CBC arena:

- What a boring person!
- He is never going to change.
- She's too old to go for that job.
- His ethnic background is an issue.
- How can she have chosen that jacket?
- How can he have said that?
- She obviously doesn't have the same political opinions as I do.

Being conscious of your own opinions, needs, and drives is an essential part of becoming a successful CB coach. None of us is perfect and inevitably we won't manage to be conscious of all these things all the time, but try to constantly review your own thoughts, feelings, and viewpoints in order to make sure that they don't get in the way of supporting your client's goals with objectivity.

Some of the thoughts that may alert you to the fact that you are focusing more on your own needs than that of your client are:

- ✔ I don't think this relationship is working, but I need the client's fees.
- ✔ I must be really good this session because I have to get a referral for my new client.
- ✔ I need to add up more coaching hours to get my accreditation.
- ✔ If this coaching programme doesn't work out, I may feel a failure.
- ✔ I need good feedback from this client.
- ✔ I don't feel comfortable talking about this subject.

By checking and evaluating your own thought patterns, you effectively develop an on-going process of coaching yourself. Try asking yourself the following questions:

- ✔ Is this agenda mine or his?
- ✔ Am I trying to make a point for my own reasons here or will it truly benefit the client?
- ✔ If I am feeling uncomfortable with what is happening, is it due to my own needs or is there a professional comment that may help my client?
- ✔ Is that thought appropriate?
- ✔ Is the comment or case study I want to share truly helpful, objective, and relevant?

By asking such questions, you become an objective analyst of your own perspectives and viewpoints, checking what is appropriate and developing the ability to be non-judgemental. The moment you have a thought, it immediately shows in a small way in your body language. Scary but true! The more open and neutral you are on the inside, the more this openness and neutrality shows in your eye movements, voice tone, and physiology. Believe in your client's success from the inside out. That means developing your own thoughts in such a way as to be confident in your client's potential to change and achieve his goals.

Considering how your client sees you

Think about your impact on your client. What impression may your client get when he first meets you? What kind of impression do you want him to have of you?

The considerations will depend upon the specific context and situation in which you're coaching. As a CB coach, you meet clients from many different walks of life and in different business sectors and environments. Flex your style in order to meet each client's needs and build a constructive working relationship. Sometimes you may want to make your client at ease, and you may choose to be informal; other times you may want to demonstrate your professionalism and be more formal. Take time to think about the following:

- Your personal and emotional energy
- Your communication style
- Whether you choose to be open, warm, and friendly or whether you need to be cooler and more formal
- The language that best builds understanding with your client, so as not to blind him with jargon or theory

Specific skills, qualities, and attributes enable you to build a successful relationship with your client. Reflect on your own competencies and keep honing your skills in the areas listed below:

- Ability to be assertive and manage boundaries of the agreement – checking the terms and practicalities
- Active listening skills – considering what your client is saying
- Commitment to your client's goals – always focusing on his objectives
- Continuous personal and professional growth and development – always finding out new things
- Creativity and a focus on solutions – finding lateral perspectives
- Empathy – understanding how your client may be feeling
- Enthusiasm and the ability to motivate – encouraging your client's progress
- Patience – the ability to flex to your client's pace
- Professionalism and integrity – knowing your boundaries
- Recognising where your client's thoughts and behaviours are limiting his achievement of goals – observing thinking errors or distorted perspectives

When you run a coaching programme, you're not only representing yourself and, where relevant, your company, but you also representing the coaching profession in general. Your own behaviour and approach therefore reflect on the reputation of the profession as a whole.

Sussing out supervision and support systems

You need support too. Coaching can be fulfilling but also demanding. Developing a support network helps you cope with the more draining aspects of CBC. You may consider some of the following ways to get support:

- ✔ A trained supervisor providing formal supervision: Someone who specialises in supporting a coach provides on-going feedback sessions to help the coach analyse and develop his approach

- ✔ Co-coaching networks: A group of coaches discuss coaching issues and share coaching tips and strategies

- ✔ Peer-group supervision: Team members provide and receive support and feedback

- ✔ Colleague support: A colleague helps with specific coaching issues

- ✔ A mentor: An experienced coach shares his strategies based on his own experience

Several professional coaching bodies now require CB coaches to have regular supervision. This supervision generally takes place after an agreed number of coaching hours have been built up. You can take supervision via individual face-to-face meetings or by telephone sessions. Alternatively, you may belong to a supervision group. Supervision generally takes place separate to the coaching session itself, although you may choose to ask the supervisor to sit in on a session if you would value his view and if your client is willing. The ratio of supervision to coaching varies from one in eight to one in 15 practice hours.

Finding a supervisor who is also a trained CB coach is preferable as he will more fully understand the implications of your approach and have had hands-on experience with clients. However, if this is not practical, a good supervisor with general coaching skills will be a good sounding board and support.

Supervision provides you with:

- ✔ An objective eye
- ✔ Professional back-up
- ✔ Analysis of your approach

✔ Focus on the client's needs and goals

✔ Suggestions and tips

✔ A process to review your own objectivity regarding the client's best interests

✔ A review of professional and ethical issues and standards

✔ A safe environment to discuss complex or difficult situations or problems

✔ Ongoing discovery and professional development

✔ Moral and emotional support

Supervision benefits both you and your client. It provides you with the opportunity to discuss your approach to coaching and gain insights and ideas as to how to provide the best service for your client.

You can find a supervisor through any professional coaching body – look at the list of websites in the Appendix. Contact the supervisor and find out how he works so that you can agree a method that suits you both.

Professional networks and membership of professional organisations also provide you with support and information. Keep up to date with the latest information on CBC when you can – continuous professional development is an integral part of being a CB coach. New books and research studies are available every day. You can make it both a responsibility and a pleasure to read up on leading-edge thinking and be able to keep yourself and your client informed and knowledgeable.

In Figure 4-2, I summarise some of the competencies that support you in becoming a successful CB coach.

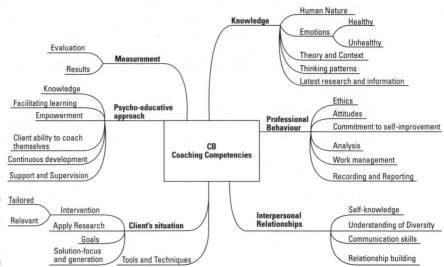

Figure 4-2: CBC competencies.

Realising that the Client Comes First

The whole coaching process is about putting your client first. You're a catalyst for your client's transformation – and being so can be enormously fulfilling. However, some days you may find focusing easy, but on other days focusing may be harder, perhaps when you don't feel well, you haven't had much sleep, or you've your own worries or preoccupations.

If you do not pay full attention to your client, your mind will wander off, and you may think about things that are nothing to do with your client, such as:

- ✔ I forgot to order bread from my online supermarket.
- ✔ I'm looking forward to going to the cinema tonight.
- ✔ I wonder if my new date will call today.
- ✔ Help, I forgot to send that email this morning.
- ✔ I wish I'd slept well.
- ✔ I can't wait to go on holiday on Friday.

You need to put the whole focus of your attention on your client. Developing this skill enables you to choose to concentrate in any other situation too. Knowing how to concentrate also allows you to transfer this skill to your client, helping him to be fully focused during the session and not worry about other things. I share tips on how to concentrate below.

Concentrating is a very sensory experience. You need to focus your mind on what you are:

- ✔ Seeing
- ✔ Hearing
- ✔ Feeling
- ✔ Touching
- ✔ Sensing

Concentrating means being right here, right now, in this room, with this particular individual, at this moment in time. You notice what room you're in, what chair you're sitting on, what table you're working at, which client you're with and what goals you are helping him to achieve.

If your attention wanders, you train your brain to come back into the room to focus on what the client is saying, what you see in his expression, what you can sense beneath the surface of what he says, what his emotional and physical state may be.

The demanding manager

Researchers from Tel Aviv University report that employees are three times more likely to perform well when their manager has high expectations of them. In other words, if you expect more, you get more. The group analysed results from 25 years of research, conducted in a variety of environments from banks and schools to summer camps and army barracks. In one study, the researchers divided bank managers into two groups: one was told that their employees were exceptional, while the other was told nothing of their employees' performance. They were then released back into their branches. The banks with the managers who were told to expect a lot from their employees were more profitable and successful. 'A self-fulfilling prophecy goes into effect' says Professor Dov Eden, who conducted the experiments. 'Managers and leaders would be well advised to expect a lot and let people know that they expect a lot. If your boss believes you can excel, you're more likely to believe in your own capacity to succeed.' This research can certainly be applied to the coach–client relationship.

The Times 3.5.2008 'Great Expectations' by Kate Wighton

Finding out how to truly put someone else first and be 100 per cent with him pays dividends. You will find that the quality of your relationships and your creativity is enhanced. By being totally present, your mind is unable to harbour distractions that may interrupt your ability to support your client's goals.

Seeing your client's potential

Your job is to support your client's ability to change and help him consider strategies to do so. This job means that you hope for his success and enable him to work out how to overcome his own doubts and blocks. Being someone who thinks that a leopard never changes his spots is not going to work! Believe in human potential.

Having positive expectations of your client will really help him to succeed. Research studies demonstrate the power of one person's expectations of another, as we explain in the sidebar 'The demanding manager'.

As Goethe said: 'The way you see people is the way you treat them. The way you treat them is what they become.'

When you treat your client *as if* he is capable of exactly what he wants to be capable of, you pass on that unconscious message to him – a message of belief that he can achieve what he wants to achieve.

You don't have to make false statements. Just maintain the philosophy that if one human being is capable of something, another human being can also be capable of that same thing. Show your client that persistence, time, and skill can help him to achieve his identified goals.

CBC is about rational perspectives. If someone who has never played the piano comes to a session and says that he wants to be a concert pianist by next year, you may well help him to look at that situation clearly and objectively in order that he makes decisions that are achievable.

The following process helps you to develop your client's potential:

1. **Identify his goals**

2. **Work out strategies to achieve those goals**

3. **Be motivated to change**

4. **Consider the journey from today to success**

5. **Identify blocks and supports that hinder or help him**

6. **Develop thinking patterns that motivate him to make appropriate behavioural change**

7. **Take actions and develop continually in order to achieve success**

8. **Take responsibility for his goals and actions**

9. **Review continuously so as to develop and adjust his approach**

Believing in your client's potential doesn't mean that he can necessarily achieve his goals without determination, persistence, and hard graft. Your client may fail a few or even many times. Try not to get frustrated or demotivated yourself. You're there to help your client check his methods and goals. He may, at some stage, decide that the goal is no longer relevant or appropriate – that's up to him. Your belief in your client's ability to make good decisions and move forward is key within this process.

The coaching process is dynamic and is an alliance between coach and client, so the pair of you develop continuously as different topics and events are raised during the sessions. You review and discover how best to help your client move forward. This process works best if you have belief in yourself and your own potential. What you discover and develop for yourself, you're better able to transmit to others. Knowing what it feels like to take yourself beyond your current position to achieve a set goal enables you to describe the experience in concrete terms to your client.

Stories and case studies of other clients who have developed their potential and achieved their goals in similar ways can also be motivational and provide clues and strategies for success. Build up a file of relevant examples.

Managing your ego needs

Sometimes you may feel tempted to show off your skills or knowledge during a coaching session. This temptation is something to assess carefully because, of course, times occur when sharing an aspect of your expertise is relevant and helpful. CBC incorporates a *psycho-educative* coaching approach, which means that you're ultimately enabling your client to become his own coach. You will therefore be sharing models and information with your client to provide practical help.

Make sure that you share information for your client's benefit and not just to demonstrate what an expert you are.

This advice goes for discussing your other coaching programmes too. For example, name-dropping of client companies needs to be handled sensitively. Your client may well want to know which other clients you work for in order to get an understanding of your experience within a certain field. You always need to check with your other clients whether mentioning their company names is acceptable, and get written permission. If such permission is not possible, try talking about the specific sector or sectors you're working within – for example: 'I have worked within legal, financial, investment banking, insurance, and health' gives a flavour of your experience without breaching any confidentiality rules.

Name-dropping of famous individual clients may be a breach of confidentiality. However, again, you may have a client's specific written permission to use his name and case history. This situation does happen from time to time when a celebrity with a specific issue is happy to have his story publicised in order to sponsor a charity or spread solutions to his particular problem for the benefit of others.

Another thing to watch out for is a temptation to drive a client through to a specific result so that you notch up some kind of personal achievement list. I have heard of coaches who boast of their coaching achievements as if they were medals of honour. The credit should really go to the client whose hard work and energy has actually been the reason for a target being reached.

We all have an ego. Within the coaching arena, it just needs to be kept in line. It is one thing to be clever and an expert in your CBC field, yet quite another to be wise and know when to share information – and when not to.

Developing Your Personal Coaching Style

You're a unique personality. Make sure that you feel comfortable with this fact because it provides a message to your client that he, also, is a unique personality. Although I give you information, tools, and techniques to apply during coaching sessions throughout this book, you must decide exactly how and why you apply these tools and techniques, and in what order or circumstances.

Try to trust your own judgement and to go with the flow of your client's needs. This self-trust tends to build with experience. You may, when you first start, get hung up on process and tools rather than trusting that you will choose the right model and the right question for the moment.

You're not there to push the force of your personality onto your client, but inevitably you bring yourself to the party – so the happier you are in yourself, the better. Notice doubtful thoughts such as the following:

- ✔ Should I use the ABC here?
- ✔ Do I look as if I know what I am doing?
- ✔ I'm not sure that she is taking me seriously.
- ✔ I don't think he is convinced by what I just said.

These kinds of thoughts can undermine your confidence and style. Work on your own negative thinking patterns and relax. This relaxation allows you to be more fully focused on your client and to bring the essence of who you are to the session without being overbearing or expressing personal opinions or advice.

Being in flow

Psychologist Mihaly Csikszentmihalyi developed a theory called *flow*. Flow is when you're so fully immersed in what you're doing that time seems to stand still. This doesn't occur if you're worrying about whether you're doing something right or wrong. Worrying just means that you're too much in your own head and not focusing enough on the communication taking place between yourself and your client. You achieve a state of flow when you're fully involved and energised in the process of the activity, whatever that activity is. Many athletes experience it as they focus on their sports.

In coaching, you may have identified the objective that your client wants to achieve. However, flow is about enjoying the journey. You're more intensely focused on the activity and the moment, not driving through the result. You're less conscious of yourself and more conscious of yourself within the activity that you're undertaking with your client.

Time can seem to stop because your awareness is so focused on the interaction with your client. In these moments, you will find that you need to make less effort because the activity itself becomes intrinsically rewarding.

Interestingly, the more you feel content in yourself and in your unique personality and style, the more likely you are to experience a state of flow, because flow tends to occur when you are relaxed but energised and involved.

Creating personal energy for mutual success

Create a positive environment for your client by being in a positive emotional state yourself. Emotions are infectious, so you feeling motivated to support your client's goals will enable him to feel more motivated too.

Walking your talk makes you a credible role model for your client. CBC is all about ensuring that your thinking is constructive and helpful to the situation at hand. A negative or doubtful thought shows immediately in the energy you create in the room. Constructive and optimistic thoughts result in an upbeat and positive atmosphere in the coaching room.

Your own health, lifestyle, and personal care are relevant too. If you're out of balance in your life, your mind and energy will be fragmented and you may feel fatigued.

Disciplining yourself to take exercise, eat healthily, and manage the work–life balance is helpful if you're to talk with credibility about such things with your clients. Equally, you will also come to understand what a struggle such things can be within a busy lifestyle! No-one is saying that you have to be perfect – just that, because you're going to be encouraging your client to take care of himself, you must do so yourself.

Being prepared

Take time before each session to consider the session and prepare yourself. Quietly tune in to the client and remind yourself of his needs and goals.

Try using the multimodal model, which was developed by Arnold A. Lazarus, that I show in Figure 4-3 to prepare yourself for coaching sessions. This preparation can include thinking constructively about the session, relaxing your body, visualising a successful session, making sure your body is comfortable and alert, and considering what behaviours will best facilitate a successful session. Preparing in this way helps you to centre yourself before you begin the session. This model is one that you can also share with your clients to help them prepare for the situations they may face.

You don't know what issues and objectives the client will want to work on until he walks into the room, but being ready and prepared sets you off to a really good start.

Being happy in yourself enables him to feel confident and comfortable with you so that he can relax, feel that he is in good hands, and focus on his goals.

The perfect coach doesn't exist. More important is using your lifetime's journey of development to help you make the most of your client.

1. **Behavioural:** What behaviours are helpful in the situation? For example do you want to be a formal, informal, patient, professional?

2. **Emotional:** What emotions help you manage the situation best? For example, feeling calm and confident.

3. **Sensory:** Noticing muscular tension, breathing that may have become shallow, butterflies or sweaty hands should you be anxious about the session. For example taking time to release any tension so as to be open, alert and relaxed.

4. **Imaginal:** Creating imagery in your mind. For example, you can visualise the session going well, with a free flow of progress, and see the client leaving you feeling motivated and energised.

5. **Cognitive:** Reviewing thoughts in your mind. For example, checking that your thoughts are constructive, such as "I have the resources I need to run this coaching session professionally.

6. **Interpersonal:** Considering what interpersonal style will help you communicate best with your client. For example, listening, empathising, being assertive with boundaries of time and topic.

7. **Biological:** Reflecting on what biological input helps or hinders your feeling of calm confidence. For example, too much alcohol the night before can leave you feeling low; too much caffeine might make you feel jittery.

Figure 4-3:
Multimodal model to prepare for a coaching session.

Part II
The CBC Process

"Being of sound, positive, secure, motivated, creative, relaxed, objective, logical, rational, responsible, reasonable, constructive, unprejudiced, & totally focused mind, I leave everything to my cognitive behavioral coach."

In this part . . .

In this part I take you through the whole CBC process starting with undertaking a coaching assignment, and finishing up with the final session. I explain the importance of the expectations and responsibilities of your client and how to develop trust and collaboration with them.

I consider the importance of communicating effectively and of working at your client's pace, and show you how to be sensitive to specific indicators that illustrate limiting beliefs. I also explain the CBC questioning process, which enables you to develop new approaches to problems. Finally, I demonstrate that no one is perfect and that you, even as a coach, are fallible and need supervision and support.

Chapter 5

Sounding Out the First Session

· ·

In This Chapter

▶ Planning and mapping out the CBC journey

▶ Agreeing the starting point

▶ Helping your client through the discomfort of change

▶ Identifying measurable milestones and results

· ·

*Y*ou can think of CBC as a process of guided discovery. You and your client travel the road together towards your client's specified goals. You may not always be sure at the outset where that road leads. A coaching programme sometimes results in radical and exciting changes for your client. At other times, small shifts make a big difference in your client's life or work. Try to trust the CBC process and believe that, wherever it takes you both, the journey has value.

In the first CBC session with your client, generate a sense of curiosity, interest, and motivation to inspire excitement about her journey of change. Help your client feel that she is in safe hands. You're there to support the process, but she is in control of the steering wheel.

Before the first session, agree the practicalities of how the coaching programme is organised. Now you start the real work, developing your relationship with your client and helping her move forward.

In this chapter, I outline the CBC process and give you ideas about how to help your client start her coaching journey on the right foot.

Explaining the Process of CBC

At the start of the first CBC session, touching on some of the key points of CBC is a good idea, even if you covered them in your introductory meeting with your client. Explain again issues such as confidentiality and the importance of a safe environment for discussion, and remind your client of the length of time agreed for the sessions.

Explain that the client and her identified goals drive the coaching programme. Your role is to:

✓ Provide the process to help your client achieve her goals.

✓ Challenge any thoughts and beliefs that may limit your client's progress.

✓ Enable your client to realise how her thoughts and emotions impact on her progress through life.

✓ Show your client how to develop thoughts, views, and behaviours that help her to be the person she wants to be and to achieve her work and life goals.

✓ Provide models that your client can apply in her own life by becoming her own coach.

✓ Reassure your client that you won't offer advice – you believe that she is the best person to answer her own questions.

✓ Discuss with your client the behaviours that will support her in achieving the objectives she has set.

✓ Enable her to identify the relationship between her objective and a positive outcome. For example, if the objective is to become more confident, what outcome would this give her? In this example, the outcome could be the ability to give effective presentations or to find it easier to make a sales call.

Your aim is to take your client from where she is today to where she wants to be, whether that goal is feeling better within herself or achieving a specific goal in the outside world, such as changing career, finding more time for her family, or becoming a better manager.

Use visual diagrams to help your client understand concepts and processes. Encourage her to ask questions if she is unclear about anything in the CBC process. Figure 5-1 shows an overview of the coaching process. You can use this diagram to explain the following to your client:

✓ The CBC process begins with her. You review who she has been up to this point and explore who she wants to be.

✓ You help her consider where she wants to go, helping her develop measurable goals in her life and work, and potentially open her mind to see beyond any fears or limitations.

✓ Together you develop a step plan to help her reach her objectives, making sure that these are realistic and achievable.

✓ Throughout the process, you explore your client's thoughts, feelings, and behaviours with a view to her letting go of negative habits and building powerful new ways of thinking and behaving.

✓ Your client integrates a process of continuous review, observing her thoughts and approaches to situations and rewarding herself for new efforts, and ultimately becoming her own coach.

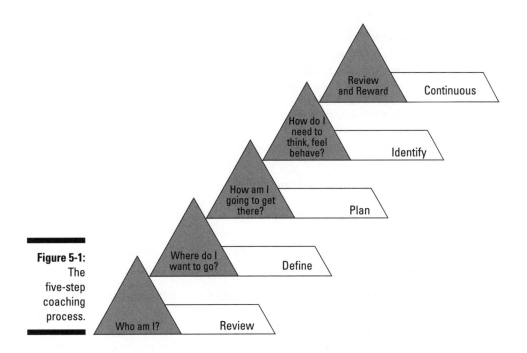

Figure 5-1:
The
five-step
coaching
process.

The model in Figure 5-1 provides a bird's-eye view. This model isn't a rigid structure, and you will likely dip in and out of the different aspects of this process as you go through the coaching programme. However, the model does help your client to understand what happens in the process of CBC.

Exploring the session structure

Each session follows a structured process to move your client forward towards her goals. The session requires movement and energy. By the end of the session, you aim to identify specific actions that your client can undertake at home.

Figure 5-2 shows a six-step process that you can follow in your first CBC session:

1. **Programme objectives:** Touching on the objectives for the whole programme whenever you meet reassures your client that she is in control of her own future and can change direction should she choose to do so. Life changes and moves on, so these objectives are not set in stone. It is advisable to revisit the objectives at the beginning of each session to check whether they're still relevant and motivating. Useful questions are:

   • You said that this was your objective, is it still relevant?

   • Has anything changed?

   • Do these goals still motivate you?

Figure 5-2:
The six-step
session
process.

1. Objectives for the whole programme
2. Objectives-setting for the session
3. Self-Knowledge and personal objectives
4. Update, discussion and exercises addressing the issues and objectives
5. Homework and Action Planning
6. Review

2. **Session objectives:** Find out your client's desired achievements for the session. Check that these achievements align with her overall objectives for the whole programme – do they take her forward in her goals? Useful questions are:

- What would you like to achieve during this session?

- Would any particular topics be useful?

- Would you like to share any recent developments?

Help her to set achievable targets for the session. Ask 'If you can resolve just one thing during this session, what would it be?' If she wants the moon, you can be a little light and humorous: 'So you're expecting to turn your life around in the space of an hour and a half?'

If your client generally seems to expect too much of the coaching session or defines goals that are hard to achieve, take time out for a reality check. Some clients expect you to change their lives around in the space of an hour, which is obviously impossible. Others have huge goals. In either case, help them look at how achievable their goals are and devise a realistic timescale of personal development and action. You play a part in helping them plan, but it is their responsibility to take action.

3. **Self-knowledge and personal objectives:** You need to check on your client's thoughts, emotions, and personal behaviours. Try to find out what else is going on in her life and how her thinking habits may impact on the success of the programme. Some useful questions are:

- How are you feeling about the coaching programme?

- Do you have any concerns or questions?

- You've stated your career goals – are there any personal changes that may make a difference in supporting your achievement of those goals?

4. **Update, discussion, and exercises:** During this part of the session, you work on your client's specific issues, challenges, and goals in order to explore negative thinking and break through limiting thoughts and behaviours. Your approach needs to vary according to the objectives and issues your client is bringing to the coaching programme. Useful questions are:

   - Where would you like to begin?

   - What is the key issue you would like to work on?

   - Have you got any major challenges or goals coming up that you would like to discuss?

   - Tell me about. . .

5. **Home tasks and action planning:** As you come to the end of the session, try to identify specific actions and activities for your client to work on between sessions. These can vary from how she is personally thinking about herself, or how she is approaching a situation or an action or behaviour that is relevant to her goals. Useful questions are:

   - What have you discovered or thought about during this session?

   - What is the most useful action you can take between now and the next session?

   - What thoughts will help to motivate you to take that action?

   - How will you reward yourself for attempting or completing that activity?

6. **Review:** At the end of the session, review how your client feels the session went. In this way, you discover what works for her and can adapt your style and the process to meet her needs. You can also mention what else, from your perspective, she can do to help the process. Useful questions are:

   - How did you feel the session went?

   - Was there anything that made you feel uncomfortable?

   - Can you think of anything we can both do to make the session work more effectively?

   - Can you bring a copy of your thinking log the next time, so that we can review it please?

Following a process helps you to keep your client on target. But a process is just that; sometimes, in the course of discussion of one goal, another issue is raised that turns out to be more pertinent, so be prepared to be flexible. You can check with your client that she realises the agenda has been changed, and make sure that she's happy with this change.

All discussion has its development points, and the process is not designed to shackle the creativity and communication that is likely to evolve during your coaching session.

Building rapport

Each client is different. People acquire knowledge in a variety of ways from the visual to the practical, from reflective to auditory. As a CB coach you need to adapt your style and approach to meet the needs of each person you deal with. Here are examples of the different styles you may encounter:

- ✔ **'I've got no time for this: prove yourself':** This person is in a hurry. She may have been sent on a coaching programme as part of a policy rather than electing it for herself. Don't let her scare you or bully you. Acknowledge her needs and introduce the concepts of CBC in a practical manner, reassuring her that she is in charge of the content and is also responsible for her own change.

- ✔ **'I've got this problem. . . ':** This client likes to talk about her problems. She sees the coaching session as an opportunity to get issues off her chest. Allow her to do so, acknowledge the problems and issues, and move her on to 'and what can you do about that?' You can help this client get her head out of the problem and above the skyline, where she can begin to develop solutions.

- ✔ **'Show me the theoretical basis for that':** This person wants academic research and theories. Provide a bibliography and handouts of relevant papers that have appeared in journals, magazines, or books. Research the origins of some of the models you're using in your sessions. Know the names of the thinkers and psychologists behind CBC, such as Aaron Beck, Albert Ellis, Windy Dryden, and Stephen Palmer.

- ✔ **'Tell me a story':** Some people like to work in metaphors. Be ready to switch into story-telling mode in order to make your point: 'Imagine if you were. . . ' or 'There was this person who. . . ' or 'What would be a positive ending in this situation?' or 'Where does/did it all begin?'

- ✔ **'Draw me a picture':** Visual images can be really useful in explaining a concept or model. Have paper and pens on the table so that you can depict your client's situation in a symbolic fashion. You don't have to be a great artist – matchstick people are fine. A picture gives you a mutual focus of understanding, so encourage your client to have a go too if you find it difficult to connect with a situation she is describing.

✔ **'I find it difficult to open up':** Shyness can be a common feature of coaching sessions, particularly as you're often discussing topics that your client would not normally discuss. Slow down, coax, and be gentle with your client. Get yourself comfortable with silence and don't try to fill the gaps. Gradually help your client to find the words she needs to describe her goals and challenges.

✔ **'Can we try that out**?': Role-play, where you actively practise specific situations within coaching sessions, can be an excellent way of integrating skills. You may have to act out the role of a significant person in your client's life and help her develop the language and body language to make the changes she wants to make.

The examples that I describe above show just a few different styles of communicating. The first session is a big development curve for you as well as your client. Listen out for clues as to how she prefers to think, find things out, and approach the topics you're exploring.

Create a bridge of communication between you and your client by adapting your style to meet hers. Don't lose who you are: being authentic is important. But being flexible also helps. For example, I pick up information visually and speak rather fast. When I first started to coach, one of my early clients said to me: 'Helen, you lost me about six sentences ago!' I have since realised that I need to be more measured and to make sure that my client and I are working at the same pace.

Applying the ABC model, which we describe in Chapter 2, is an interesting way to achieve mutual engagement and responsibility for the process. For example:

A = The Situation – a successful coaching programme that achieves agreed goals.

B = Beliefs, thoughts, or expectations that would be helpful to this process – 'We can do our best to make this work,' 'This is an interesting journey of discovery,' 'We are both going to play our part in aiming to achieve these goals.'

C = Consequence – the emotion that helps us achieve success: motivation, curiosity, and excitement. The behaviour that helps us move towards the goals: cooperation, collaboration, sharing, supporting, and openness.

It can be an affirming process to start the coaching programme off with an alignment of thoughts, views, and behaviours, applying a CBC model.

Working Out Where You Are Now

The starting point in CBC is your client's current situation. Find out more about your client: who is she, what is she doing, and hat are her values, dreams, and goals? You don't have to take a long time over this discussion, but time for self-reflection allows your client to stop and think about herself and allows you to observe and evaluate whether her thoughts are rational and helpful.

A quick and practical method to gain an overview of your client's situation is to use a *mind map,* which I show in Figure 5-3. The mind map was originated by Tony Buzan and is a visual method of organising thoughts and information. Using a mind map enables your client to look at many different aspects of her life and give each aspect a satisfaction rating. Some areas of this map are most likely not relevant to your client, so help her to personalise the branches.

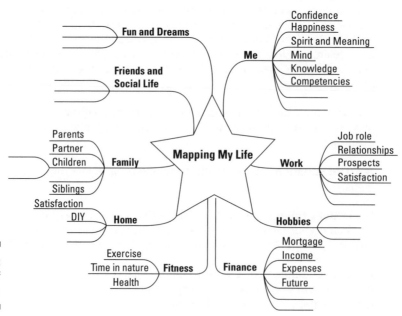

Figure 5-3:
A map of
my life.

Print off the map or ask your client to build a map during the session. The design and execution of the map is far less important than the information and the thinking process that goes on as she identifies different areas of her life and considers what aspects she wants to address.

Ask your client to start with a picture of herself in the middle of a blank piece of paper. She then builds up the branches to represent key areas of her life. Within those key areas are secondary areas that branch off it in associated groupings of information; for example, on the family branch, she may have her son John and her daughter Mary.

The mind map exercise is particularly useful when you're life coaching, which is when you are working on your client's personal life goals. A mind map can also provide a really useful overview to help someone make decisions about balancing work and life in this fast-paced world where so many people feel pressurised for time.

When your client has drawn up the different areas of her life and work, ask her to give a measure of satisfaction on a scale of 0–10 for each topic, 0 being low satisfaction, 10 being high. This measurement immediately identifies areas that she may want to work on.

You can then agree between you which of these are relevant goals to include within the coaching programme and which ones she is to address herself outside the sessions. You can use this map as part of the goal-setting process, honing down key objectives to work on together.

Seeing how you got where you are today

The mind map exercise that I explain in the previous section provides a starting point to discover how your client is where she is right now. This exercise gives you valuable information as to whether she is the sort of person who has planned out her life and achieved her goals, whether events have evolved in a serendipity fashion, or whether she feels a victim of circumstance and that things have happened to her without much control.

The areas to focus on depend on the main objectives and purpose of the coaching session, but you may want to ask some of the following questions:

✔ **Work:**

- What did you want to be when you were 7 years old?

- How did you come to be in this job?

- Were there major influences in your career choice?

- What has led you to (a) stay in a specific role or (b) change from one job to the next?

- If you could start again, would you make the same choices?

- What are some of the thoughts that have driven your decisions to this point?

- How did those thoughts make you feel?

✔ **Life:**

- Is your life today what you imagined it would be?

- How has your background and life experience shaped your thoughts and behaviours today?

- What events have influenced you in leading the life you lead now?

- How are you thinking about your life so far?

- How are those thoughts making you feel?

- What aspects of your life have you left behind and why? How happy are you about this?

Conversations arising from this type of questioning help you begin to understand what kind of person you're working with and give your client time to reflect on how she arrived where she is today.

As a CB coach, you specifically want to investigate how your client's thoughts and views have shaped her life so far. Be on the alert for thoughts or statements that signify twisted thinking, as explained in Chapter 2, such as 'Everything has gone wrong so far' or 'Things always happen to me,' because you need to address this kind of imbalanced view when you come to clarify her goals.

Entering a process of change

Charles Darwin, expert in survival of the species, wrote: 'It is not the strongest of the species who survive, nor the most intelligent, but the ones most responsive to change.' Change is a survival mechanism and a part of everyday life. Change can be uncomfortable, and many people hate it and want life to stay the same. Others get excited by it and love variety.

Challenging the fear of change

If your client finds change difficult, try reminding her of the movie *Groundhog Day,* in which the main character wakes up every day to the same situation – ask her just how boring and frustrating she thinks that would be. Suggest that if she had stayed the same as she was five or ten years ago, she would be left behind – you can bet that she has integrated mobile technology and the Internet into her life in a way she didn't know existed just a few years ago.

We all have the capacity to change, but persuading ourselves that change is worth the effort is the problem. Old habits die hard.

Investigating the brain's habit trap

The brain is programmed to build habits. This building of habits enables us to focus on the immediate situations we face rather than having to consciously pay attention to every single thing we do. Think about riding a bicycle. The first few times you tried, you wobbled, couldn't get your balance, and fell off. After a while, you probably got the hang of it and off you went, with no conscious thought required. A similar thing happens with every change you make and with every new thing you discover – and it happens for your client in her coaching programme.

To help your client understand this process, take her back over something she has become proficient at in her life. Explore with her the four stages of learning, which I show in Figure 5-4, so that she knows what to expect when she discovers new ways of thinking and behaving as she goes through the coaching programme.

The habit-building feature of the brain, whereby it helpfully files skills that you do frequently, is brilliant on one level but difficult on another. This contradiction is because when your brain stores a habit – whether the habit is the time of day you take a shower, or the way you walk into a room – immediate neurological change occurs in your body.

Your mind and body get used to doing things in a particular way. Think about how your car may have an indicator switch on the right-hand side and then when you go on holiday and the hire car has an indicator switch on the left, your right hand is flapping up and down thinking 'It should be over here!'

What happens in the mind also happens in the body. When you first start to do a task, an electrochemical message transfers from one brain cell to another (see Figure 5-4). Each time you do that task, that message crosses a similar pathway and develops neurological patterns in your brain that represent your habits.

1. **The first time you make a journey to a new workplace, you don't know the way.**

2. **Each time you make the journey, you begin to build the habit.** At first, you still need the map, but eventually you don't even have to think about where you're going: it has become an automatic habit, and you find your way along the streets and into the office without any concentration at all. Your brain has stored the process into your unconscious. In fact, you sometimes find yourself going along that route even at a weekend, without thinking!

The start
of a new habit

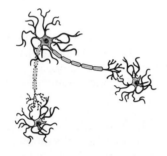

The habit
builds up

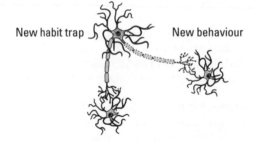

New habit trap   New behaviour

New habit
becomes easy

Figure 5-4:
The learn-
ing, change,
and habit-
building
process.

3. **Then you get a new job in a new location and have to commit a new route to memory.** You may find yourself, in the first stages, turning down the old streets that took you to your old office. And so you have to focus and concentrate to make the changes. This focusing is the hardest stage of learning because your mind and body have become so used to the old habit.

4. **Eventually, with repetition, the new route becomes automatic.** Again, you're able to relax and think about other things, finding your way on automatic pilot. That is, of course, until you change jobs or office again!

This process is relevant to changing any kind of habit, whether the habit is a new thought, skill, or behaviour. Your client may want to change various aspects of her life: the way she thinks about herself and the situations she is in, the way she communicates, her abilities within her work and life roles, and so on.

All learning can be likened to the learning and change process in Figure 5-4, and your client needs to realise that there is probably some discomfort involved between step 2 and step 3. In fact, if you have no discomfort, you have no change. So clients need to prepare themselves to try to enjoy a bit of discomfort for a while.

I find that when clients understand this change process during the first session, it helps them to persevere and accept that a CBC programme can involve hard work. Thoughts are habits, just as much as skills and behaviours are habits: they become automatic and unconscious. Therefore, changing thoughts and behaviours requires focus and repetition if your client is to integrate her new behaviours into her life. Each time she tries, she is building her pathway to success.

A CBC method called *exposure theory* is based on this habituation process. The method gradually habituates your client to situations she has previously felt uncomfortable in or been fearful of.

Karen wants to become an excellent trainer, but is nervous of her abilities. The first step may be to practise with a friend or family member, then build up to train someone who is a stranger. Karen may well be nervous and may make a few mistakes or forget to make some of the points she wanted to make. The more she practises, the more comfortable she is likely to feel. Next time, she may build up to a small group of four to six people and then repeat this a few times so that she adapts. Gradually she can build up group numbers until she can, if she chooses, give a training course or presentation to several hundred people. Each time she repeats the process, she develops and acclimatises herself to her role as a trainer, so that eventually the fear is diminished and the role is just a natural part of what she does.

Identifying Your Client's Goals

In the first session, clarify the goals that your client wants to achieve. Some clients find this process really easy; others can't imagine what the future may look like, so their vision is blocked. You ask questions that draw out your client's objectives and make these objectives measurable and achievable.

The goals your client identifies depend on the nature of the coaching programme. For example, working with a father who wants to enhance his parenting skills within a life coaching setting, and working with a businesswoman trying to influence her senior manager to give her a generous bonus is different, and these people are likely to have different goals. Your skill is to shape a tangible result in whatever situation your client brings to the session.

Try to remove any limits that exist in your client's mind, because this removal helps her generate more lateral possibilities. Try asking the following questions:

✔ If you could do anything you liked, what goals would you have?

✔ If you didn't have any fears or limits, what would you choose to do?

✔ If you didn't mind what other people said, what goals would you create?

✔ If you were to be your best self, what would change?

Notice how your client responds to these big questions. Her answers may help her think differently about herself and her life and work. Observe whether the process brings up negative thinking or resistance to change, such as: 'Well, someone else may be able to do that, but I can't', or 'I'd love to achieve that, but I know I'll never manage it.'

Damian had worked in an IT department of a construction company for over 15 years. He came to coaching because he felt demotivated in his company and wanted to explore new options. During the first sessions, he talked about possibly moving to another organisation. It never occurred to him, until his coach asked a few pertinent questions, to consider that he could transfer the IT skills to an organisation in another sector completely, such as banking or telecoms. It literally had not crossed his mind. However, once his coach broke through his limiting thoughts, he began to consider moving out of IT altogether and follow his dream of setting up his own restaurant, because he loved cooking.

When your client has limiting thoughts that stop her pursuing a goal that she identifies, you can help her gain perspective by asking questions such as the following:

✔ If someone else is able to do this task, what is the evidence to show that, given time and training, you cannot do it too?

✔ If you would love to achieve this goal, how do you know that you would never be able to manage it?

✔ Would you be able to work towards your goal if you created a step-by-step plan of action?

✔ How might someone else tackle this goal?

Narrow goals down to the specific areas that your client has brought up, so that she defines both the facts and benefits she would realise if she achieved her goal. For example:

✔ You say that you would like to influence your boss. What does this influence involve?

✔ What would it mean to you if you did succeed in influencing your boss?

✔ What would change?

✔ How would that feel?

✔ What is the first thing you need to do?

The DESTINY model, which I show in Figure 5-5, helps you work through goals and objectives with your client. Explain that her goals need to be:

✔ **Detailed:** There need to be facts and figures about what is involved, who, and where?

✔ **Exciting:** Do you really want to achieve this goal? How motivated are you? Why do you want the goal?

✔ **Specific:** What will it look like when you get there?

✔ **Timelined:** What is the step journey from here to the goals? By what date will you do. . . ?

✔ **Identifiable:** How can you measure the change from the situation today to your goal? What will be different?

✔ **Noticeable:** How will someone else know when you've got there? What will she see and hear?

✔ **Your future:** How does this goal fit into your future life and career?

The DESTINY model focuses your questions so as to sharpen and clarify your client's goals. You can work at this model in any order that comes naturally to you both. What is important is that you feel that your client has emotional engagement, because the way your client is thinking and feeling shapes whether she takes those steps towards achieving her goals.

Figure 5-5:
The
DESTINY
objectives-
setting
model.

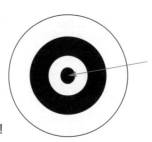

- **D** etailed
- **E** xciting
- **S** pecific
- **T** imelined
- **I** dentifiable
- **N** oticeable
- **Y** our Future!

At this stage you may involve measurement of current skill or confidence-level so that you can contrast the measurement at the end of the programme.

Moving from problems to solutions

CBC is forward-looking, but sometimes your client just needs to get her feelings and problems off her chest. That is fine – for a while! Remember that your role is to move your client, so if you feel that she is buried in the problem, take action to help her seek solutions.

Notice how the conversation goes. If your client reverts to telling you about the problem rather than the solution, be assertive and gently point this fact out. Explain that moving forwards rather than back is much more beneficial.

Listen out for the 'yes but' habit:

Coach: 'So you've said that you'd like to meet new people and go to more parties?'

Client: 'Yes, but I can't because. . .'

This exchange indicates that your client is potentially stuck or fearful, so it would be helpful to explore the limiting beliefs that hold her back. The CBC problem-solving methodology, which I show in Figure 5-6, can help you manage this situation:

Steps	Questions/Actions
1. Problem identification	What is the concern?
2. Goal selection	What do I want?
3. Generation of alternatives	What can I do?
4. Consideration of consequences	What might happen?
5. Decision making	What is my decision?
6. Implementation	Now do it!
7. Evaluation	Did it work?

Figure 5-6:
The CBC problem-solving methodology.

1. **Investigating the challenge – the aspect of life that your client wants to change.** *For example, Claudia wants to meet new people and have more fun.*

2. **Considering and identifying the ultimate goal.** What is it Claudia really wants to achieve? *Claudia says she would like to go out on Saturday nights.*

3. **Generating alternative ways of achieving the result.** Often people can only see one goal or one route, whereas in fact there may be many different ways. Help broaden your client's perspectives to brainstorm options. *With her coach, Claudia explored options: Internet dating, going to her local disco, joining a social club, going to more networking events at work, joining her colleagues at the pub on a Friday night.*

4. **Considering the consequences of potential action provides you with the opportunity to tease out any doubts or anxieties your client may be having about the options.** Here you can review your client's viewpoints and identify what may be holding her back and holding her in the 'yes but' phase. *Claudia's 'yes but' was that her colleagues might be unfriendly if she went the pub with them on a Friday night. The coach worked with her to explore what evidence she had that they would be unfriendly. She had no evidence.*

5. **Decisions are essential to change and to moving forward.** It can help if you explain that a decision may put your client on the first step to change, but she is always in control of the next decision. *Claudia's home task was to give the pub a try on the next Friday. If she only stayed ten minutes, at least she would have made a start.*

6. **Trying out new thinking, behaviour, or action can be challenging but is the only way that your client can move towards her goals.** *Claudia identified that she would think: 'Probably everyone was shy the first time, and there is no reason why I can't make a new friend.' This attitude made her feel relaxed and she decided to smile and be friendly.*

7. **Review is a constant process so that your client considers what worked and what didn't work.** This process enables her to acquire and adjust her approach so as to ultimately achieve the success she is seeking. *Claudia reported that she had stayed for an hour and had talked to a nice girl in the office next door. She decided that the next time, it would be a good idea to go early when there was not such a large crowd, because she felt more relaxed in small groups.*

The following questions can be used as part of this seven-step process to help move your client forward.

✔ What may be stopping you?

✔ Have you ever managed to break through a problem like this before? If so, what methods did you use?

✔ In how many different ways can you approach this problem/situation?

✔ How might someone else approach this problem?

✔ What may be the first step you take?

✔ What thought would help you take that step?

Your role is to give your client the ability to see through the doors of perception that she may have shut, to open up options, and help her walk through should she choose to do so.

Using actions and tasks between sessions

At the end of each session, agree with your client what actions and tasks you want her to practise at home. These can be:

✔ New ways of thinking

✔ New behaviours

✔ Trying a new skill

✔ Practising changing communication patterns within a relationship

✔ Developing body language and physiology that empower her

The tasks and actions should be relevant to the overall goals of the coaching programme and the specific issues your client needs to address in order to achieve those goals.

Once you've set the tasks, help your client to work out a strategy to ensure that she accomplishes them, by asking questions such as:

- ✔ When will you be able to do this task?
- ✔ What thought may help you practise this new behaviour?
- ✔ Will that thought generate a good feeling to help you follow through?
- ✔ How can you manage the situation if it doesn't go exactly to plan?
- ✔ How will you know when you've done it?

Encouragement works wonders. Share tips and strategies that you know have worked. Provide handouts of relevant models, theories, or articles that support your client's objectives. Remind her of the benefits of achieving her goals. Point out that you're there to support and back her up, and that a journey of a thousand miles always starts with a single step.

Chapter 6

Challenging Unconstructive Thoughts

A s a CB coach, your role is to challenge and transform your client's limiting thoughts and beliefs. You tune in to your client's *negative automatic thoughts* or NATs. We describe these negative thoughts as *automatic* because the brain shunts habitual thoughts into the subconscious part of the mind so that you no longer notice them. NATs are rather like gnats – irritating negative niggles that are difficult to see or catch – until you help your client stop and analyse what is happening.

Identifying how your client's negative thoughts and beliefs sabotage her efforts and impact on her confidence and behaviour becomes second nature to you as you develop your CBC practice.

Negative thinking occurs in many different areas of life. In this chapter, I cover the unconstructive thoughts that arise in a variety of situations. I also provide some strategies to transform negative approaches into constructive ways to achieve goals.

Accepting that Expectations Take You Up and Take You Down

The human mind creates an endless stream of thoughts, ideas, and expectations as we experience the various events of our lives. Unfortunately, the mind is just as adept at fiction as it is at fact. The following examples show how our minds can deceive us.

Sally was fed up. She had expected to receive a £5,000 bonus at Christmas, but in the end her company gave her £2,000. She had already imagined how she would spend it £5,000, and now she felt crushed and demotivated.

In coaching sessions, Sally looked back at the situation and realised that she had not received any factual information from her company that she would receive a £5,000 bonus. In fact, she had mentioned the figure to her friend as a sum that she would ideally like to receive, and somehow this figure had become fixed in her mind as something that was likely to happen. In coaching sessions, she realised that if she had expected to receive only £1,000 and had then received £2,000, she would have been delighted. Sally saw that her own expectation of the situation, rather than the situation itself, had caused her to feel stressed and demotivated.

Mary was about to celebrate her 70th birthday. She was convinced that her sons would arrange a surprise party for her and her family and friends. Instead, they arranged to take her out to a smart restaurant. Mary was disappointed: she had geared herself up for the party and seeing her friends. She had even bought the dress. She believed that surprise parties were the right way to celebrate. Her sons had given her no indication that they would arrange a party, but her imagination had created this scenario. When it didn't happen, she felt cheated, despite the fact that they treated her to a delicious lunch at a restaurant.

Mary's son Brian realised that his mother was disappointed and felt guilty. During his coaching session, he understood that he could not have known about his mother's wish as she had not expressed it. Mary had expected him to mind-read, which was not rational. Eventually he accepted that he had done his best in the circumstances.

These stories demonstrate that people frequently stress themselves by the views they take of situations. They think about an event and start to imagine an ideal scenario. If that ideal doesn't happen, they feel disappointed. Sometimes, they can imagine the worst and spend hours worrying about an event that may never happen – a loved one being killed in a accident, or the fear of being made redundant – even when they've no evidence to support the fear.

Expectations can spoil the moment. Expecting too much or too little of yourself, others, or events leads to disappointment and conflict. CBC uses a questioning process to enable clients to realise how they make themselves unhappy and then blame their misery on others. Developing rational expectations helps maintain emotional equilibrium.

In the examples that I give above, Sally could have thought 'I don't know what my bonus is this year, so I shall wait and see and decide at the time whether I feel the bonus is an accurate reflection of the work I have done. If so, I shall be pleased; if not, I can discuss it with my boss.' Mary could have thought 'It would be lovely if my sons arranged a surprise party for me, but I shall certainly enjoy and be happy with anything they arrange for me.'

One of your key roles as a CB coach is to check your client's expectations and demonstrate that she can take control of them – and feel better as a result.

Adjusting to life not always being the way you want

We would all like life to go our way. As babies, we scream if we don't get what we want. As we grow up, we begin to ask and hope that others meet our requests. Eventually, we see that sometimes we can't get what we want.

Your client likely has three main demands of life:

✔ **Of herself:** To come up to her own standards; for example:

- Managing to go on that diet

- Making the effort to get to the gym

- Feeling more confident when making presentations

- Getting around to filing her paperwork and emails

- Having a wonderful relationship

✔ **Of others:** That their behaviour comes up to her needs and standards; for example:

- Her children go to bed when she tells them to

- Her partner clears up the breakfast things

- Her boss says thank you more often

- Her colleagues do what they said they would

- Her IT department fixes her system faster

✔ **Of life in general:** That it is the way she wants it to be; for example:

- Trains run on time

- We are not at war

- The political party she supports is in power

- Global warming isn't happening

- The economy is stable and working in her favour

When things don't go our way, we can end up thinking, Victor Meldrew style, 'I just don't believe it!' or 'I can't stand it!' The result is stress, anxiety, frustration, and anger.

You probably meet these problems frequently in your CBC sessions. Exploring your client's expectations about herself and the situations she faces can be insightful – you may even share a laugh with your client about the way her brain creates these stories. Understanding the process can release your client from pain, fear, and anger, and enable her to find a way of approaching life with a more rational viewpoint, basing her expectations on facts rather than imagination.

Stella was 36 years old and believed that she was 'on the shelf', because she had not yet got married or had children. She was Internet dating, and each time she met a man she liked, her imagination took her immediately to a family home, two children on the lawn, and a happy family. She jumped from first date to marriage. The result was that she quickly – and inappropriately – became dependent on the man. This dependence led her to treat him as a husband rather than as a date, and her boyfriends found this difficult and rather threatening.

In her coaching sessions, Stella realised how her thinking led her to this panic reaction. Some of the thoughts she had were:

- ✔ 'I feel really warm towards Joe, I think we may be together forever.' Stella was allowing her own feelings to colour the fact that they had only just met and neither of them really knew one another, which is known as emotional reasoning.

- ✔ 'I'm running out of time to have children, so I must make this relationship work.' Stella was making herself anxious through focusing on time running away. The use of the word *must* was also stressing her out, because she was giving herself an all-or-nothing message about the relationship.

- ✔ 'If this relationship doesn't work, I can't stand it!' Stella was heightening her anxiety further by telling herself that it would be a disaster if the relationship didn't work.

Stella's thinking about the situation was *twisted,* exaggerating her problems. Her thoughts were making her more anxious, which impacted the way she managed the situation. There is more detail about twisted thinking in Chapter 2. Some CBC questions to use with Stella may include the following:

- ✔ How does your feeling warm mean that you may be together forever?

- ✔ Does your own feeling warm give you evidence that Joe is feeling equally warm?

✔ How does thinking that you're running out of time and must make this relationship work help you to develop the relationship with Joe?

✔ If your relationship with Joe came to an end, what would be the worst that might happen?

✔ Have you managed a relationship break-up before?

✔ What resources do you have to take care of yourself within this situation?

✔ What thoughts can help you to manage this situation more confidently?

Stella realised that her thinking was irrational and anxiety-inducing. She saw that as she became anxious, her behaviours became demanding and fearful. She saw that her expectations were all or nothing – wonderful happy marriage, or disaster through failure of the relationship. She developed new thoughts to help her take the relationship step by step:

✔ I would prefer this relationship to work, but it isn't the end of the world if it doesn't.

✔ I will allow this relationship to develop at its own pace.

✔ If this relationship doesn't work out, it does not mean that I'm never going to meet the right man.

✔ I can enjoy each day as it comes and make the most of whatever happens.

✔ I do not yet know Joe well enough to decide whether he can make me happy, so I can relax and discover how well we get along as we get to know one another.

The way people think impacts the situation. Losing perspective can cause problems in relationships and make people more anxious than they need to be. CB coaching enables your client to analyse her thoughts and develop new, more supportive ways of thinking.

Getting to the bottom of things: The downward-arrow model

Sometimes an everyday situation generates feelings out of proportion to the event. This escalation tends to be when the meaning that a person, consciously or unconsciously, attaches to the event has a more negative association than the event deserves. This negative association is because something about the situation sparks a difficult memory or stimulates a negative belief.

In such cases, you can use the *downward-arrow model* to address your client's underlying belief. In the downward-arrow model, you ask your client: 'What is so awful about this situation?' After her response, you ask again:

'And what is so awful about that?' After her next answer, you ask again, and again, and so on. After a few questions, you may identify the fundamental negative belief that influences your client's emotions and ability to manage herself within the situation. Before you ask the questions, your client may have no idea what drives her discomfort. By identifying her belief, you can work together to analyse the effect it has on her feelings and actions. Once the belief has been given a shape, you can address whether that belief is still relevant and useful in helping your client to manage her life.

Giovanni worked in the IT department of a global company. He had been within the business for some time and had been happy. However, in the past six months he was allocated a new boss, Maureen. Every time he had meetings with Maureen he felt overwhelmed. He described this thought as feeling diminished, like a helpless child, although he was 40 years old. He was demoralised and demotivated by this situation and couldn't understand his behaviour.

The situation came to a head when he completed a project report, and Maureen criticised his handling of his team. The incident left him feeling totally crushed and he decided to seek help through coaching.

Applying the downward-arrow model, Giovanni described the problem as 'feeling crushed after Maureen's criticism'.

What is so awful about being crushed by Maureen's criticism?

↓

Giovanni: It is awful because it makes me feel stupid.

↓

What is so awful about feeling stupid?

↓

Giovanni: I think other people have a bad opinion of me.

↓

What is so awful about other people having a bad opinion of you?

↓

Giovanni: I think they are laughing at me.

↓

What is so awful about them laughing at you?

↓

Giovanni: It reminds me of my mother laughing at me when I made mistakes as a child.

↓

What was so awful about your mother laughing at you when you were a child?

↓

Giovanni: It was awful because she criticised me and made me feel insignificant.

↓

What is so awful about being criticised and feeling insignificant?

↓

Giovanni: I feel my life is pointless.

Underneath every criticism Giovanni received as an adult, there was this underlying association that his life was pointless. The memory of his dominant and critical mother pervaded his life and resulted in his need for approval and harmony. The most mundane everyday situations in which things went wrong with his boss or with clients triggered the memory, and he felt disproportionately diminished.

Through CBC, Giovanni realised that the association between critical feedback and his life being pointless was irrational and out of perspective. He reminded himself that although his mother was inevitably a strong influence in his life, she was just one person with one opinion and her own problems. He understood that not managing his team in a perfect way did not, in itself, make his life pointless. He developed more constructive thoughts:

✔ 'My life has value, and if I make the odd mistake it still has purpose.'

✔ 'I can accept that I can do my best but I can't please all the people all the time!'

The downward-arrow model is a practical method to access underlying negative or disabling beliefs. If your client seems to react disproportionately to an everyday situation, work through this process to help her analyse the cause of her discomfort and develop strategies to feel more confident in these situations in future.

Thoughts don't change overnight. They need repetition and reinforcement to ensure the process of transition and change from NATs to developing what I term CATs – *constructive automatic thoughts*. (Well, cats are pretty good at looking after themselves!) A sticky note with 'CATs' written on it and stuck above a desk, beside the bed, or on the bathroom cabinet, can be a great reminder to re-focus attention on supportive and constructive ways of thinking.

Table 6-1 provides you with a model to give to your client. Ask her to keep a record of any negative automatic thoughts that she notices between one session and the next. Suggest that she identifies constructive automatic thoughts that she would like to replace the negative thoughts with. Explain that any time she is aware of having a NAT, she replaces it with a CAT, and that the more frequently she repeats the CAT, the more automatic it will become.

Table 6-1	NATs and CATs
NATs *(negative automatic thoughts)*	**CATs** *(constructive automatic thoughts)*
I'll never be able to do this.	I have the skills and resilience to complete this task.
Nobody ever listens to me.	I am being heard: my partner listens to me; my boss took notice of what I said at the last team meeting.

Observing tell-tale words and phrases

Make sure that you listen out for certain words in your coaching sessions. These words denote negativity and helplessness and, when you spot them, you can help your client to assess the way in which her life is being influenced by them. I pick out three of the most common below:

- ✔ **'Yes, but. . . ':** This is a classic block to action. It generally denotes fear and helplessness. The insinuation is that someone else may take action but she herself can't for some reason that appears to be rational to her, but may not be rational to you. The *can't* often does not literally mean *can't,* but actually means *won't.* Be gentle: you're often dealing with anxiety. However rational her excuse may be, ask for permission to investigate it. Then unpack it by asking for evidence and facts using the following questions:

- What is stopping you taking action?

- Have you checked out the facts?

- What emotions do you experience?

- Has someone you know achieved this result? What methods did she use?

- Would you be able to give it a try?

- What is the consequence of not taking action?

- What would be the worst that would happen if you did take action?

Help your client to rise above her fear and put it in perspective. Very possibly she has inner thoughts along the lines of 'I'm just too frightened to do this task,' even if she doesn't want to admit this to you.

✔ **'I'd like to do. . . , but I can't':** Fear, or being stuck in old patterns and routines, is the problem here. Enable your client to see out of the burrow in which she is hiding to discover whether the situation really is *can't* or whether, in fact, the situation is *won't*. Look at the facts and your client's feelings by asking the following questions:

- What's stopping you?

- What thoughts do you have about this situation? Are they rational and helpful?

- What would it take to do this?

- What skills might you need?

- What is the first thing you can do?

✔ **'Never', 'nothing', 'no-one', 'everyone', 'always':** These words are big sweeping statements that can sound rational, but frequently are not rational at all. 'Nobody has thought about the consequences of this policy' or 'Senior management always say one thing and do another' or 'My boss never listens to me.' You need to get specific, so try asking these questions:

- How did the policy originate? Tell me more about how it was developed, by whom, and for what purpose. Do you have any evidence that the management didn't consider the consequences at that stage?

- Can you think of a time when senior management said something and acted upon it? Is it that specific instances exist when they do act and those when they don't act, rather than 'always'?

- Has there been an occasion when your boss did listen to you?

Your client's viewpoint may or may not be justified – what you're doing is helping her to focus on specifics rather than generalisations so that she can make a rational assessment of the situation rather than an emotional one.

Seeing that logical people can be illogical

Some of the most intelligent, professional, and apparently logical people can be illogical at times. They can be quite surprised when you help them see this fact! Here are examples of words to watch out for:

- ✔ 'Should', 'must', 'ought to' – these words denote judgement and demand. This judgement can be in relation to themselves, to others, and to the events they experience. Here are a few examples:
    - • 'I'm stuck in traffic, but I simply must get to this meeting on time' – although the situation is beyond her control because of an unexpected accident on the motorway.
    - • 'Other drivers shouldn't be such idiots' – which is a totally subjective viewpoint!
    - • 'My partner ought to know that I want him to put his shirts in the washing machine' – even if she hasn't actually asked him to do so.

Enable your client to see that these statements are subjective and derived from her own need for life to be the way she wants it to be. Try asking the following questions:

- ✔ Is there a law of the universe that says that you must get to the meeting on time?
- ✔ If a traffic jam appears and you're in the middle of it, how is it your fault that you will be late, provided you left in good time?
- ✔ On what basis do you judge other people's driving?
- ✔ How is your viewpoint helping you to manage the drive to the meeting?
- ✔ How is your partner supposed to know that you want him to put his shirts in the washing machine, if you've not actually asked him to do so?
- ✔ Do you consider it fair to expect someone else to know what you want, without your having expressed it?

Attuning your ear to the words that your client uses and challenging her perspective enables her to gain greater clarity so as to be more conscious of her thinking. This perspective allows her to make more informed choices.

Checking inferences about power

Sometimes your client talks about herself in a way that infers she feels power-less. For example, she may make comments about the economy or the political situation such as: 'I'll never be able to start a business in this economic climate' or 'The Government takes absolutely no notice of people like me.'

Or the feeling of powerlessness can be in relation to another person. For example: 'It's okay for him because he just tells me what to do' or 'My boss expects me to sort out all the problems in our department, and as soon as I have solved one, he always finds another' or 'The things that have happened to me have been out of my control.'

Or the feeling of powerlessness can show in a supposition about an event. For example: '**If this** happens. . . **then** that will happen,' or '**If** I don't get a pro-motion this year **then** they obviously don't think I am management material.'

When you hear this kind of statement, it flags up an issue that we term *locus of control* – that is, how much power the person feels she has over what happens to her in life. This issue can identify areas where you can help your client feel more capable than she had previously felt of influencing events.

Some questions you can ask are:

- ✔ Do you believe that success comes through luck or personal action?

- ✔ What does being lucky mean to you?

- ✔ Do you believe we make our own luck?

- ✔ Do you feel you've any influence over the Government?

- ✔ Do you believe in destiny or do you feel in control of what happens to you in your life?

- ✔ Do you think leaders are born or made?

- ✔ Do you think success comes through who you know or through being the right person with the right skills?

- ✔ Do you think that one person has more right to power than another?

- ✔ Do you think the state of the economy ultimately dictates what happens within your business, or do you have the power to make things work within a difficult economic situation?

The answers to these questions help you to understand whether your client is making herself feel powerless as a result of external circumstances, or whether she feels that she can influence events despite the circumstances.

If you deduce that your client feels helpless, try to identify areas that she *can* influence so as to empower her to feel more in control. For example, try asking some of these questions:

- Can you think of companies that have set up and survived despite an economic downturn?
- Think of someone you consider lucky, and describe what actions she may also have taken to contribute to her success.
- Is there a law to say that one person has more right to be powerful than another?
- Can you think of a logical reason why you do not have as much right to ask for what you want as anyone else does?
- Is there any reason why you cannot influence the Government by writing to your MP about this subject?
- What steps can you personally take to influence this situation?

Research suggests that luck is an attitude leading to certain behaviours. Therefore success starts in your mind and is generated mainly through hard work and in seeking opportunities. Build up your client's ability to feel empowered to take action rather than feeling helpless.

Your client needs to identify what she really wants and what she can act upon. She needs to express her needs and recognise that she has rights, as much as everyone else. Share with her the following principles of assertive communication:

- Respect yourself and respect others.
- Take responsibility for yourself and accept a responsibility towards others.
- Express needs, and allow others to express theirs.
- Be honest and direct in communication with others, and ask clearly for what you want.
- Be able to say 'no' or that you don't understand, and allow others the right to do the same.
- Don't put others down or accept that others put you down.
- Allow yourself and others to be fallible and make mistakes.
- Treat others on an equal basis and feel equal to them – neither worse than nor better than them.

Your client may have more power than she perceives. You can show her how she can own this power and apply it in her life for the good of herself and her relationships.

Transforming Thoughts to Achieve Goals

As well as observing and challenging your client's unconstructive thoughts and perspectives, you can enable her to develop more constructive ways of approaching her goals. Sometimes, achieving a goal can be hard work, but the end result can transform a person's life or career. As a coach, you enable the client to find her way through demotivation or challenge so that she perseveres rather than gives up. It has been said that successful people take the action that unsuccessful people can't be bothered with: you help her take that action.

Mariella wanted to develop her career and decided that the achievement of an MBA would help her get promoted. She therefore enlisted in a two-year course. However, Mariella had *low frustration tolerance,* or LFT. A person with LFT gets easily bored with a situation and gives up quickly, thereby sabotaging long-term gain for short-term pleasure. This kind of person frequently jumps from job to job, house to house, partner to partner, in the belief that she can't stand to persist with something that is not immediately exciting and interesting to her. She may believe that this is the way she is, rather than accepting that she has the opportunity to overcome this tendency should she decide to do so.

Mariella came for CBC after nine months of the MBA course, complaining that she wasn't sure that she wanted to complete the course. 'The course is such hard work, and so many of the topics don't interest me. Perhaps I have made the wrong choice.' Through the coaching sessions, she reviewed her long-term goals and the lifestyle she ultimately wanted to achieve, and realised that the MBA would, in fact, enable her to achieve her goals.

Through coaching, she found out how to develop *high frustration tolerance,* or HFT – the ability to accept the hard work and discomfort in order to achieve her long-term career goals. She devised strategies to make the course more interesting, giving herself breaks to focus on other things in order to meet her need for variety. She created a coloured sketch drawing that depicted her having achieved her goals. This activity enabled her to focus on the long-term pleasure of the end result rather than on the short-term pain of the hard work. She created an affirming sentence that she kept above her desk: 'I shall feel great when I have my MBA.' Looking at this sentence reminded her of her goal and motivated her to find ways of persisting with the course.

Some people develop too much HFT – for example, someone who stays in an abusive relationship for too long. Judge whether you feel that the client has a balanced level of tolerance. If you sense that she is in an abusive relationship, either at work or in her personal life, it may be necessary to refer her on for therapy. Check out this book's Appendix for a list of professional organisations.

Redressing thoughts about a relationship

People can get stuck in a problem and not be able to see a way out of it. Sometimes this is because there is a pay-off or benefit to remaining in the problem – for example, by avoiding the risk of change, or because they gain the sympathy and attention of others. At other times, the person has become so enmeshed in her current situation that she literally can't see a way out of it. CBC provides both the opportunity for analysis of the problem and strategies to develop solutions to move forward.

Susan's relationship with her boss, David, had deteriorated significantly since he gave her negative feedback about her lack of punctuality at meetings. Her comments during coaching sessions were:

- ✔ Can't he see how much I have to do?

- ✔ He really ought to understand how much I have on my plate – turning up on time to a meeting is the least of my priorities.

- ✔ He's so tied up in his own concerns that he doesn't seem to understand that I have to respond to customer complaints.

- ✔ We're so different, we can never get on.

Susan's situation is not unusual. Many people develop the habit of blaming other people rather than taking responsibility for their part of a problem. They also become accustomed to talking about the negative situation in a way that continually attempts to justify their own positions, so that they come to quite enjoy the moan. Basically, this behaviour reflects someone who is stuck in her personal ego position and is more interested in making herself right and the other person wrong, rather than resolving the problem. The irony was that while Susan was feeling victimised by David's behaviour, he was also being victimised by her, so neither of them were happy or enjoying their work.

Susan and David needed to address the problem or move on. Although Susan got a pay-off in the pleasure she gained from moaning about David, she was nonetheless allowing the situation to continue to cause conflict. The coach's role is to help her to:

✔ Take action to address the situation. The first step was to help Susan identify a positive outcome. She started by saying that it would be for David to 'get off my back'. Where possible, however, try to identify an outcome that has a mutual benefit to both parties – what is known as a win–win. For example, Susan framed the outcome: 'David and I find a way to develop a cooperative relationship.'

✔ Develop helpful strategies: 'David gives me support in setting up my customer helpline systems so that I can feel less pressurised and I can then make more effort to turn up on time at meetings.'

To achieve this change, Susan was going to have to influence David to support her. She came to see that he would be more likely to give her the support she wanted if they had a good relationship. Through the coaching sessions, she realised that by holding on to her negative thoughts about him she was perpetuating his view of her as difficult and uncooperative. Instead of blaming him, the coach asked her to consider what she could do to alter the situation, on the basis that she could not change him but only change her own behaviour towards him.

Susan devised a strategy whereby she demonstrated to David how the customer helpline system could also be a benefit to him, and how it could free up her time so that she could contribute more effectively in meetings. She also managed to focus on some of his good points rather than focus only on the features of his behaviour that she disliked.

Gradually, over a period of three months, Susan was able to redress the relationship so that she treated David with respect rather than resentment. She no longer behaved as a victim, nor made him one, and their relationship improved significantly.

Transforming the approach to situations

The way people think transforms their approach to events and situations. Thinking is the key to change. We all have bad days and difficult relationships to manage at some stage. We can either remain stuck in the approach we have always taken, focusing on negativity and helplessness, or we can choose to switch to a new way of thinking and approaching challenges. Although thinking is the core driver, a holistic approach to change is even more effective. Draw your client's attention to:

✔ Body posture and body language – being the person who is more confident by standing taller and having more personal presence

✔ Language – moving away from talking about the problem and talking positively and constructively about solutions

✔ Appearance – becoming the person who looks as if she resolves her issues and moves forward

✔ Behaviours – assertiveness and good interpersonal communication that supports mutually respectful relationships

✔ Actions – step-by-step movement towards goals

✔ Reward – recording and celebrating success, however small, and including effort as well as tangible results

Chapter 7

Managing Setbacks and Obstacles

. . . .

In This Chapter

▶ Working through problems

▶ Re-engaging your client's buy-in

▶ Managing surprise events

▶ Accepting your own fallibility

. . . .

*I*n an ideal world, CBC sessions work brilliantly and you provide your clients with the process and tools they need to achieve their goals. However, life isn't always ideal, and most times you meet a few bumps along the way. By preparing for the occasional problem, those bumps won't faze you when they occur.

The majority of the time all works well. Indeed, I recommend that you have positive expectations both of your clients and the coaching sessions. But I do suggest that you keep a mental drawer in which you store back-up solutions in case the coaching programme does not work out quite the way that you and your client plan.

In this chapter, I alert you to some of the problems that arise in coaching, and give you tips so that you can manage the problems if they do happen. Best of all, by raising potential issues, I may also be able to avoid them happening to you at all.

Accepting that Things Don't Always Work Out the Way You Expect

The coaching relationship is like any other relationship. At the beginning, you may have a honeymoon phase where you and the client have high hopes of each other. As a CB coach, you feel enthusiastic and ready to help your client achieve his goals. Your client is also likely to be enthusiastic that the coaching programme will help him. However, you don't know each other yet. Most of the time, coach–client relationships develop easily, but occasionally you find a personality clash or the pair of you don't communicate well. Here are some examples:

Bertie was a manager in an engineering company. His boss suggested that he have coaching in leadership. Bertie was unsure about the idea. He didn't place much emphasis on personal development and thought it was a bit of a waste of time, but felt that he should keep his boss happy so, reluctantly, attended the first session.

He found the process painful. He was a man who was happier working on tasks rather than talking about things, particularly when the conversation revolved around himself. He found it difficult to see the point of developing self-knowledge and thought of it as 'navel-gazing'. He said that he thought leaders were born, not made, and didn't see how coaching would help him. However much the coach endeavoured to place the work within the context of his business, Bertie struggled to understand what it was all about.

The first two sessions were very difficult: although Bertie and his coach spoke English, it was as if they were talking different languages. Neither really understood the other. Bertie's mind worked systematically; the coach's mind worked conceptually. The experienced coach realised that he needed to adapt to the situation, but found bridging the difference between Bertie and himself quite hard. The coach despaired that he'd ever find a connection with Bertie. Meanwhile, Bertie doubted himself and wondered whether he was just not leadership material after all.

In the third session, the coach decided to take action by:

- ✔ Raising the issue honestly and compassionately
- ✔ Discussing how he perceived the problem
- ✔ Being open and ready to listen to how Bertie felt, and to receive feedback
- ✔ Deciding with Bertie whether they thought there was any purpose in pursuing further sessions

The conversation was not easy for Bertie or the coach. They agreed that they approached life and work from diametrically opposite perspectives and that this difference caused them confusion. By talking to each other, however, they accepted that they were both discovering a great deal and that the experience would be useful in other situations as well. They agreed to work together and to allocate a period of time to share and discuss problems as they arose. Bertie suggested that reading books and theories of leadership would help him to engage better with the topic, and the coach supplied a bibliography of books and articles that provided examples of the business benefits of leadership development.

The example throws up key points that you may want to bear in mind:

- ✔ **Consider coaching as a collaboration:** You don't have to take full responsibility yourself for making it work.

- ✔ **Deal with different thinking:** Be aware that your client may think very differently from you. Be prepared to ask him how he prefers to discover new things and how he likes information presented. For example, your client may prefer to:

  - Read the theory in books and journals

  - Listen to CDs or tapes

  - Discuss issues with you in conversation or in a network group

  - Role-play situations in order to practise new behaviours and language

  - Draw pictures and symbols to depict the situation

  - Use metaphors and stories to illustrate the situation

- ✔ **Don't deem you or your client a failure:** If the relationship doesn't work out, neither of you has failed or is deficient in any way. You can't win them all – accept that and help your client to do the same.

- ✔ **Let go when necessary:** If the relationship isn't working, don't force matters. Where appropriate, suggest that the client tries working with someone else. Keep a resource list of other coaches to whom you can refer clients.

- ✔ **Pick up problems as they arise:** Don't wait for several sessions to pass, imagining that problems just sort themselves out. Honesty can act as a catalyst to deeper understanding and change, and gives you both an opportunity to decide how to manage the situation.

Managing when your client doesn't follow through

However much your client looks forward to the coaching sessions, he may not realise that he has to do the hard work. Your coaching sessions are just a small part of the process of your client's development – and your client needs to do the bulk of work outside the coaching room.

Home tasks and taking actions between sessions are essential parts of the *self-directed* and *psycho-educative* features of CBC. This means that the client is responsible for initiating and driving his own development and becoming familiar with his own psychological perspectives and how to manage them. Practice and repetition are big features of behaviour change – think about how you repeated your times-tables before you finally remembered them.

Your client may not appreciate the importance of home tasks, which may lead him to become disillusioned that the coaching sessions aren't having an impact. To help your client understand the importance of his own role in his CBC, ask him to do the following:

- **Understand that real change happens when he carries out home tasks rather than in the coaching session itself:** Ask your client to talk about something he has discovered or changed previously in his life, and help him to remember how that change required action and repetition.

- **Reconnect with his goals:** What does he want to change? What does he see as the advantages of achieving those goals?

- **Identify specific actions to take him towards change:** Ensure that the tasks are in manageable steps and relevant to his goals. Make sure that he knows the purpose of the tasks and how they will benefit him or lead him towards his work and life objectives.

- **Plan exactly when he will do the assignment:** Agree on what, where, when, with whom, how, and why.

- **Make a written version of the plan:** Ask your client to record what he attempts, how things go, what he discovers, and how he may adjust his approach in future.

The coaching relationship is one of mutual cooperation and mutual responsibility. Your part is to provide the process, strategies, and tools for your client. Your client's part is to participate and practise: doing his home assignments is a part of this agreement. I don't suggest that you act like a schoolteacher, but you may need to stress that action is an essential part of change.

Overcoming unpredictable events

Things in life don't always go to plan – and the same applies to coaching. Events quite out of the control of coach and client may happen. Restructures, change initiatives, mergers, takeovers, economic and political change, family events, and world affairs can all impact on the progress of coaching sessions. As a CB coach, try to develop resilience for when the unexpected happens.

Linda's work–life balance

Linda came to coaching feeling out of balance. She regretted that she was unable to pick up her daughter from school during the week. She was the main breadwinner and her husband did the school runs. As the main earner, she was also anxious not to rock the boat at work, and to continue to look committed. During the coaching session, she identified that her home task would be to get to the school gate more frequently – she felt that she missed out on knowing her daughter's teachers and getting to know other mothers and children. She decided that she would like to leave work early two evenings a week in order to be able to do the school run. However, after several weeks, she was still not managing to achieve this goal. Each week there was an urgent work task that needed to be undertaken, or a conference call with the USA at the end of the day.

Linda needed to overcome her fears of what her peers and her boss might say. Her coach listened to her excuses and then asked her how else she might handle the situation in order to achieve her goal. Linda decided that the best option would be to discuss her needs with her boss. She knew she was respected within the organisation and thought it doubtful that the organisation would want to lose her. She needed to explain that although her work was important, this small change in her routine was also important.

She expressed her needs clearly and assertively, rather than sneaking away. The CB coach helped her to prepare for the meeting with her boss, clarifying the ideal outcome, helping her manage feelings of anxiety and guilt, and encouraging her to practise how to ask to come in early and leave early on two days a week. Linda managed to complete the task. After initial resistance, her boss eventually agreed that he would release her. Linda decided that she would start this process with just one day a week and then build up to two days as she became more comfortable leaving early.

Mike had been having coaching for some time, grooming him for an interview to become managing director (MD) of a large department within his stationery company. He was feeling confident and he and his coach had undertaken several mock interviews, which he felt sure he had handled well. He knew that the Board was looking at various options for this post, but felt he had a good chance of getting the job. The coach was also pleased with his progress and wished him luck.

However, at the next coaching session, Mike explained that the Board had just announced that the company was going to be involved in a merger with an American stationery business. This merger meant that the recruitment of the MD position had been halted while the Board analysed how it would restructure the business. Mike felt that all their hard work had been a waste. He was also disappointed that the Board had not discussed the potential merger with him at an earlier stage, rather than just announcing it to him (although it had not yet announced the situation publicly).

Mike came to understand the following:

- Although this specific opportunity slipped through his fingers, the work that he had done would always be useful. He may well be put forward for the MD position again in the future or, if things change radically, he may need to apply for another post and would need to be ready for interview there too.

- He needs to put the experience in context and work out a strategy for the future within the changed circumstances.

- Discovery and acquiring knowledge are never wasted.

Engaging the Demotivated Client

Change doesn't happen overnight. Developing new thoughts, language, and behaviour is like discovering a foreign language – which, for most people, takes time and persistence. Some clients expect too much of themselves and the coaching sessions, and get demotivated when things don't work out as quickly as they would like.

Most CBC programmes are short and focused – an average of six sessions. This short time span can give your client the impression that he will see the evidence of change quickly. Sometimes the change is quick, but sometimes it takes time – and being prepared for both eventualities is a good idea.

If your client is demotivated, revisit his demands and expectations of himself, of you, and of the coaching sessions.

Bob got frustrated when, by the fourth coaching session, he was still not managing to control his temper with one of his colleagues. He identified the following demands:

- **About himself:** 'I really ought to get this temper sussed by now. I know what I am supposed to do, but just can't seem to manage my temper. I am a hopeless case and really fed up with myself. I feel I am out of control.'

- **About his coach:** 'I thought my coach would enable me to change my behaviour easily and immediately. Perhaps he is no good. I just don't feel the coaching is working.'

- **About his coaching sessions:** 'I expected to be given foolproof systems for change. I didn't think it would be this difficult. I feel the coaching is taking away my confidence instead of giving it to me.'

These thoughts signified that Bob was beating himself up and doubting the coaching process. His coach helped him to manage his impatience with himself and the process by comparing the current situation with other challenges Bob had experienced. Bob altered his approach to allow for the fact that change can be tough, especially when it involves adjusting the balance in a relationship. He came to accept that he cannot control or predict the behaviour of his colleague, but can continue to believe in himself and the process of finding ways to manage his temper.

Bob decided: 'I can work through this change step by step and feel confident that I have the ability to achieve my goal in the long term. In the meantime, I shall stop and pace myself when I feel my anger rising with my colleague.'

This decision helped Bob get back on track and feel motivated to keep trying to make change happen.

In the example above about Bob, the coach had to work on himself so that he didn't feel that he had failed his client. The coach ensured that his thinking and perspective were rational, that he had tried his best, that he provided what models and processes he knew, and that this experience was a discovery process for him as well as Bob.

Checking the relevance of your client's goals

Sometimes your client's efforts and energy seem to stall. If this situation happens, you need to unearth the reasons why.

Martin worked in an insurance company. He was about to take his actuarial exams but was finding it difficult to get motivated and had failed his initial exam. His HR department decided that it would be helpful for him to have coaching to support him through the professional qualifications.

Martin was an intelligent young man with a good degree. However, he had lost confidence through the study process for the actuarial exams and felt crushed by failing the exam. His coach was working with him to support his strategies in gaining the qualification, but came to realise that something was blocking him. Martin just wasn't working and the coaching sessions were not helping him progress.

The coach explored whether Martin had disconnected from his original goal. He suspected that Martin had lost touch with the reason why he was even wanting to become an actuary or get the exam. It turned out that Martin was jealous that his girlfriend and flatmates were all out partying in the evenings. He resented the fact that he had to stay in to study. Martin focused on the short-term pain rather than the long-term gain. Through coaching, Martin realised that he needed to review whether this route was, in fact, what he really wanted for himself.

The coach asked Martin to reflect on his initial reasons for applying for the insurance job, and to review his values and lifestyle goals so as to see whether, in fact, this actuarial qualification would take him closer to the work–life goals that he held dear. The coach worked through the following process:

- ✔ **Finding out about future plans:** Beginning with the end in mind, the coach asked Martin what he actually wanted for his future. Martin was considering asking his girlfriend to marry him and knew that, whatever her answer, he did want to get married, enjoy financial stability, and raise a family.

- ✔ **Assessing his values:** Martin valued security, family, being interested in his work, money and financial gain, status, and reputation.

- ✔ **Reviewing his original career choice:** Martin's career had occurred due to a chance conversation with a friend of his father's. He had got a job during his school holidays and was offered a place with the company after graduating. Martin admitted that it had been an easy route and he had not necessarily given much thought to other possibilities. He decided that he would be wise to spend his next week's home task assignment researching other careers so as to make sure that he did, in fact, view insurance as his preferred route. This research led him to look at banking, accounting, and management consultancy. However, he decided in the end that he was happy where he was. He enjoyed the environment within his insurance business. He liked his boss and colleagues and felt that he was well-treated as a member of staff. He also saw that there was potential for him to go up the career ladder. This process reconnected him with his original decision to undertake the professional qualifications, and his enthusiasm began to return.

- ✔ **Action planning:** Martin decided to create a postcard to place above his desk that reminded him of the benefits of gaining the qualification. He also worked out a plan to get up an hour earlier in the morning to study before going to the office, and to set aside an hour immediately when he returned to his flat from the office. This effort would give him structure and also the opportunity to go out with his friends later in the evening if he felt like it.

Some clients make a decision to undertake a goal and then, at a later stage, forget why they did so. This forgetting can lead to a blockage in the coaching process. Reviewing your client's values and purpose can reconnect and motivate him. If, at this later stage, life has moved on and your client's changed his mind, he can change course from an informed perspective rather than a knee-jerk reaction to disliking the short-term pain.

Evaluating the approach

Occasionally, you may need to change your approach. If something isn't working, there is no point continuing with it. Be alert and be flexible to considering new ways of delivering the coaching programme so as to ensure that the sessions are as effective as possible. You can alter:

- ✔ The timing of the sessions – some people are morning people and others get going later in the day. Discuss a time that best meets your client's needs and energy levels.

- ✔ The length of sessions – observe your client's attention span – he may have a low boredom threshold, in which case you can shorten the length of the session.

- ✔ The venue and environment in which you hold the coaching sessions – make sure that the venue is both convenient and appropriate to your client's style. For example, be willing to flex should you consider that your client would prefer a more formal or informal environment.

- ✔ The methodology – if one type of exercise or activity doesn't seem to be working, try another – for example, if you have been working through the ABC model, you might switch to some role-play for a change.

- ✔ The way in which you communicate and interact with your client – see Chapter 15 for ways to bridge communication styles.

Brian always ran his coaching sessions within a serviced office block in the City of London. The location was convenient for him and for most of his clients. However, he noticed that one client, Maria, fidgeted a great deal and looked uncomfortable in the surroundings. She always went straight to the window and asked to open it, and chose to sit on the sofa rather than on the office chair at Brian's table.

After a couple of sessions, Brian discovered that Maria enjoyed walking, but had little opportunity to do so during her working week. Brian had the idea to run their coaching sessions outside, walking by the River Thames. In this way, they could walk and talk at the same time. Maria was delighted and, whenever the weather allowed, they would spend the majority of the session outside walking, only returning to the office to note down progress points. Brian found that Maria immediately became more engaged in the coaching process now that she was able to have space and fresh air: it seemed to enable her to concentrate better.

In this process, Brian also helped Maria to find ways to manage meetings more effectively when she was not able to open a window. She developed thoughts such as: 'I'd rather be outside and have some fresh air, but I can manage to participate in the meeting and can then take a walk around the block afterwards.'

Another coach, Liz, also ran her coaching sessions in a city centre. Most of the time this location worked well, but one client, James, was facing retirement and admitted that he had 'forgotten how to relax and be at leisure'. They made all kinds of plans to help him find relaxing activities such as enjoying his CD collection and taking up photography, but James was still locked into his workaholic tendencies during the working week. He got into the office by 7:30 a.m. and worked straight through, often until 8 p.m. He didn't take lunch. His coaching sessions had been arranged in the breakfast period because he liked to get on with work after 8:30 a.m. However, as he sat in the coaching room, it was obvious that he was fretting about all the emails and tasks that were building up at his desk to occupy him for the rest of the day. This worry meant he found it even harder to relax and focus.

Liz had the following ideas:

✔ To undertake their coaching sessions in the lunch hour. She encouraged him to take time to have a salad or healthy snack.

✔ To attend a lunchtime concert in a city church nearby.

✔ To walk around a London art gallery.

✔ To help James develop relaxing thoughts such as 'I can relax and be present in this situation and address my workload later.'

✔ To practise breathing exercises – to develop mental focus on the in-and-out breath and release other thoughts and concerns.

✔ To slow James's walking pace and open his senses to the environment, to observe what he was seeing and hearing, so as to slow down and relax.

By the time he retired, James felt well-prepared to manage his own time outside the workplace and had arranged to meet up with a friend once a month to visit a concert or gallery.

The benefits of visiting an art gallery

Much research has been done on the impact of the steroid hormone cortisol, which is released into the bloodstream under stress or anxiety. Cortisol is exactly what you need to protect yourself during a physical attack, but it is also a major cause of ill-health and coronary heart disease if it stays in the bloodstream for prolonged periods. A research project in 2006 demonstrated that a 35-minute visit to an art gallery reduces cortisol levels.

Source: Professor Angela Clow, Department of Psychology, University of Westminster, London

Being a CB coach often requires creative solutions. Your focus is always on helping your client develop strategies to manage more effectively the situations he faces. This focus can sometimes take a little ingenuity and the ability to see that you have many ways to achieve the outcomes you've set, beyond the coaching room.

Asking for Help

You can find many sources of help and support available for you as a CB coach. One example is formal supervision, which provides a forum for you to discuss coaching issues and problems. This is a vital resource to help you with setbacks when and if they arise. You can find more information about this in Chapter 4. Your supervisor is likely to have his own personal experiences of coaching. Supervisors also have the benefit of listening to the stories of other coaches. Supervision is a safe environment in which to share difficulties and seek professional advice.

Coaching networks also provide excellent opportunities to discuss some of the issues you may be facing in your coaching sessions. There is more information on coaching networks in Chapter 4. Inevitably, you need to bear your client's confidentiality in mind, but you can, however, raise specific themes and problems and find out what others do in similar circumstances.

Colleagues and friends can also be helpful, sometimes bringing a completely different perspective to those in the coaching profession. More brains are better than one, so take advantage of other people's solutions.

Gaining other perspectives isn't a weakness

You're not a superhero. Don't feel that discussing problems when they arise is a weakness. Dealing with people's lives, hopes, dreams, and emotions is a complex area, and inevitably sometimes things go wrong.

In the business of CBC, you may feel that you should know yourself perfectly, have developed yourself personally and professionally to the highest standards, that you should have all the answers, and that you should have the perfect solution or process to address your client's goals. You may feel a failure if things don't work out. But, however much you train and practise, you're still a human being who develops insights until the day you die. Seek help early rather than dig yourself further into problems. There may well be an emotional connection to your work that makes it difficult for you to see things rationally. Talking to others can help you to gain objectivity as well as generating creative solutions to problems.

Using difficulties as opportunities for discovery

You work with your clients on their development experiences all the time – and in so doing develop alongside them. See setbacks and obstacles in your coaching relationships as opportunities for you to stop and review your own thoughts, feelings, and behaviours. Coaching is challenging work, and you find yourself being challenged continuously through it. This challenge can be – and is, in the most part – exhilarating and exciting. However, it can also be tough to be in work where you constantly receive feedback and where your own approaches are challenged on the same levels as those of your client.

Spend time on reflection when things go wrong as well as when things go right. You may have a natural desire to put things behind you and move on, but you're unlikely to progress much if you do so without reflection. This reflection is what you're expecting of your clients, so stop and take stock. Try asking the following questions:

- ✔ What exactly went wrong?
- ✔ What thoughts, emotions, and behaviours were occurring on both parts? Were they rational and in perspective?
- ✔ Where did the responsibilities lie: are you taking too much on yourself?
- ✔ What could have been done differently?
- ✔ Is there anything you can do at this stage to right any wrongs?
- ✔ If you face this situation again, how else can you approach it?

You ask your clients to accept their own fallibility, so accept your own fallibility too. Be compassionate: being a CB coach certainly doesn't mean that you've got all the answers, nor are you expected to have. The process is a collaboration between you and your client, and we all make mistakes and have good times and bad. Luckily, the majority of the time, things go well and the fulfilment that you and your client both gain from a coaching programme is considerable.

Chapter 8

Focusing on the Final Session and Continuous Development

CBC is a time-limited approach. The aim is for your client to become her own coach by the end of the programme. You share your CBC tools, questioning techniques, models, and processes with your client so she can take these forward for herself. You help her to develop the habits of self-observation and self-coaching so she notices if she falls back into negative thinking and knows how to develop more positive and constructive ways of managing situations.

You empower your client to take control of her life. The relationship between you and your client is one of collaboration, but the client, not you, develops the methods to solve her own problems. As a CBC coach, you should not encourage dependency on yourself or the coaching process. The CBC home tasks that you set support this process, because your client applies the CBC models for herself between sessions, just as she does after the coaching programme finishes.

By participating in a CBC programme, your client is probably enthusiastic about pursuing her own self-development. Aim to help her realise that self-development makes the experience of life and work far more interesting, and that she will find the insights she gains about herself and others through CBC rewarding. Ultimately, your client develops the habit of continuously reviewing her approach, adjusting, and developing.

I usually find that this onward transition is a natural process. By setting an expectation at the outset regarding the duration of the programme, both you and your client achieve completion at that point. However, you can take certain actions to facilitate the outcome.

In this chapter, I provide information on how to prepare your client for life beyond her coaching sessions so that she feels confident in moving towards her goals without you.

Encouraging Your Client to Feel Confident about the Future

Throughout the coaching programme, you help your client develop confidence in her own ability to manage her life and work. As she takes control of her thinking and develops constructive and supportive thoughts about herself, she gains a sense of control over her responses to situations that she faces. Eventually your client develops the ability to cope by:

- ✔ Accepting life's uncertainty
- ✔ Riding the ups and downs of life with equanimity
- ✔ Using tools to manage herself more effectively
- ✔ Living with her own fallibility when she makes mistakes
- ✔ Allowing others to make mistakes
- ✔ Developing, understanding, and laughing

Your client needs to feel ready to continue developing on her own. Help her understand that CBC is not a long-term programme run over many years, as some therapeutic interventions are, but a short programme, often of only 6–12 sessions.

CBC is forward-focused, and so you discuss your client's goals throughout the sessions. In the final session, help your client plan and prepare for the events that she may face in the coming months and years.

Simon came for coaching to break through his shyness and reticence to speak up for himself. The coaching sessions focused specifically on the project he had been working on, where he had been part of a multinational team and felt himself rather overshadowed by certain US colleagues. He discovered how to put his point over more assertively and not feel nervous or overwhelmed by his colleagues' more assertive style of communicating.

As he moved on from coaching, Simon and his coach worked on a plan to help him tackle other situations in a similar way, so that he can be prepared for further eventualities. This plan included:

- ✔ Identifying likely events that would be occurring in the next few months

- ✔ Listing the skills and resources he had now acquired that would help him to manage these situations, including constructive thoughts, emotional management, assertiveness skills, and physical management of body language such as breathing slowly and standing tall

- ✔ A visualisation exercise whereby he was encouraged to develop a short video in his head, picturing various scenes of situations he was likely to experience – as 'director' of the mental video, he was asked to imagine himself managing others confidently; he mentally walked through various meetings, seeing himself speaking up and asserting his views successfully

- ✔ Role-playing some of these imagined events with his coach during the last session, practising being confident and assertive in managing people who were more extrovert than himself

Each situation is different, so you need to flex your approach to your client's needs for the specific events that she faces. The following principles apply to your approach to all your clients:

- ✔ Help her remember the goals she has already achieved.

- ✔ Reinforce her tools, strategies, and processes.

- ✔ Identify what your client has discovered.

- ✔ Urge your client to consider how she can apply all this knowledge in the future.

In this way, your client builds her confidence and realises that if she has made changes successfully in the past, she can do so again in the future.

Introducing the OVER TO YOU model

As your client moves on from coaching, she takes personal responsibility for the situations she faces. She devises her own remedial solutions. One of the most important tools to offer is the ability to retain emotional equilibrium within difficult situations. Some situations exist that your client cannot influence, and she needs to find a way of managing through acceptance. Other situations she can influence and have an impact on through her own behaviours and actions.

The *OVER TO YOU model* provides a process to help your client approach events with a specific planned strategy. The model uses a series of nine questions and activities that outline your client's desired approach:

- **Outcome:** What does she want to happen?
- **Visualise:** Help her to picture the successful goal being achieved.
- **Emotional check:** Use an 'enthusiasm gauge' – how much does she really want to achieve the goal?
- **Review methods:** Coach her to plan thoughts and methods to achieve the goal.
- **Try:** First steps – what is the first thing she can do?
- **Observe:** Are her thoughts and strategies positive and helping her to achieve her goal?
- **You:** Help her to realise that she can make mistakes and keep finding out new things.
- **Observe:** Review and adjust methods and goals to refine the approach.
- **Upwards – and onwards:** Help her to understand that success is a continuous process.

Martin had been working on his ability to influence senior management. He used the OVER TO YOU model and came up with the following ideas:

- **Outcome:** His identified outcome was that within six months, the two senior managers with whom he worked closely would be frequently seeking out his advice on his initiative to develop the organisation's sustainability policies.
- **Visualise:** Martin pictured scenes where he was escorting his managers around various parts of the office, observing changes in working practices that demonstrated new habits such as recycling and energy-saving, thus demonstrating the effectiveness of his actions.
- **Emotional check:** Martin felt enthusiastic about this outcome. He had two young children and felt strongly about environmental sustainability. It excited him to feel that he could play his own part in making it happen.
- **Review methods:** Martin and his coach reviewed the behaviours and strategies that had worked to influence his senior managers. Martin's managers had originally not been convinced by his ideas, but he had managed to persuade them that his policy suggestions could save the company money and also impact the environment in a positive way. He and his coach listed the strategies that had worked, and noted those that hadn't.

✔ **Try:** Martin planned out his strategy for the next six months. He knew that his main target for influence was the managing director (MD), who was rather old school and only played lip service to the changes Martin had made. Martin's target was to thoroughly convince him of the benefits of sustainability, leading to the point where he accepted the installation of solar panels on the roof of the office building. During the final session, Martin practised this conversation in role-play with his coach, who played the MD. In this way Martin was able to identify, through his coach's feedback and response, which words and phrases were likely to make the most impact on his MD.

✔ **Observe:** Martin wrote out a list of the thoughts that he was having about the next six months. On the whole, he was feeling pretty confident, but there were NATs (*negative automatic thoughts*) that he was having about the MD, such as 'Will he take me seriously?' 'Perhaps he can't change,' 'He is always so busy, he may not make the time to listen.' These thoughts were undermining Martin's efforts, and he identified one CAT – a *constructive automatic thought* – that he wanted to develop which would help him go forward with conviction: 'This policy is good for the environment, good for cost-saving and good for our business brand, so I am sure that I can get the MD's agreement if I take the time to explain things clearly.' This thought engaged his passion for the project and made him more convincing.

✔ **You:** Martin had been a perfectionist and had been highly critical of himself when things didn't go well. During the coaching sessions, he had started to pursue excellence, to accept that he – like everyone else – would make mistakes, and now had strategies to shrug his shoulders, smile, and objectively review what had worked and what hadn't without beating himself up.

✔ **Observe:** Martin realised that the best-laid plans can go awry, that things can change, and that there may be hurdles to go through. He therefore prepared himself for the fact that he would continually need to review his goals and strategies in order to hone his approach to achieve success.

✔ **Upwards:** Martin accepted that his own behaviour within this action would create its own energy, and that 'success' is not necessarily one defined moment but a continuous process of change and development that continues through a lifetime.

The OVER TO YOU model provides a structured approach to preparing for events both in life and work as your client goes forward. It helps your client review with a compassionate eye what she has done, what works, and what doesn't work, so that she can develop and adjust her approach on a continual basis.

Identifying steps and strategies

Your client's life is a project. She benefits from setting goals and milestones. People in business are often well practised at running projects, but people outside the work environment also have experience of projects – whether moving house, planning a holiday, or tackling DIY. Help your client set up a project road map for her own future. This involves making a detailed plan of (a) the situations she knows she will face over the next 12 months and how she will manage them, and (b) the goals and aspirations that she would like to achieve during the period. Figure 8-1 provides an example of how your client can use a Gantt chart to plan for events, and identify thoughts and emotions that motivate her. Alternatively, she could make a drawing similar to a road map or journey, with signposts to future goals, marking events, actions, and milestones she will encounter on the way. This enables her to plan both practical and emotional methods to manage the ups and downs she may face.

Left brain factors:

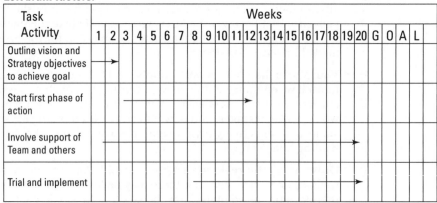

Right brain factors:

Figure 8-1:
A CBC approach to projects.

Encourage your client to take a holistic approach to her future. Many people are excellent at the 'left-brain' factors of milestones, goals, Gantt charts, spreadsheets, and timed deadlines. After all, listing tasks, times, and goals in a diary or computer calendar is easy enough. But the same people are often less good at the 'right-brain' requirements of reaching project results. There is more information on left and right-brain differences in Chapter 15. The 'right-brain' requirements incorporate the coaching aspect – seeking answers to some of the deeper questions such as the following:

- ✔ What is my vision – am I clear about it?

- ✔ Why do I want it?

- ✔ What thoughts can help me? What may hinder me?

- ✔ Who else do I need to involve? Are they clear about the vision and rationale?

- ✔ Who can help me with support, skills, and strengths?

- ✔ What skills and behaviours can help me achieve these goals?

Your client can apply this project approach to her personal and professional goals. Figure 8-1 shows a timed approach outlining tasks and actions and the coaching questions that your client needs to answer in order to engage not only her own emotional energy, but also the hearts and minds of other people whose support she may require for the successful completion of life and work projects. Her future success will inevitably involve the people with whom she interacts. These could be team members at work, and family or friends at home. She can share this planning process to motivate others as well as herself.

Your client needs to feel empowered to make her own decisions and take her own actions. As a CB coach, you exist not to flatter her or build up a false sense of her capabilities, but to help her recognise and acknowledge the skills and achievements she has already made and to identify how to apply these as she goes forward after her coaching programme.

You may want to use the *helps and hinders model* to help your client manage the steps she takes. This model encourages your client to list the factors that work for or against the achievement of her goals. The model considers aspects such as the following:

- ✔ **Actions:** What actions help or hinder the achievement of my goals? For example, picking up the phone to make a call will help me; procrastination will hinder.

- ✔ **Behaviours:** What behaviours help or hinder me? For example, being assertive will help me; not speaking up will hinder.

✔ **Emotions:** What emotions help or hinder me? For example, courage and confidence will help me; fear or anxiety will hinder.

✔ **Habits:** What habits help or hinder me? For example, building new habits will help me; old habits will hinder.

✔ **People:** Who helps or hinders the achievement of my goals? For example, certain people support me moving forward and help me; others like me the way I am and don't want me to change, so will hinder.

✔ **Thoughts:** Which help or hinder? For example, constructive and supportive thoughts will help me; negative or fearful thoughts will hinder.

In Table 8-1, I show an example of the helps and hinders model in action.

Table 8-1	The Helps and Hinders Model	
	Hinders	*Helps*
Thoughts:	'This will never work'	'I can make this work'
People:	My Mum, my old schoolmate	My partner, my PA, my boss
Behaviours:	Being unassertive	Expressing my needs clearly
Actions:	Distraction activities	Attending key meetings
Habits:	Not projecting my voice	Standing tall, maintaining eye contact
Emotions:	Fears and concerns	Enthusiasm for change

Identifying problems enables your client to prepare for potential difficulties before they arise. Burying her head in the sand doesn't work: having strategies to manage herself and the situations she faces does.

Seeing Self-Coaching as a Way of Life

See self-knowledge and self-observation as the key to moving forward. Add in a sense of humour also. If the inner voice of your client's internal coach is bad-tempered and critical, your client may soon be back where she started. If that inner voice is encouraging and supportive, she may make developmental self-observation a regular feature of how she operates.

The client's internal coach

The psycho-educative nature of your coaching programme provides your clients with models and strategies that she can apply as a thinking toolkit to help her manage situations for the rest of her life. CBC techniques support her appreciation of the good times and her ability to manage the difficult times, showing her how to:

- ✔ Set achievable, measurable, and timed goals
- ✔ Observe her thoughts, expectations, and language to ensure that they're rational and constructive
- ✔ Develop assertive behaviours
- ✔ Continuously review the process

Without regular coaching sessions, your client needs to integrate this process as a habit in her life. Warn her that the easiest thing in the world is to go back to where she began and forget all about it! Remind her that humans are deeply habitual creatures and what they do often then becomes an automatic part of their lives. If she is committed to continue the coaching process for herself, she really needs to motivate herself to do so frequently, particularly in the early weeks after your coaching programme finishes.

To encourage your client to self-coach, suggest that she does the following:

- ✔ Put regular self-review and self-coaching sessions in her diary over the first month so that she builds the habit of continuous development.
- ✔ Subscribe to some of the excellent websites that provide inspiring talks, information, and quotes on related subjects.
- ✔ Arrange to share her progress with a friend, partner, or colleague.
- ✔ Coach or mentor someone else – the best way of developing further is to teach others the process.

People can get downhearted when things don't go as planned. Your client needs to seek excellence, not perfection, so as to accept her fallibility when she makes mistakes. Refer to Chapter 1 for more information on this.

Part of the secret to your client's success in developing an 'inner coach' is for you to ensure that the inner voice sounds positive and encouraging. Check this matter out – you sometimes discover that she has her critical mother or father, headteacher, or ex-boss in her head instead of her own supportive voice. So you may need to help her develop this supportive tone for her inner dialogue by asking her to imagine a voice, preferably her own, encouraging her progress – like someone on the touchline of a sports field calling out motivational thoughts. She can practise this with you in the session.

If your client faces a situation that she finds difficult, one option is for her to go into 'neutral'. To find neutral, she disengages from the personal emotions she is feeling about the situation and acts a part that helps her manage. In this way, she stands outside herself and her problems and adopts a more objective perspective. She packages up her emotions and leaves them outside the door so that she can focus on being more in her head than in her heart. She can pick up and acknowledge the emotions again after the event, but this method enables her to remain more cool, professional, and detached during a difficult situation.

This method can be useful if your client has to do something within her work role that she does not feel comfortable with personally, such as giving negative feedback or making someone redundant. Your client focuses on being in her professional role, with the specific professional actions she needs to take, and disconnects from her personal feelings about the situation. In this way, she develops the ability to choose the approach and develop the 'inner coach' voice that fits a specific situation or requirement. She can also review her approach and challenge personal doubts or inhibitions so as to be flexible and try new methods.

The continuous journey of adjustment

We never get there – wherever 'there' is. Our current corporate and social environment tends to focus on measurable targets and goals. So does CBC. Although we may achieve one goal, there is always another to achieve. Life is a continuous journey of development and adjustment. We have peaks along the way, but we are in this process until the day we die.

Many people are fixed on the idea that they are too old to change or that they've not got the right skills to make any more changes in their lives. I have worked with clients as young as 30 who come to coaching sessions saying that their opportunities are over. Show your client how this belief is not true: many people make changes late in life. Life expectancy has increased radically in recent years, and people of all ages start businesses or develop new skills – my mother studied Egyptology in her 80s and found it thoroughly rewarding.

The idea of further change and continuous development frightens some people. They consider the word *change* to be a threat, despite the fact that everyone's life changes every day. Ask them to think back over the last ten years to remember how much they've changed and adjusted to circumstances, so as to build their confidence in the ability to manage change in future. Some people have negative thoughts about anything educative, thinking back to their experiences in the classroom at school. During the coaching programme, your client likely discovers that finding things out can be fun and that classroom experiences play only a small part in her story of success. Discovery through coaching is self-directed and rewarding.

The support of colleagues, partners, and friends is invaluable as your client goes forward. Ask her to identify people on her side to help her build a network of support. Then ask her to write a list of those people she can call on. Be specific: each one of us gets different input from different people. I offer a template in Table 8-2.

Table 8-2	Example of a Network List	
Who	*Why*	*Skills/Strengths to Share*
Tom B	Was supportive when I changed career and I value his wisdom and perspective	30 years' work in banking; he then set up his own consultancy so can help me consider whether self-employment is a good option for me

Support from a diverse group of people is a real bonus. Your client needs a few like-minded folk who understand her, but finding people with different perspectives and experiences who can open her mind in ways she may not achieve otherwise is also really valuable.

Some clients create a formal network of people with whom to have informal co-coaching sessions where they can continue their discovery and adjustment by shaping their ideas and approaches with others. I cover this in Chapter 4, and you will find contact details of professional bodies who organise coaching events in the Appendix.

Your client can also create a personal development log to review her progress over a period of time and track her personal changes and achievements. This can take the form of a paper journal, or computer or mobile technology, where she lists the events that she has been experiencing and reflects on the way she managed them, what has worked well, and what hasn't. She sets herself new goals for how she can manage situations differently in the future, so that she continually observes her development progress.

Completing the Coaching Process

Take time to stop and think about the ending of your coaching programme. This end is a transition point for you too, and with it can come a period of adjustment and a space that may yet need to be filled. This period may feel uncomfortable – you may like your client's company and enjoy the sessions with her. Acknowledge and value these feelings: the passion you have for your work is important. Then let go and move on.

You need to bear in mind certain formalities at the end of a coaching programme. You may need or want to:

✔ Invoice the client for work done

✔ Provide a written report on topics covered and actioned

✔ Give feedback to your client's boss or HR department

✔ Look for a new client

✔ Ask for a referral or testimonial

✔ Log the number of hours you've completed for your own continuous professional development (CPD) requirements with your professional coaching membership

Reviewing the coaching programme

Make time with your client to review the coaching programme. Provide each other with feedback – how did the programme go? What worked for her and what didn't? Be willing to listen and take her views on board. Your client may also want feedback with regard to her engagement in the process: be honest and supportive.

As discussed in Chapter 3, formal measurement may be appropriate here. For example, you may have done a prior measurement before the coaching session so that you can assess the impact of the programme. This measurement may have been a 360-degree feedback within your client's organisation, or some other informal measurement or feedback such as a phone call or email. You may need to send a report or arrange a meeting with your client's boss or HR department so that you can feed back development results. Make sure that your client completes any further post-coaching assessments that may be required.

It can be useful here to refer back to:

✔ A review of original objectives and gauge of achievement

✔ Issues raised

✔ Coaching reports that you may have taken or written after each session

✔ Activities, models, and strategies introduced and undertaken

✔ Mood and thinking logs, journals, recorded events, and discussion.

✔ Results: what worked, what didn't?

✔ Development points that are there for you both.

✔ What your client can take forward as having being discovered when coaching herself.

This review session is valuable for you both. It allows you to reinforce key messages and to clarify the scope of the programme – how much you've covered and its relevance to your client's objectives. It represents closure of a particular set of targets and the realisation for your client that she can take that process on for herself.

As a CB coach, you have to accept that many of the real changes that have occurred are on the inside – inside your client's head. These changes can be both subjective and intangible – not like a quantifiable measure of manufacturing a product or calculating a profit. You may never *see* the real difference that you've made, but what you can know is that you're bound to have sown seeds of change and growth whose fruits are realised sometimes for many years after the programme finishes. For example, one of my clients whom I had not seen for two years called me up and told me he had just got the promotion he had been working for in our sessions. Out of sight does not necessarily mean out of mind.

Agreeing future access and actions

Clients often contract for a certain period of time – say six sessions. When you come to the end of that period, you can confirm whether you are available for the occasional top-up session should clients want or need this help in the months to come. You often find that your client goes away and manages her self-coaching process well for several months, but that something may occur in her life that unsettles her – possibly a restructure or change at work, or a relationship problem at home.

You can also be available via:

✔ Phone or text message

✔ Email or instant messaging

✔ Skype or conferencing facilities

Keep the notes and records you made on file for at least five years, because sometimes people can turn up several years after your original sessions. If you've got the notes, you can refer back to the original issues that you dealt with, and also to any knowledge you have about the client's background, personality profile, and learning styles. You do, of course, need to be aware of data security and ensure that records on your system are kept confidential.

You may choose to define post-programme access within the contract. Make sure that you make it clear that although the programme has finished, you will be thinking of your client and supporting her future success. Also, make sure that she knows that you would like to have news of her achievements.

Chapter 9

Managing Self: Developing Self-Confidence

In This Chapter

▶ Seeing how beliefs limit your view of yourself

▶ Gaining a balanced view of strengths

▶ Realising how your experiences create skills

▶ Developing constructive thinking about yourself

....

*L*ack of self-confidence is one of the most common problems your clients bring into their coaching sessions. When people doubt themselves or lack the confidence to take action to improve a situation, their self-esteem and their sense of control over their life deplete. As a CB coach, you can explore how your client may be holding himself back by thinking in an unconstructive way and negating his personal strengths and qualities.

CBC provides a great framework to balance perspective. You can help your client focus less on negativity and more on recognising and valuing his strengths, personal qualities, and achievements. Through this recognition he can begin to accept himself as a unique individual. Your client builds an understanding that everyone is fallible, with both strengths and weaknesses. You can reassure him that, although you're there as his coach, you're also a fallible human being.

In this chapter, I include exercises and suggestions for you to apply in coaching sessions when your client raises confidence as an issue. You may be surprised by how a seemingly successful person with a sophisticated demeanour can be full of self-doubt underneath the surface. No-one is confident in all areas of his life, but you can transform how your client views himself by using these techniques.

Building Self-Confidence

Self-confidence is fundamental to success. It provides the drive required to face fear and pick up the phone in a sales call, or to go to a networking group for the first time. People who lack confidence tend to avoid occasions that may provide opportunities to meet key clients or promote their businesses. In personal life, lack of confidence can prevent a person going up to someone he finds attractive and asking her out.

Your job as a CB coach is to help your client to review his opinion of himself. Your client may be stuck in an outdated perspective of himself or may focus only on what goes wrong rather than what goes well in his life. In this way, your client may be his own worst self-critic, destroying himself with thoughts such as 'How could I be so stupid?' 'Why couldn't I get that right for goodness sake?' or 'There I go again, I always screw up.' Your role is to help your client:

✔ Identify negative or critical thoughts

✔ Check whether his views are based on evidence

✔ Develop self-supportive thoughts

Worrying less about others' opinions

Some clients put far too much store by other people's opinions. For example, I have met several clients in their 50s who harbour damaging comments made by critical parents or a bullying boss years ago. Your client may mistakenly believe that a comment is the truth rather than simply one person's opinion. As a CB coach, you can help your client:

✔ Check whether the person's comment was justified – if so, to consider what action to take; if not, to file the comment as interesting but not actionable

✔ Put the comment in the perspective of *other people's* comments

✔ Develop the ability to detach from the emotional content of a comment and view it objectively

CBC seeks to develop more rational and constructive ways of approaching situations.

Exploring limiting beliefs

Change begins in the mind. Thoughts either build confidence or deplete it. You provide your client with the opportunity to reflect on whether his thoughts are limiting his action towards his goals, by investigating the way he is thinking. Then you check the evidence of whether his self-doubt is based on fact or conjecture, and help him develop more constructive and supportive thoughts that raise his esteem and motivation to action.

Lisa is a salesperson responsible for achieving specific sales targets in her department. As her coach, you ask her what thoughts she has about the challenge. She identifies that she recently went to a conference but did not introduce herself to a prospective customer because she thought: 'I know that person is the buyer at a major retail store, but he won't want to meet me because I am so new to the business.' When she reflects on this incident, she begins to see that her thought made her feel helpless and insignificant, undermining her confidence to introduce herself. The consequence was that Lisa did not grasp the opportunity to promote herself or her business.

As Lisa's coach, you continue to explore with Lisa what underlying thoughts and beliefs may hold her back, asking her what evidence she has that the buyer wouldn't want to talk to someone new to the business.

By opting out of her challenge to introduce herself to the prospective customer, Lisa further depleted her esteem by not even having a go. This not trying results in her thinking: 'Why on earth didn't I go up to him? What a wasted opportunity! How can I have been such a wimp?' You can begin to help her to see that if at least she had had the courage to introduce herself, she may have been able to congratulate herself for being brave enough to try, even if the meeting had not resulted in a potential sale.

Many people have conflicting thoughts within challenging situations. For example, someone may express frustration with his current work role, but equally demonstrate that he doesn't feel confident enough to move up his organisation. One part of his mind is saying 'Go for it' and the other is saying 'You aren't good enough.' And so he doesn't try.

The key to building confidence and overcoming these doubts is to help your client see that he has control of which thought he chooses to take account of, and that eventually he will have control of the thoughts he generates about a situation. I call this skill *discovering how to become the controller of your mind*.

A good way to help your client identify his limiting beliefs is to provide him with the *beliefs–feelings log* that I show in Figure 9-1. Ask your client to take a situation where he experienced doubt or lack of confidence and remind himself of the thoughts he had during the event. Ask your client to write his thoughts in the log and reflect on how the thought or belief influenced the way he felt. In doing this, your client may see how his feelings of inadequacy derive from his thoughts and stop him taking action towards his goals.

In the example in Figure 9-1, the client wanted to go for a promotion but doubted his ability to do so. He convinced himself that he was not good enough. The doubts led him to feel fearful, inadequate, and isolated.

Beliefs: I can't go for promotion because:	Leads to Feeling:
• I haven't done that kind of work before	• Doubtful of own ability
• No one in my family has become a manager	• Doubtful and isolated
• I might be shown up for being stupid	• Fearful
• I might fail	• Fearful and blocked
• It will involve budgeting and I was useless at Maths at school	• Incompetent

Figure 9-1:
Beliefs–
feelings log.

When a person lacks confidence, he may fall into a negative loop of thinking that then becomes his reality. He literally can't see other ways of approaching the problem or understand that his beliefs may not be realistic. The more the person reminds himself that he isn't good at maths, for example, the more fearful he becomes at the prospect of budgeting in the workplace. His fear paralyses him. The thought itself has an impact on his behaviours and actions.

Checking for evidence

In your coaching sessions, try probing your client's thinking to reveal how it is impacting his confidence and behaviour. You are seeking fact and evidence of where he may have made assumptions or suppositions about a situation or person. The questions you ask focus on specifics so as to build a balanced perspective from which he can move forward. Apply the following questions:

✔ Are these beliefs based on fact?

✔ Where is the evidence for the belief?

✔ Is the belief helpful?

✔ Is it up to date?

✔ Is it your own belief or someone else's?

✔ When you say you haven't done that kind of work before, has there ever been a time when you did something similar?

✔ Just because no member of your family has become a manager, is there any logical reason why you can't do so?

✔ Have you met other managers whose parents were not managers?

Help your client move beyond his limits by enabling him to see that his thoughts may not be reality.

Sensitivity pays when you're exploring and challenging your client's thoughts. If you tell your client that the way he thinks isn't rational, he may get defensive. Such comments can deplete your client's confidence further by making him aware that you realise his approach is flawed. As a CB coach, you need to take your client through a process of reflection designed specifically to make him think for himself, generate his own ideas and solutions, and form his own decisions. Use questions as the most powerful method to help someone move beyond his self-limiting beliefs.

Be compassionate and sensitive when you challenge whether your client's way of approaching a situation is rational. A sense of lightness and humour can also work – especially when you make it clear that you're human too and also experience moments of doubt. Doubt is just part of being human but *can* be managed.

Managing Tamsin's fear of presentations

Using the PROVOKE model, Tamsin began to overcome her fear of public speaking and giving presentations. Below is a record of her progress.

Probe: Facts – four unsuccessful sales presentations, two successful sales presentations. Thoughts and beliefs – 'I'm no good at this;' 'I hate presenting;' 'They'll never buy anyway.'

Reflect: Evidence of her ability – two successful sales presentations, reflecting on what made those presentations successful, achieving a sales prize in her previous job.

Objectify: Another person may say that she is doing well, because sales meetings always have a success ratio. You never win them all, and she had won two.

Visualise: What Tamsin would look like if she were feeling capable and confident: walking taller, breathing more deeply, talking more slowly, and being charming, relaxed, knowledgeable, and friendly.

Own: Tamsin owned her past ways of thinking and started to identify strengths and decisions that she had been pleased with.

She had worked in different jobs around the world and was now pleased that she had landed her current post near her home town.

Know: Tamsin identified knowledge and skills she had. Knowledge: product knowledge, customer research. Skills: good planning, excellent teamwork, achieving most of her targets.

Encourage: Tamsin's coach helped her to take the first step: Tamsin planned to walk into the next sales meeting remembering how she felt when she was capable and confident. She froze a picture of herself in her mind – at her peak and wowing her audience. She decided that she would walk in thinking: 'I've won sales before, so I can win them again. If I don't win this sale then I can always try again. I have the skills.'

Tamsin reported a marked increase in her confidence when she tried out her first step. Although she did not win the sale, she said that she felt more relaxed and managed to quell her doubts. The client had given her good feedback, although the firm did not currently have the budget to buy her products.

The *PROVOKE model,* which I show in Figure 9-2, can help your client work through a problem and take steps towards his goals. You and your client work together to probe facts about the situation. Take the time to reflect on your client's approach and consider what works and what doesn't. Ask him how someone else might approach the situation, and generate alternative ways of managing it. Suggest that he imagine what it would look like if the situation were going well. Check that he owns his decisions and actions and doesn't blame them on others, that he acknowledges his skills and knowledge, and that he encourages himself to take steps forwards.

The PROVOKE Model

Probe – help the person really think about the facts and their beliefs about the situation

Reflect – help the person reflect on experiences and events that could demonstrate their ability

Objectify – help the person look at the situation from an observer's perspective

Visualise – help the person imagine what it would be like to feel capable and confident

Own – help the person own their beliefs, strengths and past and current decisions

Know – help the person consider what they know, what knowledge and skills they do have

Encourage – help the person to encourage themselves to take the first step

Figure 9-2: The PROVOKE model.

Checking evidence can be an enlightening experience for your client. He comes to see that his fears and doubts are not necessarily reality, but frequently based on supposition and imagination. Through questioning and reflecting, your client can come to see which beliefs are rational and factual and which are based on errors of perception or on the opinions of other people who may have had their own agendas. He can then develop more balanced and constructive ways of approaching his goals.

Updating self-perception

Your client may block out the thoughts and beliefs that energise him to take action. He may forget how he has managed situations successfully in the past. He may negate the skills that he has gained previously. Instead, he continues to hold a negative emotional association with an event long ago. For example, when one presentation goes badly he assumes, irrationally, that all presentations will go badly.

Often people in the workplace fear and dislike change, but forget that they've successfully managed changes many times before – moving schools, going to university, finding a job, starting a family. That is quite apart from the endless change initiatives they're already likely to have experienced in the workplace!

Enable your client to reflect on past experiences and remind himself of strengths and achievements that he has forgotten or not acknowledged. Try to move him towards options and thoughts to build his sense of confidence and capability. Include checking with your client what experiences, skills, and talents he already has that may provide him with the means to move forward. Although physical or practical achievements are not, in themselves, enough to build confidence, they do certainly help. You can help your client to move along the four-step process that I show in Figure 9-3. You start with the facts and beliefs about how your client sees the situation currently, develop optional ways of approaching the situation, consider past experiences and talents that can help and support him to move forward, and then take the first step towards his goal.

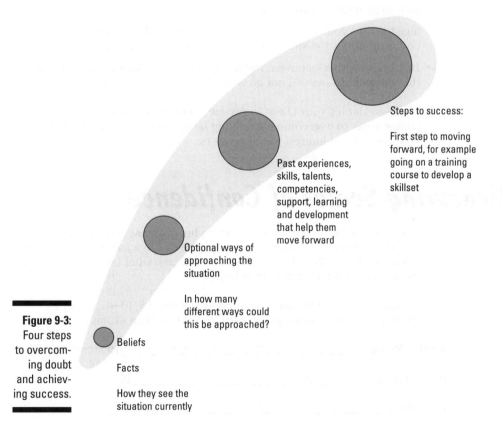

Steps to success:

First step to moving forward, for example going on a training course to develop a skillset

Past experiences, skills, talents, competencies, support, learning and development that help them move forward

Optional ways of approaching the situation

In how many different ways could this be approached?

Beliefs

Facts

How they see the situation currently

Figure 9-3:
Four steps
to overcom-
ing doubt
and achiev-
ing success.

When working within this four-step process, you may consider asking the following questions:

- ✔ What similar situation have you faced in the past and how did you tackle it?
- ✔ What changes have you experienced before and how did you manage them?
- ✔ Just because one person said you were stupid, how does that make it the truth?
- ✔ What skills and competencies do you have that are relevant to this situation?
- ✔ What feedback have you received that demonstrates that you may be able to manage this situation?
- ✔ Imagine that you're standing in someone else's shoes: what might he comment about the situation and your ability to manage it?
- ✔ Just because this last event did not go well, how does it logically follow that all such events will not go well?

This process enables your client to review his perceptions of himself and his capabilities so as to overcome his limiting beliefs and gain a more positive and balanced view of himself based on facts.

Measuring Scales of Confidence

Measurement can help your client to assess his progress. Your client analyses how he is perceiving his level of confidence within a particular situation. Measurement also enables you to identify and agree what level he would like to achieve and within what period of time.

For example, a person may have a confidence level of 8/10 when writing reports, but 2/10 when making a presentation. Here is an example:

Writing Reports 0_____8_____10

Presentations 0_____2_____10

Delegating 0_____6_____10

Accounts 0_____9____10

Creativity 0_____4_____10

By introducing a scaling mechanism, you enable your client to realise that being less confident in one area does not make him lack confidence in all areas. You help him gain perspective.

Your client can also decide priorities: what is more important to him? In the example above showing confidence level scores, the client had just become head of audit. Previously, he had not been required to present results, but, because he had recently been promoted, it was now important to become confident in presenting to the board. He was therefore content to leave his creativity score at 4, but decided that he would like to take his score on presentations from 2 to 7 within the next two months. So he set action steps to improve his presentation skills.

Journaling practices to acknowledge and record achievements

Journaling is a process similar to writing a diary, but it focuses specifically on development progress. A journal can either take the form of a diary which has space for notes as well as appointments, or can be a blank note-book or computer document.

A journal helps your client track and record his responses to current situations. Journaling can also be used as a process to record past successes. The pace of life today is so fast that people often complete successful projects without fully recognising or honouring their achievements. The focus is always on the next task, and therefore people forget the breadth of accomplishments and skills that they've developed during their lifetimes. Journaling is designed to provide space for reflection and review of events from an emotional and behavioural perspective. It can also be a place to list goals and objectives. I generally suggest that the client spends five to ten minutes each day on this task.

Sue was a housewife returning to the workplace. She felt very low in self-confidence and nervous about the prospect of looking for a job. 'I have no skills that are relevant to the workplace at all,' she said. Her coach challenged: '*No* skills?' This belief needed to be explored. So Sue went away and started to create a journal specifically to record her strengths, skills, and achievements. This record, shown in Figure 9-4, was in six sections:

- ✔ Her past, childhood, and early adult years
- ✔ Current family life
- ✔ Personal qualities, the type of person she was
- ✔ Skills, strengths, and achievements through her lifetime
- ✔ Difficult times she had managed, and the strengths she had gained
- ✔ What she might offer in the workplace in future

Childhood to 25	Today's Life	My Personal Qualities
• Head of my form at school	• Organise the house, kids and David.	• Patient
• Achieved GCSE and A levels	• Keep tabs on kids' homework and help them when needed.	• Organised
• Played in netball team		• Kind
• Lots of friends		• Curious
• Ran the Photography Club	• Arrange food and supplies for the house, including finding, retaining cleaner and delegating what I can to her!	• Fun
• Got to be quite good in the Computing Room — Excel spreadsheets to arrange Photography Club competitions.		• Sociable
		• A good networker
		• Persistent
	• Liaise with my sister to put my Mum in sheltered home near us — liaise with the Warden each fortnight and my Mum every day by phone or visit to make sure all is well.	• Creative — games with the kids
• Uni— did History of Art at Leeds. Managed hone and study projects; gave seminars; moved flat; had fun! Got a student loan and managed not to get in any more debt.		
	• Cook for the family and for friends too.	

My Skills and Achievements	Hard Times	What I can offer
• 8 GCSE	• Moved house several times when young — Dad in army.	• I can write well
• 4 A levels		• Able to get a group of people together to run projects
• 2.2 History of Art	• Learnt to manage in different places and get along with different cultures.	• Good at organisation
• Passed driving test		• Social abilities = good teamworker
• Won a few matches at school	• Came to senior school just before GCSE — had to make friends and catch up with work. — Managed this and got reasonable grades.	• Can lead and motivate (If you can get a teenager to clean a room you can do anything!)
• Got a job as soon as left Uni— for art magazine		
• My kids!	• Leeds — didn't know anyone. — Managed to get away from home okay and made friends.	• Creative — always thinking of new ideas
• Good relationship with sister and mother		• Can work with computers ok
• Loving marriage	• Married young — took some adjustment. Still good now.	• Possible jobs I can think of — fundraising team for a chairity.
• Hold the fort together!		
• Arranged the team ballot for the local election	• Dad died young — had to look after Mum just when having baby. — Sad time — mixed sadness and joy. Learnt compassion and patience.	• Social work?
• Part-time/occasional work on local newspaper		• Working with kids?
• Cooking, cleaning, tidying, organising, delegating, dog-walking, secretary, telephone receptionist, teacher, carer...		• Work in art gallery
		• Do a further arts or antiques course and set up gallery

Figure 9-4:
Sue's achieve-ment log.

The journal is a method to remind your client of the many transferrable skills and talents that he has developed through his lifetime but may have forgotten that he had. When your client records daily tasks and skills, he becomes consciously aware that he may be computing, organising, filing, team-working, influencing, running meetings, and delegating every week, but simply operating on automatic pilot and not valuing these skills.

Personal qualities, such as being kind, patient, or organised, are features of your client's personality and behaviour that he can discover how to value.

Both successful and difficult moments in a person's life enable him to reflect on the strengths he has built up through life. For example, if he had to move house many times during his childhood because of his parent's work commitments, he may also have acquired the ability to be flexible and adaptable to new situations.

The journal is a visual record that focuses on practical experience. This focusing can help your client to acknowledge his strengths. Acknowledging strengths propels him forward to gain more confidence and take more control of his life.

Bringing in the Big 1 and little i model of perspective

If your client has self-doubt, he may describe himself as a 'complete failure' or 'totally hopeless'. He negates himself as a person rather than simply considering himself as someone who has had one or two bad experiences or made the odd mistake.

Your client may have been through a divorce and ended up with a view of himself as 'an unlovable person' instead of someone whose relationship with one person did not work. Or he may have fallen out with his boss and feel unable to perform his role properly because the situation overwhelms his ability to think well of himself.

As a CB coach, don't minimise the emotional impact of an experience such as a divorce or a redundancy, but try to help your client build up his sense of self-worth beyond the external events that have befallen him. If he comes to you with a goal of building self-confidence, seek to help him appreciate himself as a human being with intrinsic value.

Self-acceptance is a fundamental principle of CBC and involves helping your client to come to terms with the fact that he is not perfect – but nor is anyone else. Work with your client to understand that everyone has strengths and weaknesses, quirks and qualities, and that he is just another part of the human race. Most people relate to the fact that a baby has an intrinsic value and uniqueness before he has ever developed any skills. Encourage your client to see that he was that baby once. He does not have to judge himself on his achievements, but can acknowledge his own sense of self-worth.

I use a model called the *Big I little i,* which I show in Figure 9-5, and which was developed by Arnold Lazarus, to help explain this concept of acknowledging self-worth. In this model, the Big I represents your client as an overall whole, encompassing all the little i's that make up that whole. Suggest that he fills in as many of the little 'i's as possible with details about personality, personal qualities, skills, talents, family, friends, work, skills, and hobbies.

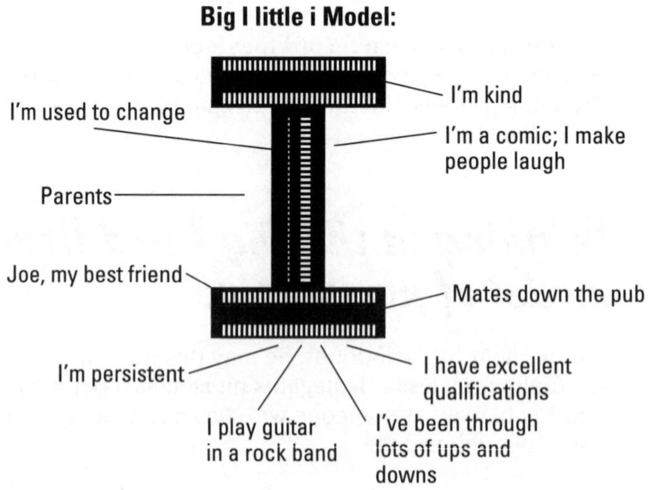

Big I little i Model:

I'm used to change

I'm kind

I'm a comic; I make people laugh

Parents

Joe, my best friend

Mates down the pub

I'm persistent

I have excellent qualifications

I play guitar in a rock band

I've been through lots of ups and downs

Figure 9-5:
Big I little i
model.

By completing his own Big I, little i diagram, your client builds a view of himself as a more holistic human being and begins to focus his attention on the areas that function well. You gradually enable him to develop a more balanced perspective of himself.

Generally, if one thing goes wrong in your client's life, even if this thing is an important event, plenty of other areas of his life remain intact. For example, being made redundant does not remove a person's skills or experiences, neither does it negate family, friends, and social network. Getting divorced does not logically mean that there is not another person out there to love in addition to those already in his life.

Using Constructive Thinking to Boost Confidence

One of your aims as a CB coach is for your client to realise that his doubts are often self-made and that he allows his thinking to undermine his confidence. Discovering that he is in control of situations can be an empowering revelation for your client.

Help your client identify what thoughts would be more constructive in developing self-acceptance and a view of himself as a confident individual. Ask him to identify specific thoughts that would build his self-worth. Without deciding on useful thoughts, his brain will go back down old and well-worn negative loops, just like falling back into old habits after making New Year resolutions.

Contrasting unhelpful with helpful thoughts

Your client has to become ace at spying on himself. Encourage him to listen in on the private conversations that go on in his head. He needs to create a warning alert for any thoughts that may undermine his confidence. As soon as he becomes aware of a negative thought, he needs to have a constructive thought ready to replace it.

These replacement thoughts must be supportive and rational – not unrealistic positive thoughts that have no basis in reality. For example, 'I am brilliant at everything I do' is unlikely to be realistic because no-one on earth is brilliant at everything.

Examples of rational and supportive thoughts are:

- ✔ 'I have succeeded at this skill in the past, so I am quite capable of succeeding again now.'
- ✔ 'I am finding out how to love and accept myself.'
- ✔ 'I can focus on my strengths.'

Self-criticism can be a difficult habit to break, especially if your client had a very critical parent, teacher, boss, or partner. The negative-obsessive loop can run on like a record stuck in a groove, pouring criticism on the client to the point of self-hatred. Your client must break this cycle and accept that even if someone else is criticising him, he does not have to take those opinions as facts.

Tuning in to notice which thoughts are helpful and which are unhelpful can sometimes be uncomfortable. It can certainly take practice, but it does develop confidence. Clearing the mind of negativity and doubt is like spring-cleaning an attic – it can be hard work, but feels great when you do it.

The link from thought to feeling needs to be emphasised frequently. How we feel shapes our experience of life. As your client tunes into his thoughts, he notices how those thoughts impact his emotional state. A thought such as 'I'll never get this right' is likely to incapacitate and demotivate him, increasing his sense of helplessness. A thought such as 'I shall work at this step by step and do my best' sets him up to persevere and pursue an excellent outcome, not necessarily an unrealistic 'perfect' outcome.

The following questions can help your client gain perspective and develop a habit of thinking more constructively:

- ✔ Is this thought helping me feel good?

- ✔ Is there any evidence for me believing this thought?

- ✔ Is this thought propelling me forwards or backwards?

- ✔ Is this thought really what I think about myself or is it just because x told me so years ago?

Your client can decide to metaphorically chuck old thoughts away into the dustbin. You may even suggest that he does this chucking out literally – by writing a page of negative thoughts and then throwing the paper in the bin.

Gradually, your client sees that he can control his thoughts. No-one else is inside his head – he has the control switch. The metaphor of a radio can be helpful – which of the following radio stations does he listen to?

- ✔ Negative FM – 'This is never going to work.'

- ✔ Critical FM – 'I am so hopeless.'

- ✔ I hate me FM – 'Why can I never get anything right?'

Or switch to:

✔ Positive FM – 'I can discover how to look on the bright side of life.'

✔ Constructive FM – 'I can do my best to make this work.'

✔ Optimistic FM – 'There are plenty of clients out there wanting to buy my products.'

✔ Encouraging FM – 'You can do it!'

✔ Music FM – if no constructive thought comes to your client's mind, ask him to have an uplifting 'signature tune' in his head. This tune can be any kind of music that makes him feel upbeat. It can stop the thought and put him in a more positive emotional state.

Developing new ways of thinking

Your client is finding out how to train his brain to focus on constructive and confidence-boosting thoughts. An effective way of helping him integrate these habits into his life is for him to develop several *affirmative thoughts* that he can call on in different situations. Affirmative thoughts are short sentences and words that provide constructive and rational ways of thinking, such as the following:

✔ 'I've got this far with my life and I have the potential to improve my situation.'

✔ 'I have the skills and resources to be successful.'

✔ 'I am noticing and honouring myself and my achievements.'

✔ 'I am loved and valued by. . . x, y, z. . . and can love and value myself.'

✔ 'I am a unique human being – just like everyone else!'

✔ 'I am developing from my experiences and becoming more confident every day.'

Ask your client to write down a maximum of six sentences to boost his confidence. You may need to help him work these out, because people who have got into the habit of thinking negatively lose the language of positivity. Make sure that the thoughts are constructive but also realistic. You're not pretending that life is always a bed of roses. The reality is that life can be difficult and unpredictable. What you're doing is helping him to build up his own resilience and belief system so that he has the capacity and resources to manage this ebb and flow, the ups and the downs.

Simon's networking event

Simon was a telecoms consultant working within a large organisation. When he was promoted to a line management role, he was expected to go to conferences and networking events to build relationships with people in other industries and raise the brand of his business. However, he was a desperately shy man, full of self-doubt. He dreaded this type of event because he hated having to introduce himself to strangers. He dried up and couldn't think of anything to say. In his coaching sessions, he discovered how to change his thoughts from 'I can't think of anything interesting to say to this person' to 'I can ask them questions about their businesses and then they will be doing most of the talking!' At the same time, he practised standing taller, taking more space in the room as he did so. Although he was a tall man, he had previously tried to draw as little attention to himself as possible. He found that when he stood tall and acted confident, other people came up to him and assumed that he was someone interesting to talk to. This change meant that he didn't have to make the first move as often. He was delighted with his new persona.

Suggest that your client places his affirmative thoughts on sticky notes around his house and workplace as a visual reminder. For example:

- ✔ Beside his bed
- ✔ On the bathroom mirror
- ✔ Above his desk
- ✔ In his wallet
- ✔ In his desk drawer

He needs to make reading and repeating the affirmations a routine habit, like brushing his teeth. The more often he is able to repeat the affirmations, the more he is building up the neural pathways to new and more constructive ways of thinking.

Becoming the change: Acting practice

As your client focuses on self-affirming thoughts, he begins to feel differently about himself. This feeling different also impacts on his physiology and body language. When he is self-critical or lacking confidence, he is likely to literally take up less space, physically and energetically, in a room. People who are full of self-doubt tend to bend over, look down, and not stand tall.

As your client develops the ability to feel more confident, he adopts more powerful body language, which increases his presence and impact. I give an example of this progression in the sidebar 'Simon's networking event'. Help your client to practise this process in coaching sessions and at home. Ask him to show you how he feels when he is confident. Guide him to stand to full height with his spine upright and shoulders back – not stiff like a soldier, but in a relaxed and flexible way. Explain that posture also influences blood and oxygen flow through his body, regulating his breathing and providing energy to both his brain and body. Building a constructive thought, positive emotion, and powerful physiology and body language helps your client to develop a greater sense of self-confidence. Figure 9-6 provides a visual reminder to your client: he can recall the three arrows building up the stages of confidence.

Figure 9-6: Three-step thoughts– emotions– physiology model.

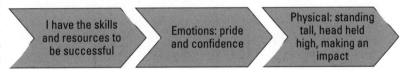

I have the skills and resources to be successful

Emotions: pride and confidence

Physical: standing tall, head held high, making an impact

As your client practises acting the part of a confident person, combined with the practice of monitoring and filtering his negative thoughts, he builds up what I refer to as the *inside–outside* method. The *inside* thought-filtering changes the way he responds to the different situations he faces and has the *outside* consequence of changing the way he stands, walks, and relates to other people.

CBC can transform the view your client has about himself and give him a totally new way of being. By adopting more powerful thoughts and body language, his mind and body become accustomed to these new thoughts and behaviours. As he lets go of his self-doubt and stands taller, he becomes a more confident person.

Part III
The CBC Toolkit in Work and Life

"There — now you've lost all your negative thoughts, <u>nothing</u> is impossible."

In this part . . .

This part takes you through the specific aspects of coaching that you may encounter as you progress in the CBC process. These include enabling a client to understand and manage themselves and to develop the confidence to broaden their goals and perspectives. I cover the all-important area of relating to others, and show you how to help your clients respect their own needs and those of others. I offer hints about helping your clients develop choices for work and life within the long-term context of their whole lives, and I show that CBC is a lifetime's journey that your client can continue on their own, as their own coach.

Chapter 10

Exploring Your Client's Potential

. . . .

In This Chapter

▶ Developing life and work goals

▶ Helping your client see beyond limiting expectations

▶ Biting off only what you can chew

▶ Applying the power of the mind to achieve success

. . . .

An exciting aspect of CBC is that it can enable your client to explore her potential more fully than she may have been able to do without you. This exploration is a key theme that runs through every session. Many people limit the goals they set themselves by holding on to outdated or irrational beliefs about what is possible and achievable. You can use CBC questions and processes to identify negative or doubtful thoughts so that you can investigate whether these may be narrowing your client's perspectives.

Everyone has been influenced by the events they've experienced in their lives, by the successes and the failures and particularly by the messages received from parents, teachers, and influential others. Our views of ourselves and our potential have inevitably been limited by what we have been taught to expect, and what we have experienced. Our social and cultural environments also shape what we see as possible.

Your role as a CB coach is to explore how these conditions have influenced your client, and whether she realises how many different directions may be available to her. The world is constantly changing, and opportunities are opening up in a way that our grandparents could not have conceived. Technology and globalisation are literally transforming the way we live and work, expanding the arena of what is possible.

In this chapter, I offer you tips to help your client see beyond any limitations she perceives of herself.

Thinking About Possibilities

CBC provides your client with more options than she previously thought she had. Each one of us is limited by being inside our own heads, and therefore by our own doubts, concerns, and anxieties. One person wouldn't think twice about selling up and moving to the other side of the world, whereas another wouldn't even begin to conceive of it as a possibility. Don't push your client further than she wants to go, but ask her questions and share stories to open up more perspectives than she held previously.

Humans are creatures of habit. Many people adhere to roughly the same lifestyle as that in which they grew up. This lifestyle includes:

✔ Geographical area

✔ Choice of political party

✔ Social community

✔ Religious belief

✔ Choice of education

✔ Choice of work

Social mobility in the UK is quite low. Among the many reasons for this fact, one key aspect is that people have limited expectations. Many loving parents still say things like 'Well, it was good enough for me, so it is good enough for him (our son)' or 'How can she (our daughter) imagine that she can ever be an actress?' without realising how such statements influence their children's decisions. Sadly, teachers still exist who tell pupils 'You will never amount to anything' or 'You're stupid,' which has a long-lasting detrimental effect on the young person's self-perception.

Due to technical change, a number of work opportunities are available today that didn't exist even five years ago. Those who counsel others on careers, such as parents and teachers, may not even be aware that these new opportunities exist. Therefore, there is generally work that you can do to develop your client's perception of her potential and the opportunities that may be open to her.

You're likely to be working on specific goals during your coaching programme. Your client benefits from understanding how these goals fit within her overall life goals. This understanding ensures that the aims she works towards in coaching take her nearer the lifestyle that she seeks.

Brainstorming your client's life

Encourage your client to brainstorm her ideal life. Try using the mind map that I show in Figure 10-1 to help your client move through aspects of her life and consider what she wants to achieve.

Together, negotiate the period of time that she wants to consider – does she want to project forwards to what she wants to experience in one, two, five, or ten years? To help your client set her goals, work through the mind map and ask her what she would like in an ideal world for the following:

- ✔ **Family:** Do you want children? If you already have some, what do you ideally want them to be doing and enjoying in two years' time? What do you enjoy doing with them? How would you like your relationship with your parents, siblings, and other family members to be?

- ✔ **Finance:** What do you need to take into consideration? What do you want to be earning? How much do you want to be able to save? What situation do you prefer with regard to mortgage, debt, finance, pension, and so on?

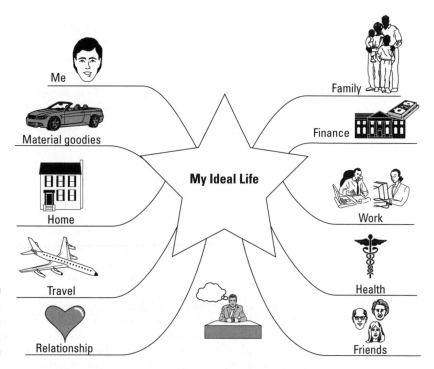

Me

Family

Material goodies

Finance

Home

My Ideal Life

Work

Travel

Health

Figure 10-1:
Possibility
thinking.

Relationship

Friends

✔ **Friends:** Do you want to give more or less time to friends? Do you want to develop new friends or new networks? What would you like to be doing with your friends?

✔ **Health:** What kind of health do you want to be in? What can you do to take care of yourself and those you love?

✔ **Home:** Are you happy in your current home? What improvements do you want to make to it? Are there various DIY tasks or building tasks that you would like to have achieved by this time? What would they look like? What about your garden? If you want to move, where do you want to move to? What does the house look like? What sort of road and area? How much land, how many rooms?

✔ **Material goodies:** Are there certain items you would like to have purchased by this time? For example new furniture, clothes, car, machines, or labour-saving gadgets? Are there ways you can start to save for these today?

✔ **Relationship:** What is your ideal picture for your relationship? If you're in one, in what ways can it be enhanced? If you're looking for one, how can you do so? What would you like to be contributing in your relationship? What would you like to be sharing with a partner?

✔ **Travel:** Are there specific places that you'd like to visit on business or for leisure? List these and consider the reasons why you want to go there. On a daily basis, are there any other ways to improve your travel arrangements to work, and so on?

✔ **Work:** What do you want to be doing in two, five, or ten years' time? What are the various options open to you: would you prefer to be in your current role, company, or sector, or would you like to have moved to a new position? What would your ideal day look like? What type of people do you want to have as colleagues? Do you like a routine job or variety? Do you want to be travelling? Do you like to work in a town or in the countryside? What part of the world do you want to work in?

✔ **You:** Goal-setting is not only about external goals, but about who you want to be on the inside too. How would you like to be feeling in yourself? Fitter? More confident? More accepting of who you are? More relaxed? Taking more time for hobbies and pursuits? Reading or studying more? Meditating, exercising, or spending more time in the countryside? What does this changed you look like and feel like?

By asking questions such as those that I list above, you start your client's mind working beyond a specific narrow focus. Start with these suggestions, but try tailoring the topics and questions more specifically to your client's situation. After you explore the various facets of your client's life, you can begin to go deeper and ask some of the following questions:

✔ Why? What is it about this goal that excites you?

✔ What difference would this make to your life?

✔ Have you taken your thinking as far as it can go with regard to options here?

✔ Are any aims conflicting – for example, have you listed 'stable home' on one branch but 'lots of variety and travel' on another? Which is more important?

✔ What does 'success' mean to you?

✔ What is it you really want – first, second, third?

✔ What values do you want to underlie your decisions?

This model can begin to open up possibilities for the future, and can certainly give your client goals to work towards.

Going beyond today's limiting perspectives

In an ever-changing world, your client needs to consider what else may change over the next few years, and what she may need to do to keep up to date and stay ahead of the game. Ask your client what may change in the following situations:

✔ **Economic environment:** What changes may take place in the political and economic environment, with emerging markets and financial influences? How can these impact upon you?

✔ **Home life:** Are your children growing up? What is your partner doing? What technological changes might you experience that would transform the way you live and work?

✔ **Society and culture:** What changes may occur in your own society, culture, or community? How can these impact on you?

✔ **Work sector:** What are your competitors planning? Is your company seeking to retrench or expand? What opportunities do you see? What actions might you need to take to stay ahead and be a leader in your field?

Again, these are suggestions, and you can apply them or not as you see fit. Some clients get excited by the pace of change, others get fearful. If your client is the former, then she is likely to relish considering these things. If she is the latter, then you may need to ask more focused questions so as to take her thinking gently forward to the future. Change is inevitable, so considering options does help your client to prepare for potential eventualities as and when they come.

To expand your client's perceptions, ask her what would she choose to do if she had seven parallel lives. In this kind of imaginary exercise, she is more likely to take risks beyond her normal safety zone. You can then explore whether your client can incorporate any aspects of these parallel lives into her future plans.

As your client begins to develop a vision of the lifestyle she wants to achieve, explore whether she has any limiting thoughts that may sabotage her efforts. For example, you may find that the following sorts of concerns hold her back:

- If I go and do something different, will family, friends, or colleagues think I am being arrogant?

- That job is rather posh compared with my friends' jobs.

- What will other people think of me?

- What happens if I fail and it doesn't work out?

- That decision is fine for Ahmed, but he's brighter than I am.

- I don't think I can possibly do that.

- That's scary!

- I'd love to, but. . .

These limiting thoughts undermine your client's ability to change, and prevent her from moving beyond her current position. She is unlikely even to consider new opportunities when her mind is so full of doubt. So work through her issues with her, taking each concern into account with sensitivity, and ask questions such as the following:

- What evidence do you have that other people may think you posh or arrogant if you make these changes? This kind of thinking is known as *mind reading*, because unless your client has any real evidence that other people will react in a particular way, she is making assumptions rather than basing these ideas on fact.

- What concerns you about what other people may think?

- What's the worst that can happen if you fail? What would be so awful about it not working out? This kind of thinking is known as *catastrophising* or *all-or-nothing* thinking: your client is imagining her action as totally successful or a complete disaster.

- What makes you think that you don't have as much potential to succeed as Ahmed?

- Why don't you think you can do this?

✔ What exactly scares you? Are you making the decision on the basis of an emotion rather than fact? We call this thinking *emotional reasoning*. Does feeling fearful preclude you from achieving your goal?

✔ Let's look at each fact that can stop you: are these facts reality or supposition?

✔ What thoughts and approaches can you apply to overcome these concerns?

One of the aims of CBC is to empower your client to value her uniqueness and make her own way in life. To benefit from others' experiences can be helpful, but to compare or limit herself because of assumptions about what other people may say is not generally useful.

Often, people hold perspectives that are actually those of previous generations and not necessarily relevant to today's world. Recently, I asked a group of young bankers in their 20s and 30s what their grandmothers had said about the nature of men's and women's roles in life. Despite the world having changed, old messages persisted such as 'A woman's place is in the home' and 'Men know best.' Young children predominantly brought up by their fathers still tend to talk about their mothers being the ones at home, despite the visible evidence to the contrary. The voices of our grandmothers take a long time to fade, so help your client update her perspectives to be relevant to today's world. Help your client to analyse whose belief is driving her: her own, her parents', her grandparents', or her teachers'?

Your client creates her own future, so give her permission to identify exactly what kind of world she wants to live in. That way she can begin to take steps towards that world.

Following the examples of other people's success

Think of some of the many stories of people who have started with nothing but nonetheless achieved success. Your past does not have to be a determinant of the future. CBC is about helping people to accept the situations they've experienced, but make the best of moving forward in strength to fulfil their potential. Some people may say that because they've had a difficult childhood, not achieved academic success, or suffered abuse or an act of violence, that their lives cannot move on. But their lives can move on! And you can help them to explore the realities of their situations so as to overcome their limiting perceptions.

Sadia came from Somalia. She suffered years of violence and abuse at the hands of her husband. Her parents and sister died in local troubles, but Sadia managed to escape to England. When she arrived, she was determined to make a success of her life. Instead of remaining a victim of her past, she thought that becoming successful in her own right was her best revenge on her ex-husband. She studied at night school and, with the help of her local social services, managed to find work as an administrator in an accounts department. She found it hard to stick to the discipline of work life at first and nearly lost her job. But, with the support of a job coach and a mentor in her workplace, she managed to be punctual and gradually developed the confidence to feel that she deserved the job and success. After a year, she was given a promotion to supervisor.

Interestingly, many successful people throughout history have had difficult beginnings and late starts. Think of the following:

✔ Richard Branson left school without academic success, but built up the highly successful Virgin brand.

✔ Jeanne Calment lived to the grand age of 122 and took up fencing at 85.

✔ Bill Gates dropped out of Harvard to start Microsoft and is now one of the wealthiest men in the world, and also a generous philanthropist.

✔ Dominic O'Brien was not considered to be an academic genius at school, but later became World Memory Champion.

✔ David Ogilvy set up the Ogilvy Mather advertising company at the age of 40, having started his life as an Aga salesman and chef. Ogilvy Mather became one of the most prestigious advertising companies in the world. He later discovered that he only had an IQ of 96 – but realised that his IQ had not precluded him from his success.

✔ JK Rowling was a single mother living in a bedsit, but it didn't stop her from writing the Harry Potter books and becoming a successful author and philanthropist.

You can probably think of many other examples yourself. Human beings find it easy to make excuses as to why they don't further develop their potential, but the fact is that human potential is pretty infinite and there to be tapped. Sometimes this tapping happens by design, sometimes by accident, but virtually always through hard work. Picking up on what other people have made of their lives may be inspiring to those who feel they can't succeed because of a limit of perception. So gather stories to share with your clients.

Setting Achievable Goals

You need to find the interesting balance between helping your client feel that she has unlimited potential and then actually setting a goal that is realistic and achievable. This balance is the two-step process of:

1. **Divergence** – brainstorming as many different possibilities and options as possible and taking someone beyond what she would originally have thought about, leading to

2. **Convergence** – bringing the options down to a small set of achievable goals

For the first stage, you stimulate your client's imagination and creativity, taking a few more risks than perhaps your client would take alone. In the second stage, you stimulate review and analysis of the options, bringing them into the context of your client's life, work, skills, and resources.

Perfectionism can sometimes creep into this process. Your client may desire a 'perfect' result, setting up a fear of making any decision in case the decision is not the 'right' one. The idea that someone can find an absolutely 'right' solution or goal can paralyse. One person's right can be another person's wrong: right and wrong decisions are subjective. Help your client to accept that she may have to live with a period of uncertainty as she starts to pursue her goal. Explain that even if she makes a decision and starts along a particular road, she can still change her mind in the future.

Making a decision, however small, has a certain energy to it – the disturbance of the mind that is created by confusion in the 'Will I, won't I?' phase is cleared and results in a greater sense of control.

Check your client's reality and enthusiasm for her goals by asking the following questions:

✔ If you were given this goal today, would you take it: yes or no?

✔ Do you have the skills and resources you need to make this happen?

✔ If not, what skills and resources do you need? How can you gain them?

✔ Can you make a start immediately? Let's set a timescale.

Setting change in motion is exciting, but do make sure that your client picks goals that she can measure and achieve. If she sets impossible goals, she may be demoralised later. Help her find the balance between believing in her potential and setting realistic goals that she is enthusiastic about putting into action.

Applying models for change

Change generally involves letting go. One way of life is replaced by another. This letting go can sometimes be a difficult transition. Acknowledging and letting go of the past is an important part of successful change. There can be a tendency for people to undermine past achievements rather than build on them. Many clients I have worked with have felt hurt that new change initiatives in their businesses have been brought in without adequate acknowledgement of people's efforts in the past. They see the initiatives as implying that what went before was not only outdated, but no good.

The past is the foundation stone for achievement of future goals. Nothing that has been discovered and experienced previously cannot be of use in the future. I give an example from my own life in the sidebar 'Transferable skills'.

Your client can develop the ability to give each transition a moment of acknowledgement, reflecting on what she can value and build on. Every change is also an ending, whether you're moving house, getting married, starting a family, getting a promotion, or beginning a new job. In each case, life changes in some way. Many of your clients are probably keen to leap forward. I suggest that you use the *LEAP model* to encourage your client to stop and reflect before leaping. With the LEAP model, you question the following aspects:

- **Letting go:** What is being released in order to move forward? What can be valued and built on?

- **Ending:** What has to end? How can you acknowledge emotions about this ending?

- **Adjusting:** What adjustments have to be made? Adjustments can include those to sense of self, thoughts, language, behaviours, way of life, or work.

- **Positive beginnings:** What is coming in? What does the new way of life look like?

Transferable skills

I had been married for 20 years and had been working part-time as a researcher for a historian while bringing up our two sons. I enjoyed the work, but realised that I would like to progress. However, I had not gone to university when I left school and decided to brave the prospect of three years' study in order to gain a history degree, which I completed when I just turned 41. It was hard work, and during the process I realised that I wanted to explore new work options rather than return to research. I retrained to became a business trainer and coach. This retraining was a completely new role. However, when laying up the room for my delegates, I came to see that I was applying all my old skills: researching information on the topic I was to train and the delegates who would attend; setting up the training room and welcoming the delegates to make them comfortable, as I had done as a corporate wife entertaining my husband's clients; dealing with people, philosophy, education, and concepts, as I had done when studying history; and, through my own experience at university as well as my sons' experiences of education, knowing that I must try to make the training interesting in order to be successful.

Allocating time for reflection helps your client to understand the transition she is experiencing more clearly. Change can be uncomfortable, but by realising that she can plan to take relevant skills and experiences with her, she is better able to leap to the next step confidently rather than crawl nervously into the future. This gives her a sense of continuity during the transition phase. Sharpen your client's approach by helping her to define the details of the goals she wants to achieve:

- ✔ How will you know when you've got there?
- ✔ How will others know?
- ✔ By what date do you want to have achieved the goal?
- ✔ In what way can you measure success?
- ✔ What are the benefits of this change?

Prepare your client for a period of confusion as she starts to make changes. Adults often expect to be able to move from one thing to the next and be totally competent immediately! Inevitably they are dealing with new situations, and it can take time to find out how to manage them. Taking time doesn't mean that the individuals are stupid or inadequate: finding out how to manage change is the natural process of acquiring new knowledge. The more she can accept this process, the more likely she is to succeed.

Biting one mouthful at a time: The step-by-step strategy to success

Goals require action, so your client needs to work out exactly what she has to do in order to achieve results. Progress is an evolving process. Make sure that your client sets measurable milestones that can help her move step by step towards her goal. Too great a task can be overwhelming.

A friend asked his 10-year-old son to sweep the leaves from the garden path one autumn day. The boy put on his wellington boots and anorak and disappeared enthusiastically into the garden. About an hour later he came back inside disconsolate. 'There are so many leaves, I shall never finish!' he grumbled. His father went out and showed him how to divide the path into manageable segments, lifting a small proportion of leaves into the wheelbarrow each time, leaving a visible clear space that signified a result. Gradually, bit by bit, his son finished the job and the path was clear.

A client, Wendy, was starting up a business, but she was overwhelmed by what she needed to manage. She was having sleepless nights about all the varied tasks she needed to fulfil to become successful. During the coaching sessions, she chunked the tasks into four activities: 1, Setting up the business; 2, Identifying the market; 3, Finance and accounting; 4, Client development.

Wendy made a plan to start with the administrative requirements of setting up her business with Companies House. Secondly, she moved on to identifying the market, working on her website and marketing materials. This work gave her a better understanding of the financial requirements she would need, so, thirdly, she arranged a loan with her bank. Fourthly, when she had her message, product identity, and branding clear, she began to have meetings with potential clients.

The human brain likes to see results, so help your client to structure her goals in such a way as to be able to get a few quick wins if possible. Putting reminders in her diary, computer calendar, or mobile phone to alert her to specific tasks usually works well. Suggest that she identifies a reward for each step achieved. This reward can take the form of personal acknowledgement of her effort, or she can give herself a treat.

Resist the temptation to set too many goals at the same time. Too many goals can dissipate energy and pull your client in too many directions. Focus on first things first: what is most important now? What can make the most difference to life? Then add new goals as each one is achieved.

Overcoming Hurdles

Be prepared for hiccups. Your client may be full of inspiration at one meeting, ready to take action, and then come to the next session in the doldrums. She has perhaps tried to develop a new behaviour or action and not had the result she wanted, or perhaps she has lost faith in herself and her ability to move forward and become the person she wants to be.

Some actions are more enjoyable than others, so find out how she can find a way to enjoy otherwise boring or challenging tasks that are nonetheless essential to her success. Here are a few suggestions:

- ✔ Undertaking the activity in a different environment – for instance at home or in the garden
- ✔ Connecting to the benefit of the end result and how good it will feel to get there
- ✔ Deciding to be in a good mood and find a way to enjoy the task
- ✔ Acting as if she has already overcome fears and anxieties and is the person who has achieved the goal
- ✔ Eliciting help from a friend or colleague

Try to move your client away from the pain, dissatisfaction, or discomfort of the past and move her forward towards the pleasure of the future. The *STEAM AHEAD model,* which I show in Table 10-1, can help you. In this model, the left-hand STEAM column reminds your client of how she steamed up at the discomfort of the old situation. The STEAM AHEAD column reinforces your client's thoughts and emotions to motivate action to reach her goals.

Table 10-1	The STEAM AHEAD Model
STEAM (pain)	*STEAM AHEAD (pleasure)*
Situation: Current/past situation	**S**ituation: Positive outcome
Thought: Negative thoughts	**T**hought: Constructive thoughts about the future
Emotion: Feelings around the old situation	**E**motion: How will you feel when you get there?
Action: What do you want to change?	**A**ction: What steps can you take?
Motivation: Why do you want to change?	**M**otivation: How can this help you?

Another reason why people get demotivated is that they've chosen a goal that is not in alignment with their values. Values are really important drivers of both conscious and subconscious action. I have known clients who have set a goal but found they sabotaged their efforts because the goal contradicted something they believed in. For example, this can happen when an individual succumbs to pressure from someone else. A client of mine was persuaded by a friend to book on a singles holiday. She agreed in order to please her friend, but she was not enthusiastic about the trip. Her own belief was that fate controlled whether or not she met a partner, and that the holiday was a waste of time. On arriving at the airport, she discovered that her passport had expired: she had consciously or unconsciously sabotaged the holiday.

Bruno took a job in a large organisation. He had spent many years as a manager in another company where staff and customers were well-treated. In his new role, he was put in charge of developing a new technology help desk where people were rewarded for the speed of the call rather than addressing customer needs. This focus on speed cut against his belief that the role of the help desk was first and foremost to take care of customers rather than to measure the time of the call in minutes. He found his physical energy diminishing, and became ill. He came to realise through coaching that he had been overlooking the impact on his well-being of how his actions in this role were contradicting his fundamental values about customer care. He decided to raise his discomfort with the HR department, and this led to strategic changes around measurement of the customer calls.

Developing resilience

Preparing your client for knocks is no bad thing. The *planning ahead model,* which I show in Table 10-2, focuses your client's mind on some of the things that can possibly go wrong or block her progress.

Table 10-2	The Planning Ahead Model
Predict: Events That Can Block	*Prepare: Actions That Can Be Taken*
My partner doesn't support my goal.	Be ready not to be defensive but to listen to his points one by one, see if I can see something he is threatened by, be ready to give reasons for my decision, and ask for his support.
My father comments that 'You haven't got it in you to do that.'	I accept that this is his opinion but his opinion is not necessarily the truth. I find a way to continue to believe that I can achieve my goal.

Life and work can be tough. Developing resilience and the ability to weather the storms is essential. Achieving goals and becoming the person your client wants to become takes perseverance and flexibility. The methods your client decides to use may not work. She needs to continually review her methods and may have to adapt her approach. Maintaining constructive thoughts and keeping the vision of the successful future in mind are key to success. When your client manages this process and achieves just one goal, she is likely to realise that many more doors than she thought previously are open to her.

Visualising success using imagery

With *visualisation,* you help your client to build pictures, like a video, in her head, of the successful achievement of her goals and potential. Interestingly, visualisation seems to trick the brain into thinking that your client is really experiencing the situations that she imagines. Even physiology is influenced: muscles twitch, hormones such as cortisol, adrenalin, and noradrenalin are regulated, and blood pressure impacted as if the events were actually occurring.

You can create a script that relates specifically to your client's future goals. Here is a suggested script to lead her through, which can take between 5 and 10 minutes, depending how long you allow your client to stay with the images she builds up. (There are more visualisation or imagery exercises in Chapter 21.)

Sit comfortably in the chair and close your eyes. Take a deep breath and relax your shoulders. Allow yourself to feel relaxed and peaceful for this period of time. You don't have to do anything at the moment, so we will use the time to visualise your success.

Start by visualising your positive outcome. (Note: this outcome may be a promotion, a new relationship, a new job, moving home, or whatever, so if you have the details, elaborate them at this stage by saying 'See yourself in your new job/house, and so on.) Picture the scene and feel that you're successfully standing within it. Walk around and imagine the people you may be talking to – how are they responding to you? See people congratulating you on your achievement, feel the pat on the back, and hear the words they may be saying. Stop and enjoy the deep sense of achievement of having become the person who has achieved what you wanted to achieve. Take a moment to build as many images, sounds, and experiences as you can.

Now, in your mind, bring yourself back into today. Keep your eyes shut and start to build the pictures of the journey that takes you from today's situation to the achievement of your goal. Picture yourself leaving this room confident and energised to make these changes; build scenes and images of the next few weeks – who are you talking to, what actions are you taking? Accept that there may be challenges, but see yourself managing them calmly and confidently. Take your mind through time and events so that you see your progress towards your goals, notching up every small success, rewarding yourself, developing and adjusting your approach as you go through time. Then find yourself back in the scene you created of your positive outcome, and again revel in the feelings of having achieved your goal. Notice the physical feelings you experience as you think of yourself being successful in developing greater potential in yourself and your life. How do you feel in that place? How do you look? How may things change? Build as many scenes and experiences as possible: be in the scene, be yourself, and really experience it. Then, when you have the image really colourful, strong, and focused, caption it with a word or short phrase to remind yourself that you're achieving your goal.

Visualisation is a powerful method for change. One client I worked with had previously had an image of herself as being stupid. This image was left over from her experiences in the classroom at school. She came to coaching to build her confidence to return to the workplace after maternity leave. During this visualisation exercise, she built images of leaving the 'stupid' image back in the school of her childhood, and of her emerging from the coaching session as a confident adult. She built images of herself going to interviews feeling intelligent and successful. She called back a few months later to say that this visualisation exercise had made a phenomenal difference to her self-image and been really helpful to raise her confidence level just before going in to interviews.

Suggest your client practises visualisation for herself as often as possible – preferably each morning when she wakes up, so that she starts each day motivated to make change happen. With each day, she reinforces her personal development. She breaks through limiting beliefs and doubts to support the personal achievement of her goals and to release her potential.

Chapter 11

Working with Relationships

- -

In This Chapter

▶ Understanding patterns of relating

▶ Feeling able to express needs and allow others to do the same

▶ Understanding hidden drives and fears

▶ Acting one's best self

- -

*O*ther people can be both a mystery and a frustration as well as a joy and a support, sometimes in equal measure. Many of the problems and goals that your clients bring into your CBC sessions are likely to involve their relationships with other people.

How a person manages his relationships with other people is often a reflection of how he is relating to himself. This link is what I call inside-outside communication. If his internal dialogue – the way your client talks to himself as he goes through life – is supportive and accepting of his fallibility, he is likely to understand the fallibility of others. If your client is a demanding perfectionist who forever criticises himself for not coming up to his own high standards, he may also be demanding of other people.

Each person is unique, but it can take a lifetime for people to become comfortable with that uniqueness. Finding out how to reflect on who he is and how his internal state impacts on his external relationships can provide a breakthrough to building rewarding relationships.

CBC provides a framework to help your clients understand their roles within relationships and to build strategies to develop assertive communication. In this chapter, I introduce you to a few communication models and give you examples of how you can apply them in your coaching sessions.

Understanding the Relationship Dance

Communication is like a dance. Within a relationship, sometimes the dance steps flow easily and both parties are happy. At other times, one partner pushes the other back against the wall or steps sideways so that the other trips up.

Interestingly, even when this kind of pattern develops, people can become acclimatised and discover how to play their part, even if that part is uncomfortable.

Through CBC, you can help your client to understand the part he is personally adopting within his relationships. You can share theories and models that help him to identify the patterns he plays out in his relationships and to devise strategies to change the steps in order to seek a pattern that works for all those involved.

Your client can change himself but he can't change other people. However, you can show him that when he changes, other people tend to change too. You can help him to recognise that his own thoughts and expectations impact on his ability to express his own opinions, and that he needs tolerance to listen to other people's opinions.

Communicating Assertively

Developing your client's ability to feel confident and assertive can overcome many relationship problems. You may be surprised by how many people find expressing their needs, feelings, and opinions extremely difficult. An apparently confident person may walk into your coaching room and disclose that he has difficulty asking for what he wants from his partner, boss, or colleagues. You may have clients who don't want to listen to other people's opinions but want to prove themselves to be 'right', blaming others for difficulties in relationships.

Assertiveness is a set of behavioural skills that can be acquired. Assertiveness enables your client to interact with others in a way that demonstrates mutual respect. The underlying intention is to reach a win–win solution. Inevitably, this isn't always possible. Nonetheless, assertiveness includes a recognition that each person has a right to express his own opinions and to be heard. Assertiveness does not always mean that you get what you want, but it does mean that you know you have articulated your own views and listened with respect to the views of others. This collaborative approach is more likely to help you to maintain good relationships with others.

The challenges your client may draw to your attention regarding assertiveness may include problems around the following:

- Saying 'no'
- Giving and receiving criticism and feedback
- Motivating people
- Influencing and persuading others
- Bossiness and dominance
- Feeling unable to ask for what he wants

✔ Shyness

✔ Managing arguments

✔ Expressing opinions

These everyday situations can provoke anxiety in your client. Through CBC he can learn strategies to develop confidence and techniques to manage both his own emotional state and communication style and discover how to bring out the best in others.

Practising the principles of assertiveness

We are seldom taught communication, we just pick it up as we go along. How effectively a person communicates therefore depends on the role models he has observed to this point. Many people can reach middle age without any formal information on the subject, so CBC sessions provide an excellent opportunity to help your client understand some of the basic principles of good communication. These include the right to:

✔ Respect himself

✔ Respect the other person

✔ Express an opinion

✔ Make mistakes

✔ Say 'no'

✔ Say 'I don't understand'

✔ Be accountable for his actions

✔ Consider his needs important

✔ Listen and respect the needs of others

✔ Set his own values and priorities

✔ Express what is acceptable and what is not acceptable to him

✔ Articulate his feelings in a way that does not infringe another person's rights

Helping your client to adopt these rights within his relationships involves working with beliefs, thoughts, expectations, and emotions, as well as behaviours such as verbal and body language. Help your client identify whether negative thoughts are limiting his ability to feel confident about communicating. Doubt will impact his behaviour. Check whether his expectations of himself and the other person with whom he is communicating are rational or whether he is demanding perfection. Observe words like *ought to* or *should,* which signify that he expects that the other person should behave in the specified way he wants him to, which may or may not be reasonable. Identify what the situation will look like when he has improved the relationship, so that he can plan what thoughts and language will enable him to transform it.

Your client can practise applying the assertiveness principles in role-play situations with you so that he builds his communication skills in a safe environment. You would adopt the role of the other person, and you both act out the likely scenario your client faces so that he practises the language and behaviours to become more assertive. Chapters 1, 2, 9, and 15 have more information on confidence and communication.

Picking out patterns of relating

Many communication models can be adapted and applied within CBC. Eric Berne introduced the model of *transactional analysis* in his book *Games People Play*. Berne describes patterns of communication, observing whether people relate as equals or from positions of higher or lower status. This model can be a useful one to apply in analysing your client's part within his relationships. The theory of transactional analysis is that each person has three *ego states* or subconscious influences on his communication style:

✓ Parent: Our 'taught' concept of life – can be Critical or Caring. Underlying thoughts tend to be 'I know best.'

✓ Adult: Our 'thought' concept of life – can be Rational, Assertive, or Problem-solving. Underlying thoughts tend to be 'We both know something; let's share and see what we can agree.'

✓ Child: Our 'felt' concept of life – can be Adaptive, Rebellious, Natural, or a Wild Card. Underlying thoughts tend to be 'I feel helpless; you know best' or ' You think you know best.'

Figure 11-1 gives an example of how a boss or manager can sometimes communicate from the 'I know best' position, talking down to his direct report and treating him as a child. The diagram argues that even though there may be a hierarchy, in the workplace everyone is adult so theoretically can communicate from the adult-to-adult assertive position of 'We both know something; let's collaborate to solve the problem.'

Many of the problems in relationships, both in the home and the workplace, occur when these ego states are 'crossed', that is when one person is communicating from a different ego state to that of the other. For example, a husband or wife communicates with his or her spouse from the Critical Parent mode. This mode can induce an Adaptive Child response, in which the spouse either adapts his behaviour to avoid criticism, or behaves in a rebellious way, rather like a stroppy teenager. Here's an example:

Spouse in Critical Parent: 'Why didn't you take the shirts to the cleaners today? You really should know that I need them for tomorrow!'

Adaptive Child response (jumping to attention to avoid further conflict)**:** 'I'll run along there now. Don't worry, I am sure that they can do them quickly.'

Rebellious Child response: 'How was I supposed to know? Take them yourself.'

Adult (assertive) response: 'Did you ask me to? Do you have another one to wear for tomorrow? What plans do you have in the morning – I have a meeting, but I can take them in later if you're busy?'

In reality, we can all switch between these ego states depending on who we are communicating with, the situation itself, and how confident we are feeling. There are times when we can be bossy, times when we need comfort or nurturing, times when we are submissive, or times when we are thoroughly unreasonable and throw our toys out of the pram like toddlers. It can be a game of power struggles.

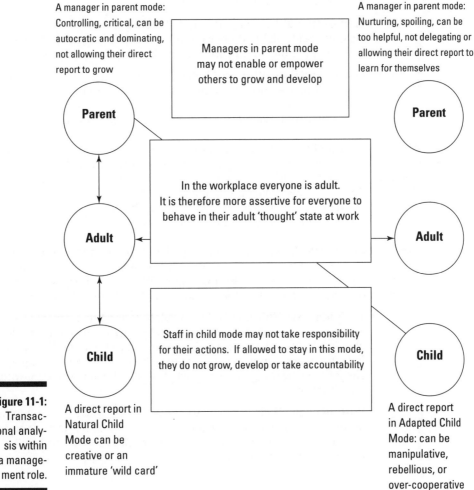

A manager in parent mode: Controlling, critical, can be autocratic and dominating, not allowing their direct report to grow

Managers in parent mode may not enable or empower others to grow and develop

A manager in parent mode: Nurturing, spoiling, can be too helpful, not delegating or allowing their direct report to learn for themselves

Parent

Parent

In the workplace everyone is adult. It is therefore more assertive for everyone to behave in their adult 'thought' state at work

Adult

Adult

Staff in child mode may not take responsibility for their actions. If allowed to stay in this mode, they do not grow, develop or take accountability

Child

Child

Figure 11-1: Transactional analysis within a management role.

A direct report in Natural Child Mode can be creative or an immature 'wild card'

A direct report in Adapted Child Mode: can be manipulative, rebellious, or over-cooperative

The trick is to help your client become aware of which state he is in and decide whether it is the most effective way for him to communicate within the situation he is managing. Only once the pattern is identified and conscious can he do something about it. I find most clients can apply this model quickly in their own lives.

You can integrate the transactional analysis model with the *ABCD model*, which I describe fully in Chapter 1, to identify the thoughts that influence your client's behaviours.

William told his coach that he was unable to state his needs to his boss. The coach worked through the first three parts of the ABCDE model with William as follows:

- ✔ **A = Activating event:** William's boss delegated a task to William at 6 p.m., to be ready for the next morning.

- ✔ **B = Belief or thought:** William thought: 'I must get home to help my wife with the children tonight. My boss really shouldn't give me a piece of work so late in the day, but I suppose I had better do what I am told.'

- ✔ **C = Consequential emotion and behaviour:** William felt frustrated with his boss and anxious about what his wife would say to him when he got home. He carried out the task quickly, presenting the document with a couple of typos, and rushed home apologetically to his wife.

When he discussed this situation with his coach, William could see that he had been communicating from Child mode and adapting his behaviour as much as possible to avoid criticism from all angles. He confessed that he almost imagined his boss as a parental figure, taller and larger than himself, even though, in fact, William was the taller one of the two. William and his coach then worked on the *D* part of the ABCD model:

- ✔ **D = Disputing the belief.** The coach helped William to dispute his thinking so that he could plan how to deal with this type of situation in future. In order to communicate from Adult assertive mode with both his boss and his wife, William needed to remember that he had a right to express the following:

  - **With his boss:** William needs to explain that while he wants to be helpful, he needs to get home to take care of the children. He checks whether the work really does need to be done that evening. If so, he offers options such as taking the work home, coming in early in the morning, or seeing whether a colleague can deal with the situation.

  - **With his wife:** William needs to explain to his wife that something urgent has come up at work and he will try to be home as soon as he can. He communicates in an adult problem-solving style with her, rather than from fear.

By explaining the transactional analysis model and how it can be integrated with the ABCD model, you show your client how to observe his own thoughts and behaviour patterns within relationships so that he can experiment with new ways of communicating.

You may choose to role-play a scenario that your client is facing. You and your client each act one of the parts in the relationship. This enables your client to practise the language he would use, so that you can give him feedback on the impact of what he is saying. Rehearsing scenarios develops your client's ability to make assertive communication a habit in his life.

Using the I'm okay, you're okay model

Another model from transactional analysis that you can apply within CBC is the *I'm okay, you're okay model*. This model divides behaviours into four quadrants: aggressive ('I'm okay, you're not okay'), passive ('I'm not okay, you're okay'), passive aggressive ('I'm not okay, you're not okay') and assertive ('I'm okay, you're okay'). Try using the template in Table 11-1 as a source of information and as a model for your client to complete to monitor his own behaviours.

Table 11-1	The I'm Okay, You're Okay Model
Aggressive: 'I'm Okay, You're Not Okay'	**Assertive: 'I'm Okay, You're Okay'**
Aggressive people get what they want through verbal or physical threat or force. They do not care about the rights of others and consider that they're right, not caring what other people think or want, and tending to blame them. Their aggressive and bullying manner can often result in other people feeling humiliated and resentful towards them and attacking back in a more indirect way later.	Assertive people respect their own rights and the rights of others. They seek a working compromise rather than a win. They express themselves directly without being aggressive. Such people have a sense of self-worth and allow other people to have different opinions, but can put their own opinion calmly and openly.
How to spot them: pointing finger, sharp; firm sarcastic voice; leaning forward. Words/phrases: you'd better; don't be stupid; your fault; you should/ought/must.	How to spot them: relaxed; good eye contact; not hostile; collaborative. Words/phrases: 'I' statements; we could; let's; what do you think?; how do you feel about this?
Situations when I am aggressive:	Situations when I am assertive:
Thoughts that trigger my behaviour:	Thoughts that trigger my behaviour:

(continued)

Table 11-1 *(continued)*

Passive Aggressive: 'I'm Not Okay, You're Not Okay'	Passive: 'I'm Not Okay, You're Okay'
Passive aggressive people act in what appears to be a passive manner while feeling aggressive and often thinking 'I'll get my revenge later.' Their inability to express their anger or resentment directly can result in their being able to manipulate other people to do what they want through emotional blackmail. They don't feel okay, so they're not assertive enough to be direct.	Passive people are timid, lacking in self-confidence, and find it hard to stand up for themselves. These people can get what they want indirectly by triggering guilt in others who may feel sorry for them or protective, because they tend to become victims or martyrs. They're often too accommodating and can be referred to as doormats.
How to spot them: body language and words similar to passive but with more negative emotional impact such as sighing, shrugging shoulders, raising eyes to ceiling.	How to spot them: hunched shoulders, downcast eyes, quiet voice, shifts of bodyweight. Words/phrases: perhaps; maybe; I wonder if you could; I'm hopeless; it's not important; never mind.
Situations when I am passive aggressive:	Situations when I am passive:
Thoughts that trigger my behaviour:	Thoughts that trigger my behaviour:

Maureen came to coaching complaining that her sister was always criticising her and undermining her confidence. When she looked at the I'm okay, you're okay model she saw that her sister was communicating from 'I'm okay, you're not okay,' and that she personally was communicating from 'I'm not okay, you're okay'. Maureen's objective was to move to the 'I'm okay, you're okay' quadrant. Here is the process of questions you can use to achieve that shift:

Coach: Imagine if you resolved this situation? What would it be like if you and your sister were getting along really well?

Maureen: I'd feel as good as her instead of the silly younger sister. I could tell her honestly if she said something that hurt me.

Coach: What stops you telling her that you're hurt by what she says?

Maureen: She'd just get nasty, like she always does, and tell me I am unreasonable.

Coach: If she is able to speak her mind to you, why can't you speak your mind to her?

Maureen: Because I fear rejection and criticism. I don't like conflict, so I have always been the one to keep things harmonious.

Coach: Does she have more right to speak her mind than you do?

Maureen: No.

Coach: The assertive principle is that you're both at liberty to express your feelings and needs to one another in a respectful way. You're also accountable for your own response to her remarks; someone else may not be hurt by her comments. How else could you think in order to communicate from the 'I'm okay, you're okay' quadrant?

Maureen: I can see that this pattern was set up when we were children. That was a long time ago! We're both adult in our 30s now, even if I am still her younger sister. I think she says these things to make herself feel better rather than to really hurt me. If I feel hurt by something she says, I shall tell her so. I shall say 'When you say that, I feel really hurt. I'd really like it if you could say something more positive.'

Using the three-step assertiveness model

Your client may need help in developing the ability to express his needs or opinions within relationships. Providing a structure to plan what he wants to say gives him a framework for articulating his response to the situations he faces. The three-step assertiveness model below is a process you can share with him:

1. **Actively listen and demonstrate what you hear.**

2. **Express how you feel and think about the statement in a non-blaming or non-judgemental way.**

3. **Say what you want to happen and suggest a win–win solution.**

For example, George became stressed when his colleague Sarah talked over him at meetings, finishing his sentences. He felt this undermined his authority and interrupted his train of thought. In his coaching sessions, George planned how he could use the three-step model to manage this situation in future.

1. Actively listen: George planned that the next time Sarah interrupted him, he would say 'I hear that you have a point to make here, and I would like to summarise what I have heard you say.' George would then précis what Sarah had said to check that he had heard her properly.

2. Express how you feel: George planned to continue by saying 'I understand that you want to share your opinions, Sarah. However, when you interrupt me I feel upset because I lose my train of thought and feel my authority is undermined.' This statement takes responsibility for his own feelings about the situation rather than blaming, labelling, or judging Sarah as unreasonable for interrupting.

3. Suggesting a change: 'I would prefer it if in future you could wait until I have finished speaking, so that I can complete the point I am making, and then add what you would like to say.'

Articulating needs: Assertive isn't the same as aggressive

Many people confuse assertiveness with aggression. They imagine that it means that they try to enforce their opinions and needs on another person. But assertive is not aggressive: an assertive person gives respect and space to his own and the other person's opinions and needs.

Where relationships are concerned, you may well find that people get stuck in the problem and find comfort in blaming other people for the difficulties they face. CBC is goal-focused, so work with your client to develop solutions to the challenges he faces. Help him to formulate a positive outcome to the relationship at the start of his coaching programme or session.

Simone came to coaching talking about how she lost her temper with her boss: 'He is impossible.' The coach realised that Simone needed to move out of the problem and focus thought and action on an assertive solution. Simone described her objective as wanting to be able to tell her boss what he could do to help her perform better, instead of criticising her for what she hadn't done.

> **Coach:** What do you expect from him?
>
> **Simone:** He should realise that I can't stand it when he never thanks me for good work I have done. He shouldn't do that – he should know better. ('I'm not okay, but he's not okay either.')
>
> **Coach:** Have you ever discussed this lack of thanks with him?
>
> **Simone:** No, what's the point? He never listens. I do get angry with him, but usually about the amount of work he's giving me rather than to tell him what my real problem is. (Indirect passive aggressive behaviour.)
>
> **Coach:** If you've not raised the subject, what evidence do you have that he won't listen?
>
> **Simone:** I suppose I don't have any evidence, as such. I make an assumption.
>
> **Coach:** This is what we call *mind-reading* or *fortune-telling* – you're imagining what his response will be although you haven't tested out your theory.

Simone's coach asked her to develop her options to manage the situation in an assertive manner. She decided that she wanted to discuss the situation honestly with her boss, without blaming him. She realised that she could not blame her boss because, she had not given him direct feedback and saw that her anger towards him had been caused by defensiveness. She identified a thought to help her keep calm during the discussion:

> *I'd prefer it if he focused on the positive, but I can manage his criticism and I can explain to him that I'd be more motivated if he could acknowledge the good things I do.*

Instead of getting angry, your client can be assertive in a calm way that allows him both to express his own needs and opinions and the other person to express his. They may not reach agreement, but there is an understanding that each of them has a right to his own views.

Acknowledging How Expectations Impact on Relationships

Expectations play a key part in relationships. The expectation that others should do what we want them to is natural but, of course, unrealistic. In CBC, you review your client's expectations of himself and other people so as to develop thoughts and behaviours that respect the diverse needs and approaches of the people with whom he relates.

A person's relationship with himself is key to how he manages relationships with other people. Many people don't forgive their own mistakes, expecting themselves to be perfect. As a CB coach, you can develop your client's acceptance of his fallibility when he is having difficulty in his relationships, by asking questions such as these:

- ✔ Many people have relationship problems from time to time. If a friend of yours had the same relationship problem as you do, would you criticise him as much as you criticise yourself?

- ✔ Is it rational to imagine that you have to be perfect all the time and never make a mistake?

- ✔ Is your idea of perfect the same as everyone else's?

- ✔ Have you ever met a perfect human being?

- ✔ How might it feel to pursue excellence rather than perfection – just do your best?

Expecting relationships to go perfectly is likely to lead to disappointment. We live in an imperfect world, and relationships are not always easy or harmonious. An acceptance that everyone is fallible leads to more reasonable expectations of yourself and other people.

If your client has perfectionist tendencies, encourage him to develop the following useful thoughts:

- ✔ I prefer it when I get things right, but I can accept myself if I don't.

- ✔ I prefer it when other people do what I want and need, but I can manage it if they don't, though I can express my feelings too.

- ✔ I prefer it when my life situations go the way I want them to, but I can manage it if they don't.

These thoughts promote a positive expectation of situations but reinforce the message that whatever happens, your client can manage it.

Checking underlying beliefs

When people are unassertive in communication, the reason is often because they fear a negative consequence such as rejection, hurting someone's feelings, or being proven that their viewpoint is wrong.

The patterns of how people relate to one another are set up in early childhood. Children observe, consciously and unconsciously, the way their parents communicate, and also experience their own interactions within their family situation. Whether someone is the oldest, youngest, middle, or a twin will have impacted on his early perceptions of how he is regarded and how he should communicate. Gender is another factor that determines how people think about themselves and how they've been treated within a childhood setting.

Getting rid of 'should', 'ought', and 'must'

In coaching sessions, listen out for phrases that denote your client's underlying beliefs. The words *should, ought,* and *must* reflect blame or judgement that someone has not come up to his personal standard of communication. Consider the following:

- ✔ 'You **should** have known what I wanted you to do.' (Example belief: in order for me to feel okay, I need you to do what I want.)
- ✔ 'You **must** listen to what I say.' (Example belief: I must be heard.)
- ✔ 'You **ought to** behave the way I want you to.' (Example belief: you've a duty to do what I want you to do.)

Try using the *three basic demands framework* to identify your client's personal rules of behaviour. To identify some of his own beliefs and demands about communication, ask your client to complete the following sentences:

- ✔ **Demands about himself:** 'When I am communicating with other people (or specific named person), I. . .
  - **Should**. . . for example, maintain harmony, listen to what they're saying, make an impact, get what I want
  - **Ought to**. . . for example, do what I am told, behave politely, not disagree, be meek and submissive
  - **Must**. . . for example, get my way, please them, get their approval, be heard

✔ **Demands about others:** 'In communication other people (or specific named person). . .

- **Should**. . . for example, listen to what I am saying, treat me with respect

- **Ought to**. . . for example, do what I want them to do, know what I want without my having to tell them

- **Must**. . . for example, take notice of what I ask of them, stop interrupting, hear me

✔ **Demands about communication situations in general:** 'Relationships. . .

- **Should**. . . for example, work smoothly, be about agreement

- **Ought to**. . . for example, be a two-way process

- **Must**. . . be harmonious, be direct

By tuning in to the words *should, ought to,* and *must,* your client can review whether his behaviour is driven by a fear that if his standards aren't met, his security will be threatened.

Using inference-chaining

There are times when you want to dig deeper into your client's beliefs and expectations around a situation in order to identify whether the way he is thinking is rational or helping him manage. The process of *inference-chaining* helps you to identify an underlying belief about the consequences of his demands not being met.

Inference-chaining is a process applying the phrase 'if. . . then. . . '. This helps to identify any unconscious fear or belief about what could happen within the situation. For example, your client asks himself 'If *x* happens. . . then what am I afraid of?' For example: 'If I don't get treated with respect, I am a failure' or 'If I don't get my way, I am not being heard or acknowledged.'

Here is an example of how inference-chaining works:

Client: I want to improve my relationship with my mother.

Coach: In what way do you want to improve this relationship? Was there an activating event that has brought this problem to your attention?

Client: Yes, my mother is moving house and is giving some of her furniture away. We had a difficult meeting on Saturday.

Coach: Can you tell me what your belief is around this situation?

Client: She just gave me the news as a fait accompli. I feel she should involve me in her decisions. I feel left out because she did discuss this with my brother.

Coach: I am going to use a process called inference-chaining and ask you a set of questions that aim to draw out an underlying belief about this situation. So, my first question is: if she didn't involve you in her decisions, what does that mean?

Client: That she's not interested in my opinion, only my brother's, because she is discussing it with him.

Coach: And if your mother discusses this with your brother and not with you, what does that mean to you?

Client: It means that she loves him more than she loves me. I feel unlovable.

Coach: So let me summarise that the inference you're making is that if your mother doesn't involve you in these discussions, she doesn't love you and you're unlovable?

The dialogue above demonstrates how a specific incident or conversation can have a far greater emotional significance to a person than it may appear to, for example that a conversation represents how much or little a person feels loved or lovable. The coach works with the client to review what other evidence he has that his mother doesn't love him, to devise strategies to review whether he has rational and helpful expectations, and to develop a plan to manage the situation directly and assertively.

Dealing with past influences

Although your focus in CBC is forward-looking, you may find that your client refers back to his childhood or previous experiences when he talks about how he relates to others. I have found that clients may make comments such as:

- I have ended up submissive because my elder brother was such a bully.
- My parents often argued, so I increasingly kept quiet and out of the way.
- I suppose I was a bit bossy with my younger sister.
- I was the middle son of three brothers, and so I became noisier in order to stand out and get attention.
- My mother was a single parent, and so I adapted to be helpful and supportive because I wanted to protect her.
- My father died when I was young, and I guess I have become rather dependent in relationships because I have a fear of loss.

It sometimes helps your client to understand how his past has influenced him, though your focus is to help him move forward to achieve his stated goals. The past, however difficult, does not need to be a determinant of his future.

There may also be times when past events and experiences are so deep-rooted that you will need to refer your client to a counsellor or therapist. (See Chapter 3 for more information on referrals.)

Developing thoughts and expectations to become more assertive

You help your client to notice the demands that he is making on himself and others. By sharing the process, language, and strategies, you're showing him how to become his own coach. Your client comes to observe:

✔ His self-talk, or inner dialogue, such as: 'I really ought to be able to stand up for myself when my partner puts me down, otherwise I am no good.'

✔ When he uses 'must' and 'should' in language with other people, for example saying something like: 'You should have known that I didn't want you to be late home tonight' or 'My manager really ought to rea-lise how much I have on my plate at the moment' or 'I must come to an agreement with my client in today's negotiation.'

Identifying the underlying expectations of a relationship enables your client to review whether the way he is viewing the situation is:

✔ Rational and logical, or subjective

✔ The way other people would respond in the same circumstances

✔ Helpful to his management of the situation

He can then transform his NATs (negative automatic thoughts) to develop CATs (constructive automatic thoughts) in future, for example changing a NAT such as 'I can't stand it, he's so selfish' to a CAT, 'I can manage this even if it doesn't go smoothly'. This is described in more detail in Chapter 6.

You cannot provide perfect solutions to relationship issues, but you can help your client to develop constructive and affirmative thoughts to support him as he experiments with new behaviours.

Being One's Best Self in Relationships

The concept of bringing one's best self into a relationship situation is a useful one to share with your client. Everyone adopts different behaviours from time to time. We can be brilliantly confident and a sparkling wit in one situation and a gauche inarticulate in another! Where CBC can help is to focus your client on being the confident communicator more often. This change takes planning.

A discipline you can encourage clients to adopt is to consider how to plan to be at their best in the various relationship situations they have pending in their diaries. Putting the meeting in the diary is the easy bit: arriving in the right state of mind is more difficult and can take preparation.

Choosing the thought and emotion to manage situations

CBC can provide structure for your client to develop a plan of how to manage a difficult situation that he may be experiencing or may face in the future. You can help him consider his goals and identify the type of thoughts, feelings, and behaviours that will help him to manage the situation effectively. The *ABCDEF model* enables your client to plan to be his best self within a situation. Here is an example:

Krishnan, a teenager, had developed a habit of being angry and in conflict with his mother on every occasion when he saw her. In coaching, he reviewed what was happening and transformed his relationship with his mother in the space of a few weeks.

- ✔ **A = Activating event** – Krishnan described the fact that every time he saw his mother, he felt frustrated and irritable.

- ✔ **B = Belief or thought** – Krishnan's thought was 'She doesn't think I'm any good. My brother is the clever one, and she thinks I am useless.'

- ✔ **C = Consequential emotion and behaviour** – Krishnan felt upset and angry that he perceived his mother didn't think as much of him as she did of his brother. His behaviour became resentful and aggressive as a method of defending his pain.

- ✔ **D = Disputing the belief** – Krishnan was asked to consider (1) what evidence he had that his mother thought him useless, (2) whether everyone would interpret her behaviour in the same way, and (3) whether his current way of thinking and behaving was helping him to be happy and enjoy a good relationship with his mother. He replied that he didn't have precise evidence that she thought him useless, and saw that this opinion was his interpretation. He also understood that his present habitual way of behaving with her was making both him and her miserable on a daily basis.

✔ **E = Exchanging the thought** – Krishnan decided to think about the situation differently in future and try a new method of behaving. 'Thinking about my strengths may help me feel better in myself and stop me being so defensive with my mum. Perhaps showing her my best self rather than my ratty self may make a difference.'

✔ **F = Future planning** – Krishnan practised being his best self within the final coaching session. The coach asked him to stand up and walk around the room acting as if he were at his best. Krishnan demonstrated how his body posture, body language, and tone of voice changed when he felt relaxed and confident. The coach encouraged Krishnan to practise this best self as often as possible so as to let go of the defensive language and aggressive body posture that he had previously shown to his mother. This switch of behaviour had never occurred to Krishnan before, but he decided to give it a try.

After a few weeks, Krishnan's mother called the coach and said that she had noticed a real difference in Krishnan and that their relationship had improved considerably. Like Krishnan, many clients are unaware that they are able to switch the focus of their mind and energy from negative to positive within a relationship, and that this switch in itself can change the relationship.

Changing the relationship dance step by step

A relationship always requires two or more people. Change does not, therefore, happen overnight, because the other people with whom your client is involved will be playing their part. Your client cannot change others but can only change himself – which may or may not change the other person's behaviour. You cannot guarantee this change. Some people have deeply entrenched behaviour patterns that they find difficult to break.

Communication is like a dance. Whether your client is in the habit of giving power to another person and behaving like a helpless child or has a tendency to be bossy, the relationship dance will have to change, and the other person may take time to practise his steps to communicate in a more assertive way. He will have become used to your client responding in his old pattern, and may feel frustrated or confused when his behaviour changes. Enable your client to accept that the perfect result is unlikely to happen immediately and that there may be moments when one or other trip up as the pattern begins to change.

Role-play can be a helpful way of rehearsing new behaviours. The coach and client act out scenarios, each taking it in turns to play both the parties involved. Encourage your client to play the part of the other person with whom he is going to communicate and literally 'sit in his chair' or 'stand in his shoes'. This method provides great insight into the emotional impact of certain words and behaviours so that he can build a number of strategies to try in future.

The more choices your client has up his sleeve the better, so that if one communication option doesn't work, he can try another. Prepare him for a journey of discovery and help him plan how to maintain his own emotional equilibrium within the various difficult relationship situations he may face. This planning gives him a greater sense of inner security and control to manage the ups and downs of relating with others.

Chapter 12

Making Choices and Decisions

In This Chapter

▶ Reviewing past decisions

▶ Accessing more creative perspectives

▶ Thinking about what's important

▶ Realising that making mistakes is okay

A person's life is made up of the decisions she takes moment by moment. Making those decisions can be hard. Whether considering what time to rise or what to wear, deciding whether to buy a house, take out a loan, extend your loft, or work abroad, or choosing which movie to see or which school is best for your child, each day is made up, from start to finish, of decisions. Some people find these decisions easy, and others fret over the pros and cons for days if not years.

People often come to CBC at transition times so as to gain clarity of perspective and benefit from an objective process of questions to help them make a wise choice about a situation or problem. Through CBC, you can help your client to consider all her options and, specifically, gain insight into how she is thinking about those options. You can check with her whether she is being driven by fear or enthusiasm and what level of risk she feels willing to take. Through this process, your client sees that how she thinks impacts on how she feels, which in turn influences her perspectives about decision-making.

In this chapter, I provide you with methods and questions to enable your client to explore her options and feel more confident about making work and life decisions.

Focusing on Factors That Influence Decisions

Sometimes people have change forced upon them externally by life events. At other times, they have an inner drive to review and change some aspect or aspects of life. In your coaching sessions, you help your client understand the nature of decision-making and see how her thoughts and expectations influence her choices. For example, a thought such as 'I must make the right decision otherwise I may look stupid' could trigger anxiety and is likely to lead to procrastination. On the other hand, the thought 'I can make a decision in my own time when I have sufficient information' may lead to a confident decision based on evidence.

Understanding why people make decisions

People have a variety of reasons influencing them as to whether to make a decision or to procrastinate and delay their choice. In CBC sessions, you provide a process to help your client understand the factors that are influencing her either to take action to change her life or decide to stay as she is. Below I list some of the causes that impact decision-making:

- ✔ Discomfort within the current situation

- ✔ Fear of failure

- ✔ Moving away from something painful

- ✔ Moving towards something pleasant

- ✔ The need for security

- ✔ The need for approval

- ✔ The need for excitement

- ✔ The search for integrity, meaning, and purpose

- ✔ The need for significance and recognition

- ✔ A clash of values in the current situation

- ✔ External change

- ✔ Restlessness

- ✔ Financial gain

- ✔ Mood – feeling happy or feeling sad can motivate people to decide to make a purchase or take an action that is emotionally driven

Uncovering decision-making styles

Everyone is different. The way people take decisions can vary, and your client may have a habitual pattern of how she approaches decision-making. Through

CBC, she can benefit from your help in understanding what type of decision-maker she tends to be. Below are some decision-making styles that may apply to your client:

- ✔ Impetuous, making decisions quickly and spontaneously: 'That looks good, I'll go for that.'

- ✔ Focused and determined: 'I know exactly what I want, so I shall go for it.'

- ✔ Pragmatic, going for the easy option: 'That looks fine, I don't want to mess around too long.'

- ✔ Security-conscious, sticking to the status quo: 'That's a safe option and won't upset the apple cart.'

- ✔ Intuitive, getting a sense that a decision feels right: 'My gut instinct tells me this way is the right way to go.'

- ✔ Logical and analytical, exploring facts, figures, and information before making a decision: 'I'll make my decision when I can back it up with evidence.'

- ✔ Hesitant, doubting their ability to make a good decision: 'I'm just not sure. . .'

- ✔ Perfectionist – no decision is ever the 'right' one: 'I've got to look at all the options – I'm not sure that this is good enough.'

- ✔ Procrastinators: 'Let me put off this decision for as long as possible.'

Inevitably, people respond differently according to the situation they're facing. However, you often find that people have habitual approaches to decisions, so it may be relevant to elicit information about your client's past decision-making habits so as to identify any helpful or unhelpful patterns. The decision review, which I explain in the following section, provides a useful process to get to the depths of your client's past decision-making habits.

Using the decision review

The *decision review* helps your client to reflect on major decisions she has made and the motivation that drove them. As the CB coach, you work through the decision-review process, shown in Table 12-1, with your client to analyse a past decision that she made. The model is designed to help her reflect on the underlying influences of her behaviours, thoughts, motivations, and actions to review how they impacted her emotions and actions. You can also use the decision review to explore whether her thinking led to action or procrastination. Your client analyses the consequences of her past behaviour so that she can decide whether the way she approached the decision was effective.

Ask your client to think of six major decisions she has made and identify what thoughts influenced her choice:

- ✔ Was she moving away from a difficult situation or moving towards a good one?
- ✔ Was her decision based on fear or enthusiasm?
- ✔ Was her decision embedded in a lack of trust in herself, life, and the situation around her?
- ✔ Did she just know, intuitively, that decision was the right one for her?

Table 12-1	Example of a Client's Decision Review			
Decision/ Action	*Motivation: Why*	*Thought*	*Emotion*	*Consequence*
Example 1: change of career two years ago	More money and financial security	I must pay the mortgage	Fear-driven – went into a job which paid better, but I don't enjoy it	Bored in my current role
Example 2: buying a holiday flat	Spontaneous impulse led by holiday mood	This looks fun	Excitement	A nice apartment we hardly ever have time to go to!

The ABC model, which I introduce in Chapter 2, is also integral within these examples. In example 1 in Table 12-1:

- ✔ **A = Activating event:** Change of career
- ✔ **B = Belief about the event:** 'I must pay the mortgage.'
- ✔ **C = Consequential emotion** (fear) **and behaviour** (taking a job she didn't enjoy)

    Through a combination of the decision review and the ABC model, you help your client to review how her thinking was impacting her emotions and behaviours and drove her decision-making. Together you can analyse whether her approach was helpful or whether she could benefit from changing her thoughts and thus changing her emotions and behaviours. For example, were she to change her belief (B) to 'there are many different career paths that would enable me to continue to pay my mortgage,' she could broaden the perspective of her career choices.

Differentiating between need and want

In the two examples in Table 12-1, I show the difference between need and want. In changing career, the client was driven by a need for money; in buying her holiday flat, she was driven by a want for an item of pleasure. Suggest that your client makes this distinction about the decisions she is facing in her own life. For example, checking whether the change she wants to make is coming from a need base such as an enforced job change, or whether the decision is driven by a sense of wanting something else rather than a specific need to change. Sometimes the sense of wanting something feels like a need, but isn't – for example, people who convince themselves they need a new car even though the one they're driving is fine.

Applying the decision review

Reviewing approaches and helping your client to understand what led her to make previous decisions can liberate her to try new approaches. She can also realise that she does not necessarily have to apply the same approach to each situation, but can choose different tactics for different decisions.

Philippe came to coaching because he felt stuck in his life and his objective was to find a new direction in his career. He wanted to change, but he was uncomfortable with risk and nervous about how to maintain his comfort zone within the process of exploring new avenues. Because he had a perfectly viable job, his decision was based on want rather than need. However, he had become tetchy and restless, and this mood was impacting on both his ability to concentrate at work and also on his relationship with his wife. Identifying that change wasn't a necessity but an option immediately took some of the pressure from Philippe's shoulders, because he had become quite edgy thinking that he really 'should' get on with his decision.

Philippe realised that many of the major decisions that he had made in his life had been driven by his need for security. He went into the public sector because there were dependable perks. He laughed at how he had started to consider his pension when he was just 17 years old. He had bought a well-built modern house in a leafy suburban area and married a reliable girl. He had been bored in his career for many years, and came to coaching as he approached his 40th birthday. Coaching helped Philippe review his approach. First, he unpacked the thoughts that had led him to make these decisions:

- ✔ I don't trust myself to find and keep a job in the private sector (leading to doubt and lack of confidence).

- ✔ My parents have always told me to create a 'solid' life for myself (leading to a focus on security).

- ✔ I am not used to taking risks (leading to anxiety about anything uncomfortable).

Philippe reflected that he had developed a fear of taking 'risky' decisions and didn't have confidence that he could make good decisions about moving forward to new horizons.

Philippe's coach suggested that rather than trying to leap into a major decision, he could plan gradual change to discover how to be more tolerant of risk and uncertainty. This method is known as *habituation theory:* clients slowly acclimatise themselves to situations that they had previously found difficult to manage.

The coach asked Philippe to take actions, away from the coaching room, that made him feel uncomfortable. In the first month, he would visit a headhunter to look at job options, and also discuss with his boss what alternative roles there may be in his current organisation. To empower himself to do these things, Philippe transformed his fearful thought 'What if he tells me I am useless and I end up with no salary' to the affirmative thought 'If someone else can make changes in her life, then I see no reason why I can't. I am adult and have the resources and confidence to move away from this dull job into something more interesting.'

This thought helped him to feel enthusiastic rather than fearful, and supported him in putting himself forward for various projects at work that he would previously have avoided. Several months after Philippe's coaching programme finished, he wrote to his coach to say that he had accepted a job in New York. He commented that a year earlier he would never have considered such a move, because it would have seemed too 'risky'. He mentioned that his wife was noticing a positive difference in him now that he was more relaxed about managing uncertainty.

As with Philippe, many people find that the decision-making habits picked up in earlier life are no longer appropriate to their needs. Once these influences have been identified, CB thinking methods can be applied to enable them to feel more confident and powerful.

Appreciating the role of values in decision-making

We all have a set of values and principles that we care about. Knowing what these values are provides a framework to guide decisions that align with personal integrity. The *values grid* in Table 12-2 provides a model to generate discussion as to factors your client may take into account when making choices and decisions.

Table 12-2	The Identifying Values Grid
People I Value Most	**Things I Value Most**
Personal life: *for example my partner*	Personal life (things I like to do): *for example keeping fit, getting home to put kids to bed*
Work life: *for example Mike, my boss*	Work life (the best use of my time, skills, expertise): *for example strategic thinking, delegating, and managing*
What I Value in Life	**Things I Value that I'd Like to Bring into my Life in Future:**
Examples:	Example: *I'd like to visit South America, write a travel book, get a job in senior management*
Security	
Change	
Contribution	
The quiet life	
Creativity and innovation	
Spirituality	
Politics	
Making a difference	
Challenge	
Personal growth	

Allow your client approximately 20 minutes during the session to start to complete the table. Suggest that she takes the identifying values grid home with her so that she can reflect further on her answers, because they're a fundamental influence on the choices your client makes in her life. As she completes this task, ask her to notice whether the values she identifies are her own or whether they are generated by a past influence such as a parent, or by a sense of duty with regard to the value she feels she should list. You are encouraging her to develop self-knowledge and be true to herself.

Identifying what is important to your client provides an excellent compass for direction of decisions. For example, if she wants a job in senior management, she can check whether the decisions she is making today lead her towards this job or not. You can also check current lifestyle decisions by asking 'If you were to lead your life in a way that reflects your values, what would it look like?' Then compare this view with her current life experience.

Checking decisions against values

You're showing your client strategies to make thoughtful decisions through understanding the internal and external factors that may be influencing her. This framework enables your client to make decisions aligned to her values. Consider the following examples:

- A management consultant who values a healthy society – does she take a piece of work with a tobacco company?

- A man who considers work–life balance and time with his family as important – does he feel happy about a career as a long-haul pilot?

- A university researcher opposed to capitalism – where does he choose to invest his money?

- A housewife who cares about ending world hunger – what decisions is she making about her own food purchases and food waste?

- A saleswoman who values honesty – how does she manage if asked to be less than truthful with a prospective client when selling a product or service?

As a CB coach, you do not exist to sit in judgement. Many people, including your clients, make choices that you may not agree with personally. As a coach, you provide your client with strategies and awareness to help her make decisions that reflect her personal values. When people neglect their values, they can become stressed or ill. Working through these topics can bring clarity of thought and perspective to complicated areas of life and work.

Getting real

People can sometimes be in denial about the realities of their current situation. Your client may well say that everything is fine whereas you're pretty clear from what she has been telling you that in fact everything is not fine.

'Just how fine is it?' is a question that can sometimes enable you to draw out whether your client's mind is deceiving her. People sometimes do not want to look at the reality, because they fear that it is more painful than their current acceptance or 'numbness'. Where appropriate, you may want to check whether your client is thinking that things are better (or worse) than they are, so that she can then go forward to make decisions based on reality rather than false perceptions.

The *cost–benefit analysis model* can be applied to decision-making to analyse risk and benefit. I introduced this model in Chapter 2 as a method to analyse a decision. The model helps your client to compare the pain or cost of her situation staying the same versus the pain or pleasure of taking action to alter it.

Martin came to coaching to develop techniques to manage stress. He began by assuring his coach that he was content in his current work role. 'It pays the mortgage, and anyway I am just waiting for retirement.' As Martin gained self-knowledge, he realised that, because he was only 48 years old, retirement was a long way off. His stress was being caused by an underlying fear that that his life was passing him by and he was 'waiting' rather than living now. He had simply got into a mindless routine. His passion was vintage cars, and he had often toyed with the idea of setting up a business supplying specialist spare parts. During the coaching, Martin completed a cost–benefit analysis to explore his options. With his coach, he drew up the matrix that I show in Table 12-3.

Table 12-3	Example of a Cost–Benefit Analysis		
Costs of Staying in My Current Role	*Benefits of Staying in My Current Role*	*Costs of Setting Up My Own Business*	*Benefits of Setting up My Own Business*
I find every day is boring.	I know the routine.	I may lose financially.	It may be exciting.
I fear I'll get ill because it stresses me out.	I can do the work without thinking.	I may be a failure.	I feel it can give me a new lease of life.
I'm wasting my life away.	I have financial security.	I'm going to have to acquire a lot more knowledge quickly.	I have saved some money that will tide me over.
I'm not using my time in the way I want to.	I have friends.	I have to work really hard to build it up.	I can meet many new people through this work.

Martin explored how his thoughts influenced his emotions and behaviours. Taking the four columns one by one, Martin analysed the cost–benefit of his options.

- ✔ **Column 1:** Martin found that the negative statements about staying in his current role triggered a stress response. In fact, he experienced a physical sensation of anxiety.

- ✔ **Column 2:** Reviewing his thoughts about the benefits of staying in his current role left him with little emotion. He found himself shrugging his shoulders and saying 'So what?' because the benefits did not excite him greatly.

- ✔ **Column 3:** His thoughts about the costs of starting his own consultancy concerned him but did not make him anxious. Martin found that he went into problem-solving mode, and he felt quite motivated that he would take action to manage these issues.

- ✔ **Column 4:** His thoughts about the benefits of starting his own consultancy created a visible and tangible state of excitement in him. He started to talk in a more animated way and talk about how his life would be improved.

The cost–benefit model can enable your client to recognise and accept the reality of the pros and cons of her current and projected experiences. It provides a framework to analyse whether new options would bring more pleasure or pain than her current situation. From that point, you then identify what actions need to be taken to achieve the change.

Generating Options

CBC can encompass a variety of different methods and models that help your client work through options and make decisions. Exactly how you work with your client depends on the goals that she brings to the coaching programme. In the following sections, I cover some of the methods you may use when helping your client work through her options.

Looking at lateral perspectives

Good decisions can arise from generating a rich set of options. One of the main problems for any of us when making choices is that we operate only in our own heads, and inevitably our doubts and assumptions limit the perspectives available. Two or more brains are usually better than one.

However, you can find ways of expanding perspectives and viewpoints so as to enable your client to go beyond her habitual ways of thinking. The following methods show how to expand the range of options:

- **Backwards viewpoint:** looking at the situation in 'retrospect' – for example, taking your client to a time in the future and asking her to look back and decide whether the decision she is considering seems to have been a good one.

- **Emotional viewpoint:** exploring how she might approach the situation in different emotional states. Checking whether the options she is generating come from a position of fear that things may go wrong or that she won't be able to achieve what she seeks to achieve, or from confidence – a feeling that she is competent to make the situation work well for herself.

- **Other perspectives:** considering how another person that she respects may handle the situation. Alternatively, other perspectives may be considering the fresh view of how a child may approach the situation, or how an older person may apply wisdom to approach the situation.

- **Success viewpoint:** imagining what solutions she may generate if she switched off her self-defeating or doubtful thoughts and believed she was bound to succeed.

These methods develop flexibility of thought and approach to generate optional perspectives for decision-making to counteract any negative automatic thinking.

Thinking about thinking styles

A fundamental difference exists between constructive critical or analytical thinking and negative thinking. The former is an objective analysis of a situation so as to evaluate information before making a decision. For example, when deciding whether to expand her business, the analytical thinker says 'We have to raise funds, and the evidence points to raising funds being tricky.' The negative thinker tends to express all-or-nothing or pessimistic thoughts such as ' It won't ever work' or 'No-one will buy in to that decision'.

Equally, be aware of the fundamental difference between constructive thinking and over-optimistic positive thinking. The former is realistic but positive: 'This situation is a challenge, but the option we have generated is valid if we work hard at it.' The latter is: 'Everything is just fine,' without taking facts into account.

CBC provides the setting for your client to become aware of her thinking habits so as to develop a greater range of solutions for decision-making.

Seeing that PRACTICE makes perfect

A well-established seven-step model for solution-seeking is the *PRACTICE model,* developed by Professor Stephen Palmer originally published in 2007 in the journal, *The Coaching Psychologist.* This model provides an excellent methodology for your client to follow and apply to problems.

1. **Problem identification:**

   • Describe the problem or issue.

   • What specifically would you like to change?

   • Are there any times when this issue is not a problem? If so, why and when?

   • What assumptions may you be making about this problem?

   • In how many different ways can this problem be described?

2. **Realistic, relevant goals:**

   • What do you realistically want to achieve?

   • By when do you want to achieve it?

   • How will you know when you have achieved this?

3. **Alternative solutions:**

   • What options do you have?

   • How many different solutions can you generate?

   • In how many different ways can you approach these?

4. **Consideration of consequences:**

   • What may happen?

   • How useful is each solution on a scale of 1–10?

   • How attractive is each solution on a scale of 1–10?

5. **Target most feasible solution(s):**

   • What is the most feasible solution?

   • What is your decision?

6. **Implementation of Chosen solution:**

   • Action steps for achieving the goal

7. **Evaluation:**

   • How successful was it on a scale of 1–10?

   • What can you conclude?

- What can you appreciate about your efforts and actions?
- What would you do differently?
- Are you ready to finish the coaching programme now?

Diana came to coaching with the objective to decide in which direction her career should go. Her coach applied the PRACTICE model to help her decision.

1. **Problem identification:** A restructure meant that her team was going to move to a different location. Diana wanted to decide whether to move or find a new post within the business. She was fearful that the restructure signified that the company would make her redundant if she didn't relocate. She had no direct evidence for this assumption.

2. **Realistic goals:** The goal was to make a decision that provided her with an interesting and secure role in future. She had to make this decision within three months and tell her boss.

3. **Alternative solutions:** Diana saw that as well as the options of relocating or finding a new role within the business, she could seek work elsewhere.

4. **Consequences:** Relocating would cause problems for her family, because her husband worked in the same business and was not being relocated. Also, her children would have to move schools.

5. **Target solution:** The solution was to move role within the business, not relocate.

6. **Implementation:** Diana took steps to talk to her boss and HR to discover what options she had within her current location in the business. She was immediately offered a position as programme manager of a new project.

7. **Evaluation:** Diana was satisfied with her decision. She realised that she had stressed herself out assuming that the company wanted to make her redundant, when in fact it already had a new role lined up for her. She decided to continue coaching for two more sessions to help her adjust to her new role and team.

Your aim is to empower your client to initiate her own options and feel confident about managing the process on her own in future.

Actioning and Reviewing

Decisions have their own momentum. I have observed clients, colleagues, and friends who hover over a decision with great anxiety for ages, fretting whether this decision is the right thing to do. Then, when they finally plump for action, they're released from the angst of 'shall I, shan't I?' and focus on making their solutions work.

Indecision can cloud the mind. While your client has uncertainty within a situation, her mind is in conflict. This conflict is not always a bad thing: some decisions have their own timescales, and solutions evolve naturally over a period of time. However, where you sense fear or procrastination, you can help your client to review her approach to see whether she feels ready to take at least a first step.

Overcoming procrastination

Fear of failure, and perfectionism are two of the chief reasons why people procrastinate or avoid making decisions. Twisted thinking often preys on them, and this thinking sets up anxiety. For example, with fear of failure, you may uncover thoughts such as 'I may screw up, so I'd better not' or 'What if I fail and look stupid?' With perfectionism, you may uncover thoughts such as: 'I can't make this decision until I can be sure that I shall make the perfect decision.'

Your client needs to assess her tolerance to risk. Life is, of itself, uncertain. We always have to accept a degree of risk in everything we do and every action we take. You're not asking her to take unnecessary or dangerous risks but to assess her situation objectively and be prepared to shift the status quo to move forward.

Being perfect is an unrealistic expectation, and your client benefits from accepting her own fallibility and ability to make mistakes – just like everyone else does. You're supporting your client to develop:

- ✔ An acceptance that no perfect human being exists on this earth, just people like herself trying to do their best

- ✔ Resilience to making the 'imperfect' decision, because it may not be the end of the world, and always presents a development opportunity

- ✔ An acceptance that she has no guarantees in life, so the most important thing she can discover how to do is to begin to trust in her own ability to manage the uncertainty and challenges

This last process is what I call finding out how to dance on the shifting carpet – reminding herself of the strengths, skills, and resources she has available to her to manage life's ups and downs and survive.

Check the thoughts influencing your client's procrastination. Explain that seeking excellence is rational and achievable whereas seeking perfection is irrational, so that she manages to tolerate making the odd mistake. Also remind her that she would never have found out how to ride a bicycle or drive a car unless she had taken the odd risk in the process!

You can introduce the *STEP model* to explore how to plan to take action. This model provides a structured process for you to work through with your client, reviewing the situation and the thoughts and emotions your client is experiencing around the decision, and planning how to develop thoughts and actions that support her ability to move forward to make a decision. I offer an example of this model in Table 12-4.

Table 12-4	Example of the STEP Decision Model		
Situation	*Thought*	*Emotion*	*Plan*
Whether to move house	I'd better wait for a while because the papers say that the housing market is slumping. I wish I could make up my mind.	Anxiety and frustration – a desire to move, an anxiety about the slump, and frustration at being unable to decide whether to go ahead	The 'perfect' time to move house doesn't exist. I can keep the slump in mind, but, if I see a house I like, I can assess at that stage whether the price is good and a manageable risk. I shall call the agent tomorrow.

Many adults have a surprisingly low tolerance to making mistakes. However, they need to take the risk of making the occasional mistake if they want to change their current situation. Procrastination not only causes paralysis but can also reduce self-esteem because the person berates herself for her indecisiveness.

Enjoying the journey

A decision is just the first step towards change. It may or may not signify an immediate result. For example, the decision to move house involves many further steps along the way. Thus there can be time both to adjust to the change and to continually evaluate the decision. Your client doesn't need to feel locked into her choice, but can review the situation as she goes along by asking whether:

- ✔ The decision is still relevant and appealing
- ✔ The strategies are working successfully
- ✔ She can think of any more effective ways of approaching the situation

Chunking the steps into measurable actions can help the anxious decision-maker find a way to enjoy the process of change and development. Many people say 'It will be fine *when*. . . I have a new home, a great relationship, a perfect job' and ignore the journey to get there. Generate ideas to help your client enjoy the ups and downs along the way without clinging to the end result. For example, thoughts such as 'It may not be immediately clear whether I have made a good decision, but I shall focus on enjoying the development process.'

It can take courage to make decisions. Rewarding effort as much as achievement acknowledges this courage, so suggest to your client that she stops to celebrate from time to time. Encourage her to reflect on what has worked as well as what she can do differently so she gets into the habit of adjusting her strategies as necessary. In this way, she can overcome her doubts, step by step, and start to make decisions with greater confidence.

Chapter 13

Achieving a Healthy and Balanced Lifestyle

*Y*ou may frequently hear 'Too much to do in too little time' in coaching sessions. Keeping healthy and achieving a work–life balance is one of the biggest challenges for people in the 21st century. Individuals across the globe are stretched in every direction, juggling commitments. Working long hours is now the norm as people struggle to manage the pressures of an ever-increasing workload alongside maintaining their personal lives.

Work–life balance is one of the most important topics you cover in coaching. Work–life balance is not a 'soft' topic but a deep one. It is the balance in how a person lives his life and where he chooses to focus his attention. Work–life balance has a huge impact on the individual's sense of happiness and fulfilment, and yet many people feel helpless to make the adjustments that enable them to achieve a better quality of life.

Thinking is at the heart of how someone experiences time. In CBC sessions, you provide a structured process for reflection on the cognitive and behavioural changes your client can make to regain a sense of control within a demanding environment. Unpacking the way your client approaches the decisions he makes about his life enables him to make more conscious choices based on his priorities.

In this chapter. I introduce CBC techniques that you can use to support your client's ability to take care of himself and to achieve a lifestyle that is meaningful to him.

Balancing Work and Life

The speed of social and economic change puts huge pressure on individuals. People struggle to keep up, reacting to changing demands and technological advances, rather than having the time to take proactive and wise decisions about their lives. Organisational structures are frequently outdated, having been set up at a time when women stayed at home to care for children, look after elderly parents, and deal with domestic matters such as deliveries and boiler servicing.

Below I list some of the problems your client may raise in CBC sessions regarding his work–life balance:

✔ I have to work these long hours because, if I don't, someone else will, and I shall lose my job/promotion/bonus.

✔ I wake up every morning just praying that the nanny isn't ill.

✔ I don't know how to keep calm when my baby's nappy needs changing just after I have spent 30 minutes getting her ready to go to crèche and I realise I shall be late for my meeting.

✔ I'd love to take flexible working, but doing so is bound to impact my career progression.

✔ What's life all about if I don't have time to enjoy it?

A few statistics

✔ Three out of four people say they work 'very hard' and cannot imagine how they can work any harder.

✔ One in five people take work home every day.

✔ One in three partners of people who work for more than 48 hour per week report that it has a negative influence on their relationships.

✔ Thirty-three per cent of people report that their company has family-friendly policies or support systems.

✔ Men and women state that they want more balance but feel under pressure to be present and work long hours even when they don't have a pressing need.

✔ Married men aged 30–49 with children work the longest hours.

✔ One in four respondents reported a negative impact on health of some kind.

✔ Most respondents reported negative effects on their job performance.

✔ Many people comment that 'quality' time with children is often not 'quality' due to fatigue.

From the Chartered Institute of Personnel and Development Working Hours in the UK Survey, from a representative sample of UK workers but with an emphasis on those working 48 hours or more per week, revised August 2008

✔ I want to spend more time with my family, but my manager and peers all work late, and by the time I get home the kids are in bed and my partner is exhausted.

✔ I have to achieve so many targets and deadlines that if I leave early I won't achieve them, and someone is always waiting to get into my shoes.

✔ I am working here, but my parents still live in my country of origin. This situation means we don't have any back-up of grandparents, uncles, or aunts to give us practical or moral support with the kids.

✔ I feel really unfit but just don't see how I can make time to go to the gym when work has a real culture of 'presenteeism' – you are expected to be at your desk from 8 till late, even if you don't have urgent work to complete.

People can lose perspective in situations such as those above and may have a tendency to catastrophise the situation. Your client may go into all-or-nothing thinking and say that 'Everything is awful' or 'If I leave early, I'll never cope or they'll overlook me for my bonus.' As a CB coach, you can unscramble the tentacles of fear that interfere with your client's clarity of focus and help him to review his approach and devise a plan to organise his life in a way that puts him in charge of the choices he makes.

Living the LIFE Act model

Clients can find it difficult to retain clarity of focus when they are feeling swamped by the demands of their lives and work. CBC enables them to stand back and reflect on their priorities so that they put their energy into the areas of their lives that matter most. The LIFE Act model provides structure to the process of achieving work–life balance:

✔ **List all commitments:** Create two columns headed 'Life' and 'Work' for the commitments he juggles. Ask your client to give as much detail as possible – for example, if your client mentions 'admin' in the work column, ask him to be specific – for example 'filing', 'bookkeeping', or 'emails'. The lists should include both activities and people.

✔ **Identify priorities:** Give each of the commitments a high or low priority. Asking the following questions may help:

• Who and what are most important to you in your personal life? (Make sure that he includes himself and activities he enjoys or needs to do to maintain his well-being.)

• What is the most important use of your time at work?

✔ **Focus on what matters most:** Decide which priorities your client wants to focus his time and energy on and identify thoughts to support this decision.

✔ **Evaluate options for change:** Apply models to review choices of ways to achieve balance.

✔ **Act:** Take action for balance. List any specific actions that may help your client achieve work–life balance. Make the life change a project. I suggest you identify no more than three actions to start with, because changing behaviour is not necessarily easy, and biting off more than your client can achieve is often demotivating.

Finding balance with the 3As model

Today's life offers both demands and temptations. People can take on more than they can chew by filling their lives with activities just because the activities are available rather than of real value. Before he knows it, your client can feel out of control and pulled in too many different directions. The *3As model*, which was developed by The Centre for Stress Management, can be applied to reviewing options for making change to achieve balance. Ask your client to list his time commitments and then review each one in turn to consider which he can alter or avoid or which commitments he needs to accept as things he cannot change.

✔ **Alter:** This can be a behavioural change to the situation, such as making time to go running, or a cognitive change such as choosing to enjoy an activity that previously he resented.

Anna, who hated completing her quarterly VAT forms, decided to enjoy the experience by focusing on how wonderful she will feel when she finishes, and arranges lunch with a girlfriend as a treat afterwards to make the experience more pleasurable.

✔ **Avoid:** People cram their life full of activities, many of which may be pleasurable but in fact leave them feeling pressurised and fatigued. These activities can include evening classes, spending time in activities or company they don't really value, and duty tasks or habitual routines that they've not reviewed. Explore whether your client can simplify his life in order to make him happier and less exhausted. 'What is enough?' is never a bad question. Ask him to consider whether the activity is:

- Essential

- A luxury or pleasure

- A hassle

You may have to challenge what your client sees as 'essential' with questions such as:

- What is the worst that may happen if you don't do that activity?

- If you were given the choice, would you still choose to do this?

- Is there a law of the universe that says you must do this?

- Is there any way you can delegate the task?

- What's stopping you giving this up?

✔ **Accept:** In everyone's life, some things can't be avoided and are an integral part of work or life. These things may include adhering to specific rules or procedures that are expected within work, or resenting the fact that a partner travels, even though this was known when the relationship started. Nonetheless, these activities can cause a sense of resentment or pressure.

Discovering enjoyment in routine tasks

Enjoying a situation that cannot be changed can, in fact, make time pass more enjoyably. Sophie was getting stressed by her daily commute from the city to the coast due to a relocation. Through coaching, she applied the ABCD model to understand how her thoughts were stressing her out. The ABCD model is introduced in Chapters 1 and 2 and enables you to review how your client is thinking about his situation and dispute whether his approach is helping him achieve his objective.

✔ **A = Activating situation:** Sophie spent two hours commuting.

✔ **B = Beliefs and thoughts:** 'I can't stand this,' 'This drive is so boring and tiring,' 'I shouldn't have to do this every day.'

✔ **C = Consequences:** Emotional stress was leading to conflict with Sophie's partner in the evenings when she got home, because she took her frustration out on him.

✔ **D = Disputing thoughts:** Sophie realised that her approach to the commute was making her daily life miserable. She discovered how to transform the experience by deciding to enjoy the time she spent in her car. Instead of resenting it, she realised that she was passing through beautiful countryside. She decided to discover Spanish through a CD training programme. In this way, she began to feel in control of the time that she was spending on the commute instead of feeling the victim of an experience that someone else had forced upon her.

Focusing on the positive can be applied to many situations. For example, many people rush from one task to the next, their heads in a spin of things they must do, rather than spending a moment to prepare their minds from one situation to the next.

The focus of thought can make a radical difference to the quality of emotional experience. One client who used to feel stressed out in the mornings getting ready for work changed her thoughts from 'I must rush' to 'I shall choose to potter about as I get prepared.' She found that it took her exactly the same time to get out of the house, but was a much less stressful experience. Another client whose walk took him across Westminster Bridge focused his mind on the view of London and the river instead of the worries of the day, and found that he arrived at work in a calmer, clearer state.

From luxury to hassle

Tom bought a new motor bike for his 30th birthday and took enormous pleasure in driving it to work every day. He felt he was fulfilling a long-held ambition. However, several years later, his sons were an age at which he wanted to take them to play football at weekends but found himself too busy cleaning and oiling the bike to give them his time. Through coaching, he decided to put the bike away and dedicate the majority of his weekends to his sons for a while, so as to take advantage of the precious years that they were living at home. 'I can always get the bike out again when they're at college.' As he commented afterwards: 'It's interesting how easy it is to know the cost of everything and the value of nothing.'

Feeling in control

Your client needs to feel in control of his life and his time – and not feel that that time is being dictated by some other 'force' of which he's the victim. Look to help him find small changes – even a few minutes a day can make a difference to life – catching the earlier train home or walking the dog.

When your client makes choices about where he focuses his time, suggest that he keeps the following questions in mind:

- Why am I doing this?
- Is this a priority activity for me?
- I'd like to say 'no' to this – is there any reason why not?
- Who am I trying to live up to?
- What does it take to have the courage to be myself and express my needs?
- Would other people act differently?
- What is enough here?
- What thought can help me manage to take the action I want to take?

Many people struggle with guilt about taking action – particularly, I find, working mothers. Juggling children and jobs requires organisational skills. An aspect that is less debated is the emotional tug that mothers can experience when leaving their children in the care of other people. One of my clients cried every day for a month when she had to put her baby in a crèche and return to work. However, in the workplace, she was expected, inevitably, to be professional and pull her weight despite acutely missing her baby. Working mothers often feel that they are falling between two stools – not coming up to their own high standards either at work or at home.

Whether your client is male or female, this guilt can be draining and requires support during your CBC sessions so that change can be achieved to alleviate the problem. Your client may consider any change in routine or attitude to be selfish or inconsiderate. Perversely, feeling guilty may make it feel as if he cares more about both work and family. It can feel uncomfortable for your client to leave something or someone out of his life or alter a situation. However, guilt is not, in CBC terms, regarded as a healthy emotion, because it stimulates a sense of deserving punishment and takes away the pleasure of the moment. Certainly others' needs have to be taken into account, but your client also needs to consider the consequences to his health if he overstretches himself. When people get tired, they can end up snapping at those they love.

Achieving quality of life = achieving quality of work

Many organisations now have work–life balance policies in place, and the Government has introduced working time regulations that lay down minimum conditions relating to weekly working time, rest entitlements, and annual leave, as well as making special provision for night workers. There are also requirements for companies to offer flexible working for parents with young children. These policies are in recognition of the fact that many staff feel stretched, which impacts performance, retention, and sickness absence. The challenge for business is that work–life balance is subjective and means different things to different people. One policy won't fit all. A single 20-year old inevitably has different but equally valid priorities to a 40-year old with a family.

Daring to ask for change

Paul and his wife both worked full-time. His parents-in-law looked after their two children while Paul and his wife were at work. As a result, Paul and his wife felt grateful to them and had got into a routine of having the in-laws to lunch every Sunday. Now that the children were older and needed more help with homework in preparation for exams, Paul found that his Sundays were interrupted by these lunches, but he didn't dare to ask for a change because he felt he'd look ungrateful and may upset the childcare arrangements. His coach asked him to consider the options and explore his fears about asking to change the situation. Paul felt that once a month was fine for his in-laws to come to lunch, but not every weekend. When he looked at the likely outcome of explaining the situation to his in-laws, he realised that it was worth asking, even if they did look a bit upset, because he thought it likely that they'd adjust eventually, and he knew that they were so fond of the children that they'd be unlikely to stop the arrangement in a huff. In fact, when Paul did make the suggestion that they come over once a month instead of every Sunday, his in-laws were understanding and supportive of him wanting to spend this time with his children. So it was worth him asking.

If your client sets an objective to achieve balance, help him to consider what balance looks like to him. Ask him, if he had balance:

- What would he do?
- How would he feel?
- What would be different?

Use the model that I show in Table 13-1 to help your client consider the consequences to himself, his work, and his relationships of continuing to be out of balance. The examples in the table reflect the comments of many of the individuals and groups of people I have worked with.

Table 13-1	What Balance Means to Me
What Balance Means to Me	*Consequences of Being Out of Balance*
Feeling in control	Exhausted and fatigued
Feeling energised	Fuzzy head
Having time for the things I really care about	Irritable – conflict with partner and colleagues, and shouting at the children at the end of the day although none of it was their fault
Not feeling guilty that I am always in the wrong place and never fulfilling everything I should be fulfilling	Bad decisions – too hasty
Being able to 'switch off' in the evenings and at weekends	Making mistakes
Not feeling I must work late or be present in the office, but able to choose my own preferred way of working – sometimes at home, sometimes at work – but with a focus on outputs not time	Getting sick – then coming into work because I feel guilty staying away, but that passes the virus all around the office and everyone gets ill, which puts more pressure on! And then our kids get sick and can't go to crèche, which means we're stuck and can't go to the office anyway. What a crazy vicious circle!
Being able to keep fit	
Remembering what it is like to relax!	

The factors regularly listed under the 'consequences of being out of balance' column demonstrate that work–life balance makes business sense. Someone who feels satisfied with his home life brings more positive energy into the workplace. Equally, if he's not worried about how children or elderly parents are being cared for, he's able to focus more fully on his work without having half his mind taken up with other preoccupations.

Work–life balance definition

✔ Being aware of different demands on time and energy

✔ Having the ability to make choices in the allocation of time and energy

✔ Knowing what values to apply to choices

✔ Making choices

Managing work–life balance by David Clutterbuck

Seeing how work–life balance impacts on motivation and retention

Many organisations are concerned with the retention rates of talented staff. Several clients I have worked with have commented that the long-hours working culture has resulted in their reviewing whether to leave the organisation in order to find a role with more balance. I have had many talented women as clients who say that they'd rather start their own businesses than have to battle with a macho culture that makes them feel guilty about having a life or needing to collect a child from school. Many men think in a similar way and want to maintain their marriages, personal health, and quality of life. Generation Y (those born around 1980 and termed 'Y', succeeding the previous generation termed 'X') perplex their employers by deciding to accept less pay in order to achieve balance. Old and young seek meaning and purpose through sabbaticals, voluntary service overseas, and travel. This situation isn't good news for businesses, because recruitment and retraining is expensive and time-consuming. You may find yourself employed to resolve some of these issues through coaching. Changing economic times raise different issues. Economic downturns result in unemployment, so you may work with clients to reassess their future directions, both in terms of employment and lifestyle.

Peer pressure is a major influence. People don't want to stand out from the norm. Also, many bosses mistakenly imagine that their own long-hours habits do not signify that their direct reports have to work late. But, of course, bosses are the role model for success, so inevitably people follow their lead.

Again, CBC questioning models enable you to dispute what is perception and what is realistically required. Here are some examples:

✔ Just because your boss and peers work long hours, how does that mean that you must too, provided you achieve your outputs and targets?

✔ What is the worst that can happen if you decide to leave at a different time?

✔ You say that your boss would think less of you if you took an hour to go to the gym at lunchtime – is this mind-reading or has she actually expressed this feeling?

✔ Can you think of anyone else in your organisation who has taken steps to achieve balance? Has this decision impacted on his career?

✔ If you're choosing to stay in this organisation, are there aspects of the work that you need to accept?

✔ What one change can make a difference to your sense of balance?

✔ What thought can help you to feel confident that you can make a change?

Deciding what is acceptable

Most people are happy to work late from time to time. The problem is that when a department has been working hard on a particular project, the practice of working late becomes the norm and people forget to slow down again. This constant overwork can lead to exhaustion, sickness, resentment, and lack of motivation. It seems incredibly easy for groups to lose touch with what is a reasonable expectation of working hours.

Try using the model for setting boundaries that I show in Table 13-2 to help your client reflect on his habits and identify what is acceptable and what is not acceptable to him.

Table 13-2	Setting Boundaries
Acceptable	*Not Acceptable*
Working late for a specific deadline	When working late becomes the norm
Helping out if someone is sick	Not being able to take time out to go to the gym
Working through lunch occasionally to cover a colleague who wants time out	Feeling I can't share my childcare or domestic problems with my manager

Traditional working patterns can become a cultural and behavioural habit but need constant review according to business demands, changing personal and economic circumstances, and technological developments. Many companies have options for new ways of working, including:

✔ Working from home

✔ Working flexible hours

✔ Part-time working

✔ Job-sharing and job-splitting

✔ Working annualised hours

✔ Term-time working

✔ Virtual team-working

Achieving work–life balance

Managers and teams need to:

✔ Clarify what is important and know business priorities

✔ Recognise and support the fact that people are 'whole', and encourage balance

✔ Continually experiment with the way work is done

Friedman, Christensen, Degroot in Harvard Business Review

It makes sense from everyone's point of view to ensure that working practices are shaped to support both business outputs and personal life.

A survey by Working Parents/PWC in 2008 demonstrated that line managers are often the biggest block to change in introducing flexible working. Despite evidence that productivity increases or stays the same, they're fearful that adjusting working methods will detract from performance. In fact, evidence in Chartered Institute of Personnel and Development research in April 2008 listed benefits such as raised morale, motivation, commitment, and engagement.

Changing habits is uncomfortable, but a coach can enable managers to objectively consider what options they have for the way in which they and their teams work. Group-think leads people to blindly continue to follow old practices even when the practices don't work, so challenge them to consider: 'Just because people have worked in this way in the past, how does it follow that work and outputs suffer if you work differently in the future?'

Small changes can make a real difference to your client's quality of life. Taking half an hour to focus on his child before bedtime, making time for a romantic meal with his partner, or shifting his working pattern at the office to relieve pressure can all improve your client's sense of control over his work and life.

Managing the BlackBerry age

Is your client a 'crackberry' – someone chained to his digital technology? Technological changes have revolutionised our lives since the mid-1990s. Have you noticed how people fidget with their mobiles as they sit on trains or planes, try to drive illegally around a roundabout with a mobile phone propped on one ear as they endeavour to steer and change gear at the same time? At the end of short plane trips, people dive to turn their phones back on again – 'Surely someone must have needed me in the last 40 minutes!' Now you see fraught executives sitting by their holiday swimming pools frantically responding to emails on their BlackBerries. Such is this obsession that even sleep is disturbed by people taking their mobile devices to bed. Not surprisingly, this activity intrudes horribly on relationships, and partners have been known to throw the wondrous machines into the pool on holiday or down the loo.

'Logging on is essential because . . .'

Your client may have a perception that he is supposed to be available for emails 24/7. He may consider he is an essential cog in the organisational wheel and even gain his sense of status from feeling that others are dependent on him. In CBC sessions, you can help him analyse whether this expectation is realistic and whether it is helping or hindering his performance. You may find that your client has a great explanation for why he's joined at the hip to his technology:

- ✔ I have at least 200 emails come in every day and if I don't pick them up over the weekend or when I am on holiday I will just be so swamped when I get back that it won't be worth going away!
- ✔ I don't like to leave my desk during the day, because people expect me to respond to emails immediately.
- ✔ I can't concentrate, because I always have an email or a call coming in every few minutes.

However, there will be negative consequences of this type of behaviour, not only in relationships at home but also in the quality of your client's thinking and attention at work. Your role will be to help him to unpack his habits and try to carve out a way to feel in control of the technology rather than feel that the technology is in control of him. As one client commented: 'I realise that I feel psychologically shackled to my email and mobile phone.'

I have come to the conclusion that this obsession with technology is about the human need to be included, to be part of the tribe. Much as people complain about having 200 emails a day, if they happen to be left off the 'cc' list one day, they can panic and feel excluded – outside the pack. This panic is about the need for significance and recognition, and the email and mobile system is an easy fix. But surely people can find better ways to feel included and significant than being a slave to technology?

Technology is clever stuff and has enormous benefits. However, being clever isn't being wise, and where you can help your client is in getting him to consider how to manage the clever beast wisely!

One of the dangers of these habits around technology is that the mind and body are on constant ready-alert. The brain gets used to high levels of stress hormones such as adrenaline, noradrenaline, and cortisol and forgets how to properly relax and switch off so as to dissipate this chemical mix. Eventually, this situation can lead to fatigue, sickness, and depression. Several of my clients have commented that they have forgotten how to relax.

One of the issues around technology is *irrational expectations,* that is expectations based on supposition rather than evidence. Only a few years ago, business functioned without mobile phones, email, or the Internet. Now, if people are out of contact for a few minutes, they panic. This panic leads to thoughts such as:

- ✔ 'I must be at my desk to reply to email immediately.' (assumption)
- ✔ 'They will think I am not committed if I don't respond to email in the evenings.' (mind-reading)
- ✔ 'I'm frightened that I will miss out on a major deal.' (anxiety-inducing thinking)

Overcoming technology addiction

Few organisations have put policies in place to manage expectations around email, Internet, and BlackBerry use. Most behaviours are based on assumptions rather than agreed statements or policies. Therefore, if your client is enslaved to his technology or resentful and fatigued by it, you can suggest that he arranges a meeting to clarify the situation with his boss or HR department. He can discuss with them what they consider to be reasonable and evidence-based and what is supposition, so that they can agree between them how he should work in future. As the saying goes, to 'assume' something makes an ass out of you and me!

Explore what access and contact your client considers reasonable and help him to set a routine that reflects this. For example, he may choose to access his email once an hour rather than having it continuously interrupting his thinking process at work. Seeing an email come in on the screen tends to make people slaves to the adrenalin of the excitement of the 'new'.

With regards to home life, review with your client how his current use of technology is impacting on his relationships. If technology has no impact, he has no problem. If he is interrupting his quality time with family and friends to answer his mobile or respond to emails, you can help him to reflect on:

- ✔ Whether this behaviour is really necessary or just a habit
- ✔ Whether being in contact makes him feel needed or important
- ✔ How he might feel if someone he was with behaved in this way
- ✔ Whether a family member has commented on the way he uses technology
- ✔ What he expects of other people with regard to access
- ✔ How he can change his behaviour to use his technology more effectively in future

Help your client to make behavioural changes by setting up his computer and mobile technology in the way he decides, for example switching off the signal for email and the 'view new email' mode, setting a time in the evenings and at weekends when he switches off totally and focuses on his personal life; planning a meeting with his boss to discuss acceptable use.

Maintaining Optimum Energy through a Long Day

Many people work long hours at sedentary jobs. The Government berates people for being unfit and obese, but the reality of most people's lives is that they have little opportunity to take exercise during the working week. However, as Aristotle wrote many centuries ago 'healthy body, healthy mind'. Being fit and strong promotes flexibility of mind and provides energy to help people concentrate.

Time management only gets you so far. If you manage to get to the meeting on time but are so fatigued that you're mentally asleep, you may as well not be there!

Energising your mind

The mind is the key to good thinking – which is what CBC is all about. The human brain needs as much care and fine-tuning as the body, if that body is to work well throughout a long day. Machine operators and long-distance lorry-drivers have their hours regulated because their companies understand that they cannot concentrate for endless hours without the danger of an accident occurring. As soon as people get behind a computer at a desk, this principle is forgotten, and many firms expect people to work 12-hour days without breaks.

Working such long hours has negative consequences on thinking and creativity, which are the skills that knowledge-based industries depend upon. Your client may be a manager trying to get the most out of his staff, or an individual trying to ensure that his mind performs at its peak. Help your client to review his existing habits and practices to work out better strategies for feeling mentally alert throughout the working day – and into the evenings too.

Taking breaks to refresh mind and body

The human body has a *circadian rhythm,* which is the innate biological clock that regulates our waking and sleeping patterns. These rhythms control the daily ups and downs of physiologic processes, including body temperature, blood pressure, and the release of hormones over the 24-hour period. Good sleep is essential to the process of revitalising the immune system and re-energising the mind. Many clients consumed by watching TV or logging on to the Internet do not allow themselves adequate time to relax and prepare for sleep. In fact, many of the clients I work with tell me that they want to get to bed at 11 p.m. but that they find themselves still on the computer surfing or responding to emails at 2 a.m. This activity both shortens their hours of sleep – most people benefit from around 7 hours rest – and also leads to them going to bed in a heightened state of stress or alertness, with their minds still full of new information that then has to be processed.

If your client mentions insomnia as an issue, help him to set goals for relaxing before bedtime and getting to bed at the time he seeks. Encourage him to challenge any 'addictive' thoughts such as:

- ✔ I must just finish this presentation before I go to bed.

- ✔ That looks interesting so I'll just see what it's about. . .

- ✔ I can only sleep if I have cleared my inbox.

Challenging habits

People are habitual creatures, and it can be hard to break through old habits. Help your client to develop new behaviours to support his personal health and energy. Ask him to identify those habits he considers unhealthy and decide what actions he will take to replace them. Suggest he sets reminders and incentives to help him achieve his objectives. These can include practical reminders such as setting an alarm clock to sound at the time he intends to go to bed, putting an alert in his computer calendar, or asking his partner or friend to call him at a specific time. He may decide to reward himself in some way when he achieves his goals, possibly simply by putting a tick on a chart or by buying himself a treat of some kind.

Prepare him for the discomfort he will feel when he makes changes to his routine, but acclimatise him to the fact that the discomfort is a positive signal that he is doing something different. Help him become familiar with the conflicting thoughts that he may be having, such as one thought drawing him back into his old habit and another thought reminding him that he wants to change his behaviour. Reinforce the message that it is him who is in control of which message he responds to, and that it is daily disciplines that help him achieve balance and quality of life. I refer to this process in Chapter 5.

Encourage your client to ask himself the following questions to challenge his habits:

- ✔ What's the worst that can happen if I don't do this task?

- ✔ Why must I finish this job before I go to bed?

- ✔ What makes it essential to answer this email tonight rather than tomorrow morning? Will anyone be awake to read it? Will it really make a difference?

Taking time out

Encouraging people to wind down in the evening is good for mind and body. The chemical cortisol, which is triggered in a stress situation, should be naturally high in the morning to wake people up, but it should dip at the end of the day to allow people to get sleepy before going to bed. However, if someone is stressed by working just before sleep, this chemical will probably be raised, influencing both his immune system and his sleep. Where possible, encourage people to allow for a period of time of relaxation before their heads hit the pillow.

Throughout the day, the brain also responds to *ultradian rhythms,* which are the body's natural cycles that occur approximately every 90 minutes throughout a 24-hour period, altering hormonal release, heart rate, and other physiological functions. When you watch a baby or puppy, it tends to have bursts of activity followed by periods of rest. Your client can find out how to respond to his own natural 'down' times with a power nap, a quiet meditation, or a walk to allow the brain to switch off for a short period of time so that he returns to his tasks refreshed and energised.

Long periods of sitting at a computer make people feel sluggish. The body slows down and, because many people lean forward to work on their desktops, their lungs are compressed, decreasing the flow of blood and oxygen to the brain. Standing, walking, and exercise all improve the pressure of blood flow through the veins, so make sure that you advise your client to set regular periods where he moves away from his desk and gets his body working again. This movement aids thinking, because the brain requires blood and oxygen to function well. Drinking water is also essential to effective thinking.

Simple changes make a real difference to a person's life. Your client can take simple and practical steps to keep his mind and body alert.

Ditching Bad Health

Books and newspapers go into so much detail about healthy diet and exercise these days that your client probably doesn't need further information from you on these topics – make sure though that you always have a bibliography of information available. Where you come in, as a CB coach, is in helping your client discipline himself to take action to *apply* the information. Many people have great difficulty changing their habits around health, exercise, and nutrition.

You can help your client in various ways, including the following:

- Identify the vision of the lifestyle he wants to achieve.
- Record the benefits of changing versus the consequences of not changing.

✔ Engage your client's emotional will to change.

✔ Set practical and achievable steps for change.

✔ Consider rewards for effort, such as treating himself to an hour reading his favourite magazine when he has achieved his health goal, against penalties for not changing, such as doing a DIY task that he has been putting off for some time, or putting money aside for a charity.

Putting yourself first

To enhance his health and well-being, your client has to put himself first from time to time. Many adults feel selfish at taking the time out required to maintain their well-being. Remind your client of the safety instruction often given on aeroplanes: 'Put your own oxygen mask on before fitting an oxygen mask to anyone else.' Using this metaphor can help your client see that putting himself first is often not selfish, but responsible. If he doesn't look after himself, he won't be around to look after or support others, whether they are babies, partners, or colleagues.

As an adult, your client is responsible for himself. He needs to take that responsibility seriously, because no-one else will do this job for him.

Personal responsibility is one of the difficulties of behaviour change around work–life balance – many people seek an 'outside' source or power to tell them what to do and when. However, because people have different needs, your client must find this discipline from within and feel good about taking time for his own health and well-being. Encourage your client to develop an affirmative statement such as 'Taking time to look after myself is responsible, not selfish, and also demonstrates to others how they can do the same.' I discuss developing affirmative and constructive thoughts in Chapter 6.

Getting off the sofa: Routines for maximum well-being

Have you noticed how many people think in an all-or-nothing way about their well-being? They start a diet on a Monday and, if they have broken it in any small way by Wednesday, they give up and wait until the following Monday. Equally, people start an exercise regime and set themselves such high demands that if they can't go to the gym for at least an hour or two they decide it isn't worth going at all. But surely even 10–15 minutes' exercise is better than none at all?

Through CBC questioning, you can help your client check out how his thinking is helping or hindering his health, nutrition, and exercise routines. In

Table 13-3, I show a simple model that you can use to start the discussion by asking your client to share his current habits and routines with you.

Table 13-3	My Well-being
Things I Currently Do to Jeopardise My Health	*Things I Need to Do to Take Care of Myself and Feel at My Best*
Get takeaway pizzas when I am tired	Get a good night's sleep
Put off going to the gym because I never have enough time	Get exercise to keep fit
Drinking too much	Stop responding to work demands after 7:30 p.m.

Identify what thoughts keep your client stuck in the old patterns and those that may motivate him to move forward to change. I show an example in Table 13-4.

Table 13-4	Sofa So Good
Demotivating Thoughts	*Motivating Thoughts*
I don't have time to go to the gym.	Any time spent in the gym is better than none.
I don't have the energy.	I shall have more energy once I have exercised and eaten healthily.
It's so comfortable here, I can't be bothered.	I have to get out of bed some time, so let's make it now!
They say chocolate is good for you, so I'll just have this piece. . .	This outfit will look great if I lost weight.

Acting healthy and energised

Knowing what you should do is one thing; doing it is much harder! Develop your client's emotional association with the person he wants to be, the one who has succeeded in changing his lifestyle and is feeling the benefit. Suggest that he acts as if he's healthy and practising his new lifestyle changes. Acting healthy leads to comments such as the following:

✔ I feel more energised.

✔ I am walking in a more determined way.

✔ I feel lighter and happier.

✔ I can imagine being healthier – and feeling really good about myself.

Getting back on track

Prepare your client to deal with blocks and limits he may face, by suggesting he keeps connecting to how good he will feel when he achieves his desired lifestyle rather than the old but unhelpful comfort zone of unhealthy habits. Take a little time to look at the consequences of not changing versus the benefits of changing his routine.

If he breaks his diet or exercise regime, help him to devise statements such as the following:

✔ Just because I have broken my objectives, does it mean that I can't start trying again straight away?

✔ Can I reward myself for effort even if I didn't achieve my target?

✔ I haven't allowed myself the desired amount of time for exercise today, but is there any reason why I can't do ten minutes or more anyway?

✔ Let me remember how good I feel when I have eaten well and exercised, so that I feel motivated to take action to take care of myself.

Constructive thoughts and statements are powerful drivers of change. Your client will also need to plan some practical actions to ensure that he integrates his new healthy behaviours into his routine. Some tips that can help him are:

✔ Plan exercise at the beginning of the day, because many people have more control of their time at the beginning of the day than once the day has started to get control of them!

✔ Plan exercise that your client can do with children, colleagues, or partners – for example bike rides, basketball, baseball in the garden.

✔ Choose exercise that he enjoys – for example dancing or Tai Chi, or whatever makes him smile.

✔ Even if he has no time to go to a gym or exercise in a formal way, suggest that he lifts a couple of 2-litre bottles of water as weights while he sits on the sofa, or does stomach crunches while he lies on the floor watching TV in the evening. Move him away from all-or-nothing thinking to taking small steps to change his habits.

When people gain control of the small daily disciplines that nurture them internally, they feel more in control of how they spend their time externally. Strength and flexibility of mind and body enable people to gain strength and flexibility in how they manage their lives, work, and relationships.

Chapter 14

Managing Career Transitions

· ·

In This Chapter

▶ Adjusting to the changing world of work

▶ Expressing your strengths

▶ Choosing your response to change

▶ Working through transitions

· ·

Many people change jobs four or five times over their lifetimes. The psychological contract between employer and employee has altered dramatically over the past 20 years, and many organisations now hire staff on a project basis and outsource functions that used to be done in house. Ease of movement within the EU and worldwide has also brought competition from an international workforce, so each individual needs to consider her career progression on a regular and continuous basis.

These changes have also brought more opportunities for changing career within one's current organisation as well as moving sideways, upwards, or out to new territories. Organisations are now commonly involved in mergers and takeovers, which may demand relocation. With this change comes the likelihood of restructuring departments and roles. Staff may be made redundant as the management seeks to streamline functions in order to make more profit. This situation takes emotional and practical adjustment for all those involved.

Your client needs to be prepared to keep an eye on her career position and direction. Whether she's sent to you by her organisation or comes voluntarily to discuss her role, CBC can help her to gain clarity of perspective and overcome any tendencies to self-defeating or limiting thoughts about her capability to succeed in this changing world.

In this chapter, I cover the various transitions that your client may experience within her career, and I introduce methods that you can use to help her to move forward with confidence.

Working through Career Changes

A career change can be both exciting and daunting. How a person thinks about herself on the inside determines what other people perceive on the outside. Thoughts and expectations impact on feelings and body language. The workplace is probably the most important place to be aware of this impact, because those who are able to articulate their strengths and appear capable are the ones noticed for promotion. Pessimistic or limiting thinking can hold a person back. Your role is likely to be to work with people to identify their unique talents and contributions and how they decide to apply them within their careers.

Bharat was a young manager who came for coaching. He was thrilled to have been promoted, and yet also felt acutely aware that everyone else at his level in the company was ten years older than him. With several direct reports now under his auspices, he recognised that he needed to change his own view of himself if he were to succeed in his new role. His focus on his age rather than his skills undermined his confidence – coaching helped him acknowledge his competence.

Considering the continuous interview

There was a time when people imagined that the first job interview they attended would get them a job to last a lifetime. These days, many companies effectively interview employees every year at their annual appraisals. Some may even be interviewed for their own jobs. Demonstrating talent and competence therefore has to become a continuous activity in how your client presents herself in the workplace, rather than one that only occurs when going for a new job.

In a way, people now need to think of themselves more as self-employed consultants rather than employees. They're only as good as their last projects! Encourage your client to review the contribution she brings to her workplace on a continuous basis so that she can:

- Know her strengths and skills
- List her achievements
- Work effectively with others
- Sell her 'added value'

Doing all the above can be quite a tough call for people who prefer to feel securely employed. You may well have to help your clients discover how to project and sell themselves, because many clients come to CBC to become more influential within their business environments.

Identifying strengths

Ask your client to list her skills, strengths, competencies, and achievements. If she doesn't know her best attributes, other people won't know them. I am always amazed by how difficult people find this task and how much they discount the positives. Self-defeating thoughts that my clients have told me include:

- ✔ 'Well, I just do my job.'
- ✔ 'Talking about my strengths is arrogant.'
- ✔ 'I haven't achieved that much.'
- ✔ 'I feel really uncomfortable talking about myself.'

You may have to be quite direct. Sit with your client during the coaching session and encourage her to make the list, or ask her to complete the task at home. You're not asking her to write a curriculum vitae (CV): you're asking her to produce the content that can be included within a CV but can also be used to build confidence in her ability to succeed. In Table 14-1, I show a framework called the *strengths chart* that your client can use to help her list her positive points.

Table 14-1	Strengths Chart
Skills and qualifications, continuous development	*e.g. degree, professional qualification, word processing, accountancy, budgeting, training course on assertiveness skills*
Life experiences that have given me strengths	*e.g. living abroad as a child gave me capability in l anguages and flexibility, ability to make new friends*
Work experience	*e.g. x company, three years, account manager*
Personal qualities and strengths	*e.g. tolerant, loyal, good team worker*
Projects and achievements	*e.g. successfully managed office relocation, including facilities and IT*
Passions and talents	*e.g. play the guitar in a band at weekends, go hiking in the Himalayas for holidays*
Travels	*e.g. Europe, USA, Asia; enjoy finding out about different cultures*
Good feedback	*e.g. boss was really pleased with my organisational skills, colleague commented what fun it was to work with me*

Your client may need to write several pages of information in order to build up an accurate picture of the strengths she has accumulated over her lifetime. Encourage her to list as many as possible positives as she can, because so much of what people achieve gets overlooked in the maelstrom that is today's fast-paced workplace.

Developing affirmative statements

In order for others to perceive your client as competent and successful, she needs to work on her inner dialogue so that she can 'walk' her strengths. Acknowledging what she has achieved, however great or small, is the foundation to building confidence. You can help your client to build *affirmative statements* so that she take these on board. The development of constructive and affirmative thoughts is also covered in Chapter 6. For example:

- ✔ 'I am one of the most experienced people in this company.'
- ✔ 'I demonstrated my creativity during the latest management meeting.'
- ✔ 'Several people have commented what a good team player I am.'
- ✔ 'I am well travelled and that helps me understand the different cultures I work with.'
- ✔ 'My boss often comes to me for advice about projects.'

The more frequently your client repeats her own affirmative statements to herself, the more she is likely to believe that they're a part of her, and the more the strengths and confidence are integrated into the way she thinks about herself. Thoughts and statements developed through CBC differ from positive thinking, which may not be based on fact – everything she articulates in CBC is based on real achievements and strengths.

Articulating strengths

Encourage your client to practise articulating the strengths that she listed in the section above, so that other people know about them. Many people assume that their bosses and colleagues know their achievements, but unless they have told them specific details, they may know little. Again, many people are fearful of talking about these things, thinking it can be perceived as bigheaded or arrogant. Certainly you need to tread a fine line here, and you're not asking your client to stand on the rooftop pronouncing that she's the greatest! However, you are suggesting that she formulates phrases, based on the inner dialogue that she has now built up, that explain to other people the contribution and added value she brings to the department or organisation.

Amy, a senior manager, was waiting at the lift when the chief executive from the USA came and joined her. She introduced herself, and he asked her what her role was. 'I'm a project manager,' she replied. When discussing this situation later in her coaching session, she realised that she had missed an opportunity to spread information about her capabilities – she had undersold herself. When the coach asked how else she may have described herself, she replied: 'I am a senior programme manager for the EMEA region. I have just overseen the integration of the IT systems during our recent merger, and it went really well. I am currently working on a systems upgrade for Europe.'

As she described her role this time, her body language changed and she stood taller and looked generally more confident. The coach asked her to consider different circumstances where she may be able to promote her skills within the new organisation. With the merger, the business had expanded considerably, and there were several members of the senior management team who did not know what she could offer them in the way of services.

The *TCP model* can be a good prompt for a client who becomes aware that she needs to promote herself within her business:

- ✔ **Thoughts:** Identify what thoughts can help you manage the situation. What thought can make you feel good and more able to present yourself in a positive light?

- ✔ **Circumstances:** What practical steps can you take to achieve your goal? What situations could become opportunities to articulate your strengths?

- ✔ **Physiology:** What body language can you adopt in order to promote your message more fully?

Whether your client is going to a formal interview, planning for an appraisal, or just trying to raise her profile within her normal role, get her to practise being the person who people see as competent and confident. How she walks to the coffee machine and what she talks about can be as important as how she behaves in a formal meeting. These actions can provide opportunities to raise her image in a structured and planned way. CBC provides your client with the understanding that the quality of her 'inner dialogue' and thinking is at the heart of influencing others, building success from the inside out.

Adjusting to a new role

Moving into a new role requires the development of new thought patterns within the brain. It is rather like moving furniture when you move house: everything needs to be re-positioned. Your client's perception of herself has been formed from the various experiences of her lifetime. Most people are too busy working on targets and deadlines to stop and think about their inner lives of thoughts and feelings. Transitions such as a job move frequently bring people to a point where they feel they need help to reflect on who they are and who they need to become. And so they come for coaching.

Changing roles

Changing role is the beginning of something but also the end of something. The process is a transition. With any transition, more things change than the physical movement to a new desk or office. Your client finishes a stage of her life with all its associations and moves to a new stage. This change can be uncomfortable, because she may not be clear about what the new stage involves. Coaching can help your client stop and reflect on this process and be prepared to enter the new stage with confidence.

When a client comes to you for help entering a new phase or role, try to make the distinction between what she leaves behind and what she may need to do to make her new role successful. Identifying your client's thoughts can give you and your client an understanding of how she feels about both situations. Try using the *changing roles model* that I show in Table 14-2 to help your client list her thoughts and feelings.

Table 14-2	Changing Roles
The Old Role	*The New Role*
I was ready for a change = feeling good.	It's a great promotion = feeling excited.
I shall miss my colleagues as they were a good team = feeling sad and nostalgic.	I hope I am up to it = feeling anxious.
I discovered a lot = feeling competent.	I don't know any of my team yet = feeling anxious.
I can't believe I was in that job for ten years, it makes me feel old = feeling anxious.	I have to find out how to manage a big department = feeling anxious.
I became really comfortable in that role = feeling good but also restless.	I'll earn a lot more money – that's good, but I think they'll expect a lot from me = feeling pleased and anxious.

The changing roles model highlights the areas that you and your client may want to work with. Her thoughts may lead to feelings of nostalgia around leaving the old role, and this nostalgia can be honoured and experienced. She needs to accept the inevitable changes. Identifying skills that she can transfer to the new role can build confidence.

In the example above, the client has anxiety that is triggered by the way she is thinking about her future role; this anxiety is certainly an area you can work through. Your client may benefit from finding out how to transform her self-doubt into more self-supportive thoughts. Questions that you can use in this type of situation are:

- ✔ What would it take for you to feel you were up to it?

- ✔ Do you have any evidence that others may not think you're up to it? Are you mind-reading?

- ✔ What is so anxiety-making about not knowing new team members?

- ✔ What expectations do you think your managers have of you in this new role? Do you have evidence for these thoughts or are you making assumptions?

- ✔ Is there any reason to believe that you can't manage a larger team?

- ✔ What skills and resources do you have that can be transferred to your new role?

- ✔ Are you prepared for a period of discomfort while you adjust to your new role?

- ✔ What thoughts can help you manage this transition?

Help your client to focus on what is evidence-based, and ensure that she has constructive and supportive thoughts rather than self-defeating or doubt-invoking ones.

Using the SPACE model

The *SPACE model* (developed by Nick Edgerton and originally referred to in an article with Professor Stephen Palmer in *The Coaching Psychologist*, Volume 1, No.2 in November 2005), can identify an overview of your client's current challenges. The table shows how negative and doubtful thoughts trigger physical and emotional responses that influence actions. The SPACE model can also help your client to prepare for a new or stressful situation by exploring her thoughts, as follows:

- ✔ **Social context:**

  - What is the social context that you're finding challenging?

  - What is the specific situation?

  - What is within your circle of influence to control?

  - Who can you call on for help?

- ✔ **Physical reactions:**

  - When you're in this situation, or thinking about it, what physical reactions do you experience?

  - Are there changes you can make to lifestyle, diet, exercise, or sleep that may be helpful?

✔ **Actions:**

- What are you doing or avoiding doing that may be inducing anxiety, doubt, or stress? How is your anxiety influencing the actions you're taking?

✔ **Cognitions:**

- What are your thought processes during or while anticipating this situation?

- Are you thinking negatively or making things worse than they really are?

- What thoughts and images can you use to help you manage this situation?

✔ **Emotions:**

- What key emotions do you experience in this situation?

- How is your thinking making you feel?

- What may be a more helpful emotion to experience in this situation?

The SPACE model enables your client to gain insight into how her thoughts are impacting her ability to manage the situation she is facing, and helps her identify specific actions. You can use the model in many situations. The following example shows how this model can work in helping a person adapt to a new role:

✔ **S = Social context** – new role

✔ **P = Physical reactions** – standing taller, breathing calmly, heart rate normal

✔ **A = Actions** – making time to meet new staff, speaking up in meetings

✔ **C = Cognitions** – I have managed new roles in the past so I can manage this transition too; I can remind myself of past successes and feel confident; I have a lot to offer this job

✔ **E = Emotions** – excited, confident

Many factors in your client's life are likely to change as she adapts to a new role. For example, she may move to managing members of staff who previously were her peers. Some people find this hard, because they want to remain friends and yet have to performance-manage their teams. Encourage your client to identify thoughts and behaviours to help her adjust to her success and find a way to maintain good relationships within a framework of respect and acceptance of her as a manager.

Keeping an Eye on Career Progress

The world of work is changing on many fronts – new industries develop, and your client needs to keep an eye on the options available to her so that she doesn't end up feeling stuck. Also, many people enter their first jobs more by chance than planning. Where a client comes to you uncertain about her future, it can be useful for her to review her career–life direction so that she makes good decisions.

Reflecting on how your client came to be in her current role or sector may provide clues as to how you may work with her. Ask your client to describe how her career choice came about. Some of the replies my clients have offered in response to this question include:

✔ I took a holiday job, and it turned into a permanent role.

✔ My dad happened to mention a vacancy in a friend's company.

✔ It just happened – I went to a recruitment company and this job was the first one they came up with.

✔ I have always wanted to go into this industry.

✔ I always admired my aunt's lifestyle and decided to follow her lead.

The first three answers above show clients who fell into a career rather than planned one, while the final two clients had distinct ideas about why they made their career choices. Try to work with your client to ensure that she takes time to make a considered decision about her future progression.

Taking steps on the career ladder

If your client wants to review her career decision, she needs to take into account several aspects of her life. Try asking questions such as the following to draw out discussion for you to work on together:

✔ What do you consider success to look like?

✔ What type of lifestyle do you want?

✔ What sectors interest you?

✔ Do you feel you have a calling?

✔ How can your career reflect a sense of meaning or purpose in your life?

✔ Do you want to travel?

✔ Do you want a job or a career?

✔ Who do you admire? What types of people do you admire?

✔ Are there organisational structures that you prefer to work within – for example a hierarchy or a more informal or flatter structure?

Listen out for answers suggesting that your client holds limiting or self-defeating thoughts or beliefs about herself that may stop her going for the career she wants. These may be:

✔ I don't think I have the right qualifications.

✔ I'll never get in there because that is such a competitive industry.

✔ I'd love to work in that sector but the pay is lousy and my lifestyle won't allow for it.

✔ I am not sure I have it in me to manage a sales job.

✔ I'd like to go for that promotion but I know several of my colleagues who have been in the industry for longer than I have are also putting themselves forward.

In order to challenge and transform your client to move from this type of thinking to being more self-supportive, try asking some of the following questions:

✔ Do you have evidence that your qualifications aren't good enough?

✔ In what way can you upgrade your qualifications to be relevant?

✔ Just because the industry is a competitive one, how does this fact mean that you personally won't get a job in it?

✔ Just because your colleagues have been in the industry for longer than you, how does that mean that you don't also have a chance of getting the promotion?

✔ If this career is the career you really want to get into, is there any way that you can manage to make ends meet even if the pay is less than you're currently earning? Have you done a budget?

✔ What would it take for you to feel confident enough to go for this job?

✔ What thoughts can help you to feel confident?

Some of your clients may want to make major career changes, but others may seek to make smaller steps. The process of helping your client consider and prepare for a career change allows you to work on several levels, including her experience and relevant qualifications, her success criteria regarding career and lifestyle, and – perhaps most importantly – her confidence to make changes. Develop a record of people who have succeeded against the odds or without relevant qualifications, and remind your client that the power of passion, persistence, and personality can move mountains.

Managing mergers and structural changes

Mergers, acquisitions, restructures, and change initiatives all exist as part of the business scene today. With each one comes anxiety and uncertainty. Inevitably, much of this mood is about the 'What's-in-it-for-me?' factor, and your client may ask some of the following questions:

- ✔ What's going to happen to me?
- ✔ Will I be made redundant?
- ✔ Do I have to reapply for my job?
- ✔ Will I like the new management?
- ✔ What is it exactly they want me to do?
- ✔ What does it all look like and how does it affect me?

People tend to feel out of control when change is forced upon them. If your client has an objective of managing a change, you can help her feel as secure as possible within the midst of change. As I mention in Chapter 12, I call this skill the 'finding out how to dance on the shifting carpet' skill.

Humans are deeply habitual creatures and like a sense of control of their own destinies. When mergers and restructures occur, they may lose that sense of control. Bring your client back to the central premise of CBC – that people become disturbed not by events but by the views they take of those events. We may not be able to control the situation itself, but we can always control the way we respond to the situation. See the change as scary and it becomes scary; see the change as interesting and something that can be managed and your client can feel more in control, if only of her own emotional state. Our emotional state is the determiner of quality of life, so this state is, in itself, extremely important.

Responding to change

When a change has been forced upon your client, she may go through various emotional states, including the following:

1. **Shock:** How can they do this and not warn us?
2. **Denial:** I don't want to think about this.
3. **Awareness and understanding:** What exactly is going to happen and why?
4. **Acceptance:** Okay, so I guess this is inevitable.
5. **Options for action:** What am I going to do about this?
6. **Integration and acclimatisation:** I am getting used to this now and see what I can gain from it.

Encourage your client to gain as much information as possible so that she works from facts rather than allowing herself to have mind-reading or fortune-telling thoughts such as: 'I bet they're planning to do. . . ' or 'It'll never work.'

Considering the options of change

With as many facts to hand as possible, you can help your client realise that she has options for responding to the change. When people are anxious, their ability to think laterally can narrow. In CBC, you help your client to approach change in a more proactive way, so that she develops a greater sense of personal control within a situation that may remain uncertain for some time. Help her consider her options, which include:

- Be proactive and talk to her boss or the new boss, and begin to state preferences: 'I'm going to let them know my skills and express my preferences for my new role.'

- Be reactive and stay to allow the process to happen: 'I'll just wait and see.'

- Consider options within the organisation and also recognise that she has the option to move into a new organisation: 'I feel confident that something good is out there for me, here or elsewhere.'

- Look around and see how the changes may impact on her and what opportunities may exist within the new framework: 'Maybe something better for me will come out of all this change.'

Your client may find it hard to be proactive when she is feeling anxious about her future. Lack of confidence limits her ability to break through her fears and take action. CBC provides the opportunity to overcome her barriers and take control of those areas of her life that are within her remit. Build her sense of confidence that she has the personal skills and resources to manage the situation.

1. List the factors she can control.

2. Remember the various changes she has managed successfully in her life before, whether going to university, starting a new job, moving house, or getting divorced.

3. Identify the skills and strengths she applied in those situations and consider how she can choose to transfer these to the current challenge.

4. Consider who she can call on for support.

5. Plan to manage the change day by day, continuously reviewing options for response and action so that she gains a sense of control of how she responds to external factors.

Managing change with the BASIC ID

The BASIC ID model, developed by Arnold Lazarus, can be a useful way for your client to uncover her current mode of response to a situation and help her plan to manage a situation. In Table 14-3, I show an example of a client planning to manage a period of change in her organisation.

Table 14-3			BASIC ID			
Behaviour	*Effect*	*Sensation*	*Imagery*	*Cognition*	*Inter-personal*	*Drugs, Biology*
Maintain performance and productivity.	Anxiety – focus on being calm and confident.	Butterflies and nerves – make time to go to the gym and get good sleep.	Banish fearful images of things going wrong and replace with image of me managing the situation confidently.	'I have managed change before.'	Be assertive.	Eat healthy food to feel good.
Keep talking to managers to gain information.				'I have the capacity to stay calm and focused.'	Don't play the victim of the change but be proactive with my boss to gain information and share my strengths.	Don't comfort myself with that extra glass of wine.
				'I have real skills and value to bring to the new structure.'		Avoid too much caffeine.

Change is an inevitable part of life. Although some people find change easier to manage than others, most people would be bored if every day were the same. Enabling your client to recognise that she has the capacity to manage change sets her on a path to feeling confident and more in control of how she responds to these challenges.

Being Ready for the Open Road

Times arrive when people have to leave an organisation or place of employment for one reason or another. This leaving is another transition, so the models I describe elsewhere in this chapter may be useful. Two of the most specific situations where your client may need support in adjusting to change in a positive and powerful way are redundancy and retirement. Both can be scary moments or opportunities to discover new aspects of her potential. CBC can support your client through these experiences by making sure that she's aware that how she feels through these processes depends on how thinks.

Making redundancy work

Downsizing, rightsizing, letting people go – call it what you will, from time to time organisations decide to make staff redundant in order to cut costs or to streamline their organisations in some way. People have become more acclimatised to this occurrence, but that doesn't mean to say that each individual case does not present challenges for the person going through it.

Some people respond confidently by deciding to switch career or start their own businesses. These people may need support to become adapted to the challenges of their new chosen fields.

Others feel that being made redundant signifies that they're failures. However, the definition of redundancy is that a reorganisation within the company makes the position redundant. This redundancy may include the job being outsourced or being integrated into another person's role. It does not, in itself, signify that the person was no good at her job.

However, the feelings can still be those of hurt, a sense of unfairness, or injustice. You want to identify the thoughts driving these emotions and analyse twisted thinking. You may hear statements such as the following:

- I've been here for 20 years – how can they do this to me? (emotional reasoning)

- It's so unfair that Susan is staying on but I have to go. (emotional reasoning)

✔ What on earth am I going to do now? (anxiety-inducing thoughts)

✔ This means I am a complete failure, no-one will want to employ me now. (labelling)

✔ I'll never get another job at my age. (catastrophising)

People can get into obsessive loops of negative thinking that deplete their ability to manage the situation. Your client can lose sight of the positives and of her own strengths, so CBC plays an important part in bringing her back to reality. You can help your client gain perspective by asking some questions, such as the following:

✔ Do you regard other people you know who have been made redundant as complete failures?

✔ Just because you've been made redundant, why should that mean that you will never get another job?

✔ Is there a reason, now that the Age Discrimination Act is in place, why you should not get another job at your age?

✔ Just because one job has gone wrong, does it mean that all jobs will go wrong?

If your client considers herself a failure and unskilled, the metaphor of the fruit bowl can be a useful one. Ask your client: does one piece of rotten fruit in a bowl mean that all the fruit in the bowl are rotten? In other words, does your client's redundancy remove all her skills?

Redundancy, especially when accompanied by a reasonable payout, can provide a valuable moment of reflection in a person's life when she can reconsider the choices she has made in her career. Many people find that they're re-employed quickly. Others find that, after a period of reflection, they feel renewed and energised to start on a completely new path.

CBC can support the decision-making process involved in moving on from redundancy and ensure that thoughts, emotions, and behaviours empower and don't limit.

Preparing for retirement

Retirement is a major change. People respond differently. Whether someone is enthusiastic or fearful, CBC provides valuable space for your client to reflect and plan how she will manage the transition to retirement in a positive and proactive way. Some of the feelings that your client may have include:

✔ Looking forward to it for years

✔ Dreading it because of lack of status

✓ Wondering how to fill her time

✓ Being disappointed that the grass was not as green as she imagined

✓ Being delighted that she can now explore hobbies and new ventures that she never had time for before

✓ Worrying about her financial security

✓ Finding that she can live happily on less than she had imagined

As you can tell from the diversity of response, the key to how people manage retirement lies in their thinking patterns. If they're prone to negativity and pessimism, the experience is likely to be a difficult one, and you need to be able to support them in finding ways to approach the event in a more positive manner.

One certainty is that someone retiring always needs an adjustment period. Some people can stage their retirements over a period of months or years so that they acclimatise themselves to the extra leisure time. Others are employed one day and retired the next, which can be quite a shock.

Partners also have to adjust. This adjustment can require honest discussion and negotiation so that both people feel that their needs are heard. Lifestyle changes need to be tailored to compromise for all parties.

Retirement can be about 'being' rather than 'doing'. Those who have been really busy and active can find this change hard and may not even be sure what 'being' means or who they are without the label of their working role. Many of the exercises that I list in this book, for example the goal-setting models included in Chapter 5 and the change models in Chapter 10, can be helpful in building up a sense of self beyond the workplace. You may find the *life grid model* useful, which I show in Table 14-4. This model puts work in the context of all the other aspects of your client's life.

Table 14-4	The Life Grid	
Relationship	*Hobbies*	*Sport*
Friends and social life	Work	Family
Voluntary or community work	Travel	Acquiring knowledge and reading
Achievements and aspects of myself I am proud of	Planned projects	Things I am happy and grateful for

As you ask your client to build up different boxes and information, she can come to see that work is only one part of her life, and that, although work has disappeared, the rest is still there. You can work together to decide in what ways she may want to spend the time that she would have been at work.

Acting as if she is happy and enjoying her retirement can also be helpful. This encourages your client to consider how she would be thinking, feeling, moving physically. She begins with acting the part, but gradually these changes become integrated into who she is. I introduce this concept in Chapter 9. In my experience, the adjustment can take a few months but, after that, people come to thoroughly enjoy the experience of being retired. Your support during the adjustment phase can be invaluable.

Chapter 15

Meeting the Manager as Coach

....

In This Chapter

▶ Laying the foundation for coach-managing

▶ Managing performance to enhance growth and productivity

▶ Encouraging success for the benefit of all

....

More and more managers are adjusting their management style to that of a coach. You may be one of them, in which case this chapter is for you.

Managing used to be about control and direction. Today managing is often about coaching, inspiring, and empowering. Many companies use a *coaching culture* in which managers are responsible for the continuous development of their staff.

Some managers find such coaching roles easy, but others find the area quite difficult. Managers who are natural coaches, working alongside their staff to enable them to grow and succeed, have always existed. Other managers apply a more directive style, and still others prefer to focus on tasks. Your personal managerial style probably depends on your own experience of being managed and the type of organisation in which you work and have worked.

Whatever your situation, in this chapter I aim to provide you with some tips on developing a CBC approach to managing your staff.

Portions of this chapter are derived from the Whole Brain® thinking model from Herrmann International and used with permission ©Herrmann International 1987–2008.

Introducing a Coaching Culture into Your Workplace

When you bring in a coaching culture, you need to clarify what managing by coaching means to you and your team. How you manage the transformation to a coaching culture depends on the type of management style you have used and experienced previously – moving to a coaching style of management may be a radical change or an easy evolution.

Your role as a manager is to achieve results. If your staff are used to you focusing on tasks and targets, they may be surprised if you suddenly show an interest in their longer-term growth and potential. The good news is that, by developing your staff through coaching, you will probably increase productivity, because coaching helps to:

- ✔ Clarify vision and identify mutual benefits to achieving that vision
- ✔ Motivate your staff to do even better
- ✔ Enhance communication skills and team understanding
- ✔ Identify problems and work through them together to reach solutions

Comparing traditional and CBC management

Traditional command-and-control management involves setting and achieving targets, directing people through telling them what to do, hierarchy and authority, and criticism with a view to performance improvement.

Managing in a CBC style uses the following approaches instead:

- ✔ Problem-solving and setting mutually agreed objectives to achieve goals
- ✔ Listening and supporting
- ✔ Asking questions rather than providing answers or solutions
- ✔ Setting your staff member on the road to continuous self-directed learning
- ✔ Encouraging and inspiring
- ✔ Believing in your staff member's ability to be more than the person he is today
- ✔ Working through faulty thinking and limiting beliefs that may block individual and team progress
- ✔ Developing new ways of thinking and behaving to achieve agreed goals
- ✔ Leading by example

Clarifying boundaries

It is important that your staff member understands what to expect when you manage him through coaching. It is also important that you agree the boundaries of how you will manage issues as they arise. Some of the questions he might want you to answer are:

- ✔ 'If I tell you something I'm having difficulty with in a coaching session, will you or somebody else hold that against me in my appraisal?'
- ✔ 'Will you share information we discuss in our coaching sessions with my team members or other colleagues?'
- ✔ 'What happens if I reveal in my coaching sessions that my long-term career path is outside this organisation?'
- ✔ 'I've only ever had a manager who told me what to do before, so what does it mean when you say that you will be coaching me?'

Make it clear that as both an employee of the organisation and a manager you have a duty of care to ensure that any misdemeanour or breach of legislation or health and safety regulations is reported. You need to agree at the outset what issues this may include and to whom you will report; this will differ from company to company. Assure your staff member that you will not share information without first alerting him to your action.

In Table 15-1, I offer some dos and don'ts to help you manage your staff in a CBC style.

Table 15-1	Dos and Don'ts when Managing by CBC
Dos	**Don'ts**
Explain what coaching is – a future-directed, problem-solving approach to personal and professional development.	Give orders. Instead: develop solutions together.
Explain the CBC approach – that you will be helping your staff member to achieve his goals and targets by transforming limiting thoughts and behaviours into constructive approaches.	Criticise or judge. Instead: give specific feedback with a view to personal and professional development relevant to the goal.
Act with integrity; sticking to your word is essential if your staff member is to understand what managing through coaching means.	Control or be authoritarian. Instead: allow the person to develop his own solutions and style.

(continued)

Table 15-1 *(continued)*

Dos	Don'ts
Build an environment of trust where your staff member can share concerns and issues without fear of retribution in his appraisal.	Be ego-driven. Instead: focus on this being a win–win for both of you with an understanding that if your staff member succeeds, you succeed too.
Reassure your staff member that you will not discuss problems raised in your sessions with other team members unless you both specifically agree that this is acceptable.	Treat your staff as a function. Instead: realise that human beings are complex and driven by emotional needs.
Agree whether your coaching style is a continuous part of how you work together, or whether you will arrange specific coaching sessions.	
Agree when, where, and how often you will meet	

Using a coaching style of management doesn't mean that you are not demanding or that you have to be 'nice' all the time. You still seek to build performance and productivity – that is part of your job. The difference is in the way you achieve that performance and productivity – through collaboration and support instead of control.

Identified boundaries of confidentiality and trust enable people to open up and develop. The clearer you both are at the outset about how this relationship works, the more rewarding you will find the process.

Making time for performance management

One of the most common problems I come across in business is that managers are often so busy with operational requirements that they do not always have or make the time for performance management.

You may have trained as an engineer, accountant, or graphic designer, but, with promotion to managerial level, often those activities go out of the window and you redirect your focus on people management. This doesn't suit everyone. Some people prefer the task-focused approach. No right or wrong way exists, other than that it is important to adapt your style to bring out the best in your staff. Acknowledging your own preference does help. For example, if you are uncomfortable dealing with people issues, you may procrastinate in, postpone, avoid, or rush meetings where you are expected to focus on 'soft' topics.

Giving feedback

You can give feedback in various ways. The aim should be to get the best intention from the person receiving the feedback, not to get frustration off your own chest. You may offer comment from observable facts, but make sure that you make it clear that these are your own views, from your own perspective and opinions. Your views are not necessarily fact, but they can be helpful when sharing your own experience of a situation.

In a coaching style of feedback, you may ask questions such as the following:

What was your intention and aim in this situation?

What results do you think you achieved?

Where was the focus of your attention and effort during the experience?

What skills and approaches were you applying?

How do you think it went – what worked and what didn't, from your point of view?

What might you do differently in future?

Such questions enable the individual to reflect, review, and learn from his progress, and are unlikely to lead to defensiveness.

You may not value these meetings, but some people do. The psychological contract between employer and employee has changed, and less loyalty and job continuity exists these days. Staff satisfaction and productivity per head are low in the UK compared with in other EU countries. The manager's role in boosting staff morale and improving the employer–employee relationship is key. Management style influences issues such as sickness absence, staff turnover, and performance. You can play a real part in providing an environment that encourages retention of talent and staff personal development and growth.

In a survey for Best Companies Ltd, of those employees who felt strongly that their jobs are good for their own individual development, only 4 per cent would leave tomorrow. Of those who felt strongly that their jobs are not good for their personal growth, 73 per cent said they would cut and run.

Self-knowledge and skills are transferrable from one company to another. Development builds confidence and strengths, which benefits both the individual and the manager.

One of the reasons that managers avoid appraisals and performance review meetings is because many people perceive such meetings to be an opportunity to criticise. Criticism is seldom comfortable for either party, and many people cringe at the thought of sharing feedback on issues and mistakes.

Steve's elusive appraisal

Steve had been working within a construction business for over 20 years. He was excellent at his job and had been promoted to managerial level at quite a young age. Like many others within the business, his focus was on operational results. He was a friendly and sociable man, but he didn't really see the point of soft topics such as motivation, training, or development. It wasn't that he didn't care about his staff, it was only that he couldn't understand the tangible benefit in spending time talking about personal growth.

Steve's boss, Bruce, took the same attitude and so, despite the efforts of his HR department, Bruce had only undertaken an appraisal with Steve three times in 18 years. Steve hadn't pushed it because he was equally uncomfortable in these discussions – the more so because he knew that Bruce didn't value these subjects.

However, as Steve had gone up the business ladder, he had begun to realise that these meetings did, in fact, matter, because he wanted to know what expectations Bruce had for his career progression. In many ways, Steve came to realise that by postponing meetings and not taking the time to prepare or think about the issues that were important to Steve's career, Bruce was subtly undermining his development. It left him feeling undervalued, thinking, 'If Bruce doesn't make time for me, it's obvious he doesn't care about me.'

Experiencing this himself, Steve realised that he had also neglected to support his own staff too. He vowed to make sure that he made time for an annual appraisal meeting from now on, changing his thinking to, 'Even though I am uncomfortable running appraisal meetings, I shall make time and do the best I can for my staff.'

The problem is that by not sharing information, a manager limits another person's growth because of his own attitude and discomfort. Consider the following examples of limiting factors:

- ✔ Magnifying a problem through criticism – William has made one mistake so his manager ends up thinking 'William is stupid,' even though it was just one thing that he did wrong. Treating William as if he is stupid will probably result in his loss of self-confidence, leading to reduced performance. A CB coach manager would think: 'William has made this one mistake, but that doesn't make him stupid. He has potential and can develop. How can I move him forward?'

- ✔ Allowing emotional reasoning to take precedence – 'I do it this way so Fred should do it this way too, and when he doesn't, I get so frustrated.' Your frustration could well make Fred fearful and paralyse his natural style and creativity. A CB coach manager would think, 'Fred has a different style to me. I wonder what I can find out from this? As long as he achieves outputs and targets, he can work in his own way.'

- ✔ Mind-reading – 'Dina won't want to hear that feedback; she'll probably be hurt,' even though to withhold information means that Dina will continue to make the same mistake, and this may limit her career progression.

A CB coach manager would think 'I shall share this feedback with Dina in a constructive way, because it is for her own benefit to adapt and develop so that she can be more successful in future.'

✔ Shoulds, musts, and ought tos – 'You really *should* have completed this project by 1 March;' 'You *ought to* have spoken to the client to agree the change in budget;' 'You *must* take more care with detail.' In an appraisal situation, this ends up sounding like blame – rather like a schoolteacher telling off a pupil. It can lead to stroppy or rebellious behaviour, because people don't like being talked down to or treated like children or teenagers. In the workplace, everyone is adult, so it is better for the manager to use the coaching style of questions. A CB coach manager might ask: 'What stopped you completing the project?' 'What could you do differently next time?' 'How can you make sure you include clients in budget discussions in future?' 'Do you need any support from me on detail?'

✔ Only seeing things from your own perspective – 'Nancy, I don't see why you are so anxious about this problem. It's straightforward and should take no time at all to resolve.' This shows a fundamental misunderstanding and lack of acknowledgement of how Nancy is feeling. The manager is viewing the situation through her own eyes rather than teasing out what it is, exactly, that is making Nancy anxious. A CB coach manager could ask 'What is it about this situation that makes you so anxious?' 'What thoughts are you having that are creating this sense of anxiety?' 'How else might you think about this situation that would make you feel more confident of your ability to manage it?'

Making time for your staff-coaching sessions is important and builds trust. Each time you postpone or cut short a coaching meeting, you chip away at your relationship. By avoiding the meeting, you give the message that you don't consider the person to be important, and that you don't care about his development. However difficult it may be, find a way to motivate yourself to approach the meetings with enthusiasm. Comfort yourself with the fact that if employees have support and development, they are more likely to achieve their targets faster and more effectively.

Managing privileged information

Keeping information in the right place involves a difficult balance. As a manager, you are often privy to certain information before your staff members are. Equally, they may share information with you in a coaching session that has an impact on the business in other ways. Managing such situations isn't always easy, but trust is at the heart of coaching, so give careful thought to sensitivities on both sides.

Consider the following situations where the issue of privileged information may occur:

✔ **Mergers and acquisitions:** You often receive certain information before your direct reports, so take time to consider how you manage this. You may be able to prepare them for some news without telling them what that news is. For example, it is likely that rumours will be buzzing around the organisation, so you could ask:

- What have you heard?

- What are you imagining?

- What do you know to be fact?

- What ideas do you have to manage this uncertainty?

✔ **Change and restructure:** You may or may not have more information than your direct report, but you can help build his confidence in managing change so that, whatever happens, he is well prepared:

- When have you managed change?

- What are some of the negative or limiting thoughts that you are experiencing?

- Are they rational? Are they based on fact or imagination?

- What resources do you have to manage change and uncertainty? What skills and strengths could you draw on? What can support you?

- How can you approach this situation constructively going forward?

✔ **Privileged information from your staff member:** It may be that your staff member has confided some personal information to you that they have not given you specific permission to share. When that person's name comes up in a meeting with your boss or peer group, it is important that you remember not to share the information, even if it seems relevant.

Understanding How to Ask, Not Tell

In your CBC managerial role, you help your direct reports to achieve their set targets and to grow and develop personally and professionally. This may be a continuous process – for example, you adopt a coaching style on a continuous basis – or you may arrange specific coaching sessions.

In coaching sessions, you will be following the CBC process mentioned in Chapter 5, tailored to your own corporate environment.

As a manager, you may well share some of your own solutions and particular case stories of what has worked for you in similar situations. The difference is that you won't be presenting these as 'THE solution' or 'THE only way', but as suggestions from which your staff member can take what they want and apply as they choose. This enables your staff to grow, take responsibility, and make their own learning mistakes, and eventually – hopefully – achieve great success, possibly in different ways to you.

A CBC manager session focuses on his staff member's part in achieving departmental and organisational goals. Within the meeting, you seek to help your staff member to develop the thoughts, behaviours, skills, strengths, and confidence he needs to achieve more than he may do without your support. You both win!

Adapting your coaching style

Different people have different priorities and preferences. In order to get the best from your staff, stop and consider what type of people they are. A useful and practical model is the *HBDI®* or *Herrmann Brain Dominance Instrument,* developed by Ned Herrmann which is a model that reflects thinking preferences in what Herrmann describes as the Whole Brain® model. See Figure 15-1 for this model in full.

- ✔ **A. Theorists (Left Brain):** People who are rational, logical, analytical, and critical, and like facts and figures, technology, and detail. Priorities are on factual and analytical tasks rather than discussion.

- ✔ **B. Practical Planners (Left Brain):** People who are procedural, systematic, and organised, who are planners, and who like to follow through a step-by-step process to an end result. Priorities are on systems and safe-keeping rather than innovation or new ways of working.

- ✔ **C. People-oriented (Right Brain):** People who are interested in people and like to consider what makes people tick, how to keep team morale high and what makes customers happy. Priorities are people-focused, building relationships, keeping in touch, talking and being helpful.

- ✔ **D. Innovators (Right Brain):** People who are big picture, future-oriented, who like to adopt new methods and variety, will take risks and innovate. Priorities are on trying new ways of working, on change and look for 'what's next?'

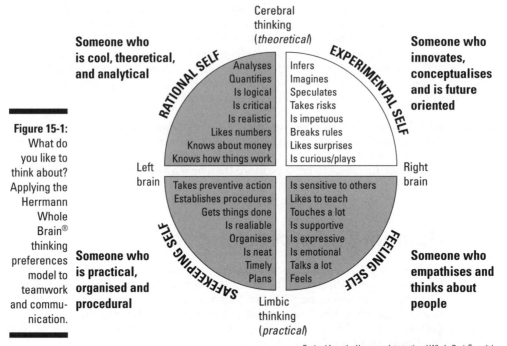

Derived from the Herrmann International Whole Brain® model.
Used with written permission.

Figure 15-1: What do you like to think about? Applying the Herrmann Whole Brain® thinking preferences model to teamwork and communication.

Consider whether you are one or a mix of some or all of these. Do you spend more time in one particular quadrant area? Are you more comfortable working in a particular way? Then think about your direct reports and whether they fit within one or more styles. Sometimes relationships are more difficult with people who are very different from you. Similar styles can lead to 'blind spots', and even competition.

Unfortunately, we can all be seen from a negative perspective as well as a positive one. Figure 15-2 demonstrates perceptions that people may have of each quadrant type. Consider whether other people may use any of those words about you. People who are different to you are more likely to get frustrated by your approach than those who are similar, just as you may become frustrated with them. Once you consider how other people may see you, you can take action to counteract this by using language that fits some of their preferences.

Figure 15-3 provides some clues as to how to engage with someone who is different to yourself. If you are a left brain organiser and your staff member is a right brain creative strategist, you may want him to work in a systematic way because that is the way you work personally. Or if you are a left brain analyst who likes to work with facts and figures, but your staff member is right brain feeler and people-focused, you may prefer that he puts information into statistics or spreadsheets instead of discussing the situations.

Where possible, allow people to be themselves, and acknowledge the diversity of their approaches. Every team needs the strengths and qualities of diverse talents to function well and to cover all aspects of problems and challenges. Trying to make someone adapt to your own style can frustrate and limit them. Find a way to meet in the middle by recognising and valuing their approaches. This allows you to benefit from a Whole Brain® approach, getting thoughts and solutions that you may personally never generate yourself. Use the Whole Brain® model as a template for problem-solving and communication, because it provides a structured and holistic approach.

Analytical theorists can be seen as: Nerd, geek, uncaring calculating, unemotional. power hungry, number crunchers	Innovators can be seen as: Reckless, can't focus, unrealistic, off-the-wall, undisciplined, woolly, head in the clouds
Planners can be seen as: Stick in the mud, unimaginative plodder, picky conservative boring, pedantic	Empathisers can be seen as: Not business-focused Bleeding heart Touchy-feely A push over, soft touch gullible, over-emotional

Figure 15-2: How others could perceive you.

Differences in Processing Modes, © 1987-2008 Herrmann International. Used with permission.

Does it use facts? Are they quantified? Does it show clear analysis? Is it to the point? Is it logical?	Does it show the big picture or overview? Is it visual and colorful? Does it use metaphors? Does it look at the future?
Does it provide details? Is it organized? Is it legible? Is there an action plan? Does it anticipate questions?	Does it relate to audience? Is it interactive? Is it helpful and friendly? Does it acknowledge emotional issues?

Figure 15-3: Bridging the difference. Applying the four preference approach to enhance communication.

Whole Brain® Walk-Around CHECK LIST, © 1987-2008 Herrmann International. Used with permission.

Making the most of diverse approaches

A project finance group were mainly technical left brain analysts and were excellent at ensuring that figures were calculated to perfection. A new member of staff, Ron, came in who was more people-oriented. His manager, Estelle, spent several months trying to encourage him to work in the same way that the others worked, completing record sheets and spreadsheets. But she came to see, through their coaching sessions, that whereas his colleagues preferred to work at their computers, Ron enjoyed phone calls and meetings. Estelle therefore decided that Ron could be responsible for ensuring that client contact was maintained. This was an area that had previously been neglected. He also arranged social events for the team that enabled a free flow of information and knowledge-sharing. This raised team morale and performance. Estelle challenged her colleagues' limiting thoughts such as 'He should do his work our way' or 'He is obviously no good at his job if he can't put that information into a spreadsheet' and helped everyone to develop thoughts such as 'Ron is great at doing the tasks we don't enjoy that much' and 'we can value Ron's approach.'

Motivating and encouraging your staff

Generating the will to achieve goals and succeed is part of your job as a manager. Play to your staff's strengths and preferences to stimulate their enthusiasm for the task. Watch out too for demotivation and procrastination, and address the problems as they arise.

Procrastination is generally associated with one or more of the following:

- ✔ Anxiety – concern about the task and the person's inability to achieve it to the standard required

- ✔ Lack of clear priorities

- ✔ Low frustration tolerance – boredom, discomfort, or lack of persistence or desire to work hard to complete the task

- ✔ Rebellion – irritation at being given the task or at the way that the task was delegated, which makes a person respond more like a teenager than an adult

- ✔ The inability to say 'no', resulting in someone getting overwhelmed and unable to see clearly what to focus on

- ✔ Lack of skills and resources

- ✔ Distraction habits – going on social networking websites, habitually clicking into emails, surfing the Internet

- ✔ Not seeing the rationale or benefit of the task

When your staff member procrastinates, he may have a limiting thought about achieving the task he is meant to be doing. In coaching sessions, explore blocks to progress with your staff member and encourage and support his actions towards achieving his goals.

Ensure that your staff members are clear about what you ask of them. Do they have a clear and aligned picture of the vision and direction in which you want your team to head? Check assumptions: many managers assume that others know what is expected when in fact they don't. Check mind-reading too, on your part and theirs. Is a staff member imagining that a colleague has taken responsibility for a task when in fact the colleague hasn't? Does he know exactly what steps he needs to take first, second, third?

Motivating others requires flexibility and creativity. You need to find the 'hot buttons' that turn people on to enthusiastically pursuing goals. Different people are motivated by different things: for example money, results, harmony, good relationships, variety, values, change, and innovation.

When people have to do tasks that are not their preference, they can end up feeling challenged and lacking in confidence. To motivate, help the individual to find an aspect of the task that does relate to his own priority and preference. For example, demonstrate to a theoretical analytical person that talking to a customer will get them better bottom-line results; or to a practical planner that there is a step-by-step journey within a change programme and that they will achieve greater results at the end of it; or to a people-person that he is being helpful to others if he presents information in a factual format; or to an innovator that he will achieve his new solutions better if he develops a systematic plan of action. Figure 15-4 provides some hints with regard to diverse motivators.

Theorists are motivated by: Figures, statistics, evidence, evaluation, technology, details, critical thinking, challenge, solving tough problems, working solo	*Innovators are motivated by:* Vision strategy. taking risks, creativity, intuiting trends, identifying themes and links, having variety, experimenting, playing around, breaking rules
Planners are motivated by: Systems and procedures, getting and driving results, risk control, quality focus, organisation, administration, structure, detail, order	*Empathisers are motivated by:* Working with others, communication, teambuilding, client relationships, talking, phone calls, helping people, arranging social events, intuiting team morale, coaching, counseling, supporting

Figure 15-4: Strengths in each quadrant. Flexing to diverse motivators.

Whole Brain® Strengths of Each Quadrant, © 1987-2008 Herrmann International. Used with permission.

Some other questions you can ask during coaching sessions that can help people to feel motivated include the following:

- ✔ How will it feel when you get there?
- ✔ How can you do this task and enjoy it?
- ✔ What thoughts will help you to feel enthusiastic about this task?
- ✔ What's your plan of action?
- ✔ How will you reward yourself?

 One of the primary functions of a CB coach is to support and motivate others to achieve his goals. When you enable someone to break through concerns or lethargy, it is a rewarding experience for you both.

Developing a Coaching Culture

Coaching can become a way of life for you and your team members. Every day becomes a part of a development experience, and this makes working life more interesting for everyone. It stimulates an environment in which everyone grows and shares their experiences. Successes are rewarded and discussed and, if judgement and blame are put aside, mistakes are readily shared, so that everyone understands what works and what doesn't.

Team members can *co-coach,* each acting as a coach to one another, and coach their direct reports. It can be an equal way of encouraging an atmosphere in which everyone is curious and continually discovering new and more constructive ways of thinking and approaching work challenges.

Discovering the journey of continuous development

You can foster a coaching culture environment by sharing the processes, tools, and questions of CBC with your colleagues. In this way, each person becomes his own coach as he checks whether his own thinking is rational and helpful to his work and life goals.

 Create time for skills training and development. Encourage people to share their experiences of acquiring knowledge, both on the job and in the meeting room. Make the time to stop and collect ideas and solutions for what works and what doesn't. In this fast-paced world, people tend to finish one project and move on to the next without considering what they can do differently in future to build on success and achieve even greater results. This sharing can be done in a formal setting – in coaching sessions or team meetings – or by encouraging people to arrange lunch or a social event where informal conversation can lead to sharing stories and creative solutions.

Knowing when to let go

Trust in others is key to being a successful CBC manager. This means letting go. It isn't always easy, because inevitably you are accountable for the results of your team and responsible for achieving targets. However, once you know that your team member is working on overcoming limiting beliefs, you have to make sure that *you* don't hold on to limiting beliefs about that person. Once you are sure that a person has developed a constructive strategy and approach to goals, trust his ability to achieve those goals. Just like the duck who pushes her chicks into the water, you need to let your reports swim and make their own mistakes.

Sometimes you need to make decisions even if you do not have consensus within the team. Part of your coaching is to help others realise that no-one has his opinion heard and considered in every situation – decisions are taken from time to time that are not what we would choose.

Equally, support your team in being prepared to take decisions that could be unpopular with their peers and staff if they believe something to be right. This is about stepping up to leadership and accepting the responsibilities that come with it. This includes performance-managing their own staff who may need to become more accountable for follow-through on tasks and goals.

Growth and success are as challenging as failure. Personal growth sets people apart from those who were previously their peers. Business success leads to the need to adapt to additional workload demands. Generating a culture of personal empowerment within your team better enables people to rise to these challenges.

Encouraging growth can require you to let go of your own needs too. For example, if an excellent team member brings you results and is in line for promotion, you may be tempted to hold on to him for your own sake. But, as a coach, you need to encourage his own success and trust that you can manage without him. In this way, everyone is willing everyone else's success.

Chapter 16

Addressing Performance Issues

'More for less' is today's mantra in business. Businesses are under pressure to provide excellent service for lower cost. The success of an organisation depends upon finely tuning the brainpower and emotional will of its staff to increase performance and productivity. This situation in turn drives a trend to measure human output to ensure that each employee is as productive as he can be.

From a CBC perspective, how an individual thinks about his job impacts on how he feels about his job. Both competence and emotion influence productivity. Emotional engagement to work is key to driving personal performance. Thoughts shape how a person focuses his energy, manages his time, and communicates with others. As a CBC coach, you can help your client identify what peak performance means to him and develop thoughts, behaviours and actions to help him maintain this level of performance through a long working day.

In CBC sessions, you can work with your client to take an objective view of feedback and accept personal accountability for his own performance, productivity, and development. In this chapter, I cover a variety of methods that you can introduce when coaching your client on performance issues.

Managing Feedback and Assessment

From the moment we are born, we receive feedback. We discover how to walk, talk, and behave within the cultural expectations of our society by receiving feedback. We achieve and develop at school through feedback. Unfortunately, however, feedback can also make us afraid of failure, paralysed, and unable to take the risks required to move forward.

We require feedback in order to develop, succeed, and perform well. We give ourselves feedback – some people are their own greatest critics – and we receive feedback from others on our performance. Feedback can be a useful process in personal and professional development, but different people respond differently to feedback. Your client may respond in one of the following ways:

✔ Listen and obey so as to achieve

✔ Rebel and do the opposite of what he has been told

✔ Get defensive and not listen, saying that the feedback is unreasonable

✔ Get competitive and determined to prove himself to others

✔ Feel crushed and criticised

✔ Accept the advice and willingly take it on board

People can get stuck in some of these habitual behaviours, so through CBC you can enable them to review their response to feedback and see whether it is helping them address their performance issues. Often people come to see that they have developed an automatic response as a result of what a teacher said to them at school. They can now decide whether this is still appropriate.

Practising performance and assessment

In the business world, assessment is a fact of life today. Your client may be having to give or receive feedback – or both. Understandably, organisations want to measure performance – 360-degree feedback (which I explain in Chapter 3), annual appraisals, targets, and performance management feature regularly in most organisations today. These measures of performance can be effective motivators or stressful and sometimes even damaging experiences.

CBC can provide an opportunity to review strategies for giving and receiving feedback in a way that is constructive and developmental.

Measuring human performance is a complicated business. Humans are not machines but vulnerable to internal factors such as whether they're feeling physically and emotionally well, and to external factors such as whether they have problems in their personal or work lives that impact on their ability to focus and concentrate on their outputs. Producing maximum human brain output is not the same as manufacturing widgets.

Performance appraisals can have an impact on people on many of the following levels:

✔ Sense of self

✔ Perceptions and reputation within their group

✔ Career promotion

✔ Bonus and financial reward

✔ Recognition and acknowledgement – or lack of it

✔ Personal and performance development goals

How effective feedback is in determining and raising performance depends on the relationship between the person giving and the person receiving the messages. The kinds of issues you may experience in coaching sessions with clients include the following:

✔ Clients who are ambitious and seek to increase their targets and gain the best marks

✔ Clients who want a quiet life of routine work and feel the pinch of having to push themselves further than they naturally want to go

✔ Clients who perceive that they work hard but have not attained the grades they feel they deserve

✔ Clients who are managers and have to performance-manage their staff to perform ever harder

The giving and receiving of feedback is an essential part of life, and your client can develop the resilience required to listen to feedback objectively without being over-sensitive to what is being said. Your client can also find out how to deal with her inner critic, who may exaggerate the feedback to be 110 times worse than it really is!

Giving feedback

Many people feel awkward about giving feedback, even if the feedback is positive. An endless moan of staff is that management so seldom acknowledge their efforts. Everyone likes a pat on the back. Your client may need to find the words appropriate for giving feedback by developing thoughts that support this process. Try sharing some of the following tips with your client:

✔ **Be clear exactly what you're giving feedback on.** This avoids labelling a person as stupid or inefficient. For example, if someone has low marks in certain areas of her performance appraisal, is he, in fact, achieving in other areas? People can label an individual as a low performer without taking into account that he is a positive influence within the team, supporting the efforts of other team members. Or a sales person who has not hit her targets may, nonetheless, have created a relationship with a new client who may bring reward in future. Be aware that just because one presentation went badly, it does not mean that all presentations by that person go badly. Make sure that you don't generalise, but be specific about what works, what doesn't, and what you want the person to work on.

✔ **Give feedback on the behaviour, not the person.** For example, rather than saying 'You're not a communicator,' you can say 'When you don't join in discussion, you may be withholding vital information from the other team members that they require in order to be able to perform well.'

✔ **Share feedback to help the person to develop, not to get something off your chest.** Be focused on her future and what he can do about it, rather than on what didn't work well.

✔ **Always praise what is going well.** You can sandwich the critical or developmental message by starting and finishing with acknowledgement of positive performance. This makes the other person more receptive to hearing what you're suggesting he works on and develops than it would if you only focused on the negative. A character assassination is not what you're aiming for, because it will not be a balanced perspective. No-one is totally hopeless in every way.

✔ **Put yourself in the shoes of the person receiving feedback.** Consider how you can phrase the feedback in a way that is constructive and useful. Consider how you might personally feel if you received the feedback in the way you're planning to give it. Can you say the same thing in a different way to be more acceptable and motivating?

✔ **Listen to the background reasons for work performance that is not up to standard.** Was there more that could have been done to support the individual's efforts? Is there more support, skills development, or resource that he now needs in order to perform well? Does he feel that the measurement criteria are fair and, if not, what other factors can they suggest? Take these factors into account so as not to negate the positives.

✔ **Give criticism in a way that is meaningful to the other person.** For example, if the person is mainly motivated by bottom- line issues, but you want him to develop his customer focus, phrase the feedback to demonstrate how the focus on customers will ultimately deliver a better bottom line. Or for someone who is more people-oriented but needs to develop his ability at completing his monthly budgets, phrase the feedback in such a way as to demonstrate how the completion of budgets is helpful to his colleagues.

✔ **Remember that feedback is essential to growth.** Holding back on praise or criticism is not necessarily in the other person's interests. Holding back is not being kind, because the other person cannot change what he does not know. Help your client to check what thoughts may hold his back from addressing specific issues. For example, 'I can't give this feedback because it may hurt his' denies the other person the information he needs. 'I can give this feedback sensitively for his own personal development' is more helpful.

Giving feedback to bullies

Giving feedback to people who bully or dominate can be difficult. The person being bullied is often too fearful to stand up to the bully or give them feedback. But those who dominate may simply not know the impact that their words or actions have on other people. I find it interesting how seldom even colleagues give feedback to bullies – people end up walking on eggshells around them so as to avoid the bullying behaviour rather than addressing it. So the person with the power never becomes aware of the consequences of his actions. For example, instances happen where a child's life has been made totally wretched by the bullying of another pupil and yet, when the two people meet as adults, the bully has no recollection of his behaviour, nor understands the impact it had on the other person. The person with the power is oblivious: the person who perceives himself to be without power is the one who is finely attuned to every nuance and may need support to address these issues.

Your client may be on either side of a bullying relationship. Use role-play to help him experience the emotional impact of his own behaviour so that he develops adult-to-adult communication. Introduce the person who is being bullied to the assertiveness models that I use in Chapter 11, and help him practise giving feedback. Suggest also that he asks for support from colleagues or the HR department if the matter is serious.

Receiving feedback

Receiving feedback is not always a comfortable experience. Some people feel awkward receiving positive feedback; many feel uncomfortable receiving critical feedback. Your client may have a tendency to do some of the following when receiving feedback:

- Be defensive or aggressive
- Blame others for his own shortcomings
- Make out that he was powerless within the situation because of the inefficiencies of the system or process
- Sulk and say little but appear defensive
- Brush off praise as empty flattery rather than really listen to what other people see as strengths and skills that can be focused on to build further success

To help your client maintain perspective and gain benefit from feedback, try sharing the following tips with him:

- Listen and take on board comments that may be useful.

- Recognise that it may just be one person's opinion, and that does not make it the 'truth'.

- The other person may have his own perspective and agenda.

- Your manager may have developed his own way of carrying out a task which he considers to be the 'right' way, but this belief does not mean that many different ways don't exist to achieve the same or even a better end result.

- Don't personalise the feedback by labelling yourself a failure or incompetent in some way just because you received one piece of feedback about a situation or because you made one or two mistakes.

- Don't imagine that you can't change because you're too old or change is too much effort: everyone can change and develop.

- Listen to the specific behaviours and skills discussed and be willing to develop and experiment with new ways of behaving.

- Don't feel helpless: take accountability for what you've done and what you can do to improve or enhance the situation. Take control of those areas of the situation that you've got control of – which are often personal attitude, energy, and effort.

- Maintain objectivity and evaluate the criticism or feedback in an unemotional way so as to consider what you can discover from this situation.

- Don't magnify the awfulness of feedback: put it into perspective and assess it within the specific context of the situation in which feedback is given.

- Don't delete the positives: accept them and build on them.

Through CBC, you help your client review his behaviours so that he can judge whether his response to feedback is reasonable and helpful to his situation. You may want to unpack his thoughts and expectations, so consider using the ABCDE model, which I introduce in Chapters 1 and 2, to help your client assess how his thoughts are impacting his emotions and behaviours:

- **A = Activating event:** for example, annual appraisal – 'My boss says that I haven't come up to expectations.'

- **B = Belief:** 'How can he say that when I have worked so hard. He's being unfair.'

- **C = Consequential emotion and behaviour:** Hurt and depressed, feeling useless, which has resulted in a negative attitude to work and demotivation.

✔ **D = Disputing the belief:** Ask your client to consider whether any aspects of the feedback were fair and just. Also dispute his emotional and behavioural response – is he doing all he can to maintain his own emotional equilibrium and take action that is self-supportive and does not compound the problem? For example, a few disputing questions you can ask are:

- Did your boss explain what his expectations were? Were specific targets, behaviours, and goals clear?

- Can you think of any instances when you feel you exceeded those expectations and did really well? If so, did you share that information with him? If not, how do you expect him to know about these successful moments?

- Can you think of any reasons why he may feel you've not come up to expectations? If so, can you identify the reasons for this situation? What was happening?

- Are there any development needs that you've identified to help you maintain a better performance in future?

- Is your current emotional and behavioural response to the criticism helping you manage the situation and actively change your boss's opinion of you for the better? If not, what thoughts, emotions, and behaviours can help you to move forward in strength?

Accepting personal accountability

Your client is personally accountable for his performance. No-one else is responsible for whether your client focuses on a particular project, or whether he has too many glasses of wine the night before a major presentation. Your client is an adult: he makes his own choices. As a CB coach, however, you can help your client accept that responsibility so that he doesn't blame other people or the system for his failings.

How people respond to managing their own performance can be influenced by the following:

✔ Working hard for the approval of others

✔ Fear of failure

✔ Competitive determination to win and be the best

✔ A sense of need – both financial and for a sense of security within their roles

✔ An 'if I must' dragging of the heels

✔ A 'play them at their own game' determination to say the right things to gain grades

✔ An 'all-or-nothing' response that if one aspect of the appraisal is not going well, then it means nothing is going well

✔ The self-critic who berates himself more than anyone else does

If your client has the objective of developing or maintaining his performance, first identify what peak performance means to him within his specific work context. What precisely is his own contribution to the organisation: is he responsible for increasing sales, maintaining systems, or raising brand awareness? Ask him to clearly define his role.

 To support your client in raising his performance, reconnect him to his sense of purpose about work and why his work is meaningful to him. Try asking questions:

✔ What is peak performance to you?

✔ If you perform at your peak more frequently, what may you be able to achieve?

✔ What would that mean to you?

✔ What actions do you need to take to perform more effectively?

✔ Who do you ultimately answer to?

✔ Who is your worst critic – you or others?

Evaluate the benefit to your client of high performance, and define who ultimately judges your client. Remind him of the following:

✔ He can never please all people all the time.

✔ He can never be perfect, and nor can anyone else, but he can pursue excellence.

✔ He is bound to make mistakes because he's human and fallible.

✔ If he does his best in his own terms, he meets his own standards and can choose to develop additional skills.

✔ To have made an attempt and put his energy into working hard to improve himself is, in itself, commendable.

✔ What he develops in one area of his life is transferable to other areas in future.

✔ He can identify specifically what it takes to raise the bar and reach the next level.

Whatever level of his organisation your client is at, help him to understand that he's accountable for his choices and actions.

Reviewing personal performance and development

Some people love to develop, find out new things, and become accomplished in new skills. Other people prefer life to stay the same. To support your client in achieving his objectives, you may need to engage his motivation around his personal development plans. Try applying the five-step performance review model that I show in Table 16-1.

Table 16-1	Five-step Performance Review Model			
Performance: *What Do You Have to Achieve?*	*How Do Others Know That You're Performing Well?*	*What Are the Ultimate Results of Peak Performance?*	*What Does it Take For You to Perform at Your Peak?*	*Why Does it Matter?*
e.g. design advertise-ments for clients	e.g. good feedback from clients and others re. my ad design	e.g. client sales up	e.g. feeling energised, mentally alert, and creative; having a clear desk; working at major tasks in the morning; switch-ing off my email to focus	e.g. I gain a sense of satisfac-tion that my work is worth-while and helping others

The questions that I include in Table 16-1 can help your client reconnect to the meaning and purpose of his work. You can then identify specific thoughts, behaviours, and actions to create the environment that supports his performance needs.

Motivation issues

Motivation is key to performance: the will to perform, develop, and succeed drives mental, emotional, and physical energy. You can help your client iden-tify his personal motivators using the model that I show in Table 16-2, based on the Whole Brain model®, which I introduce in Chapter 15. Ask your client to tick or insert relevant information about activities that motivate him.

Table 16-2	Motivation Gauge
A. Blue	D. Yellow
Financial reward	Innovating
Problem-solving	Finding new ways of working
Analysing and evaluating data	Art and design
Creating financial systems and structures	Pushing people's thinking
Completing accounts and spreadsheets	Spotting trends and relationships
	Intuiting the 'next idea'
B. Green	C. Red
Achieving quality results	Building team morale
Producing systems and procedures	Recognition
Writing	Helping others
The prospect of career promotion and status	Raising morale
Doing a good job	Developing oneself and others
	Bringing people to work together
Dotting the 'i's and crossing the 't's	Customer satisfaction

Copyright Herrmann International 2008, adapted by author.

You may find secondary motivators worthy of discussion. For example, what does 'financial reward' mean to your client – a holiday, security, a new extension? What makes the money meaningful? What is meaningful about 'quality results' – a sense of achievement? Dig a little deeper to help your client understand the underlying motivators of his work behaviour too.

Performance-interfering and performance-enhancing thoughts

Performance depends on how a person thinks about the task. Discipline and persistence play a part in maintaining performance, but people can allow procrastination and distractions to interfere with their efforts. Investigate the types of thoughts that help your client to achieve peak performance and those thoughts that interfere. The model that I show in Table 16-3 is known as PITS and PETS (performance-interfering and performance-enhancing thoughts).

Table 16-3	PITs and PETs
Performance-interfering Thoughts (PITs)	*Performance-enhancing Thoughts (PETs)*
e.g. 'I think I'll just look on eBay before I start to write that presentation.'	e.g. 'I shall allocate the morning to writing the presentation as that is the time when I feel most alert and energetic.'

Suggest that your client identifies three PETS and records the statements in a visible place to focus his energy and attention on affirmative thoughts.

Your client must have health, rest, and refreshment to maintain motivation and performance. Fatigue or stress deplete brain function and can lead to ill health. Help your client to develop a plan of practical steps to achieving the performance levels he identifies. You may need to ask the following questions:

✔ What will you do differently now?

✔ What actions do you need to take to support your goals?

✔ What lifestyle changes can help – for example breaks, exercise, healthy diet?

✔ What first steps can you take to maintain peak performance before the next session?

Visualisation imagery can help your client to 'see' his success by visualising himself taking the necessary steps, breaking through problems and difficulties to achieve his goals. See Chapter 21 for lots of interesting imagery suggestions.

Managing Time

Many of your clients probably have objectives around time management. How someone spends his time has a direct impact on his performance. It also impacts on relationships with colleagues and customers, because delays or demands put pressure on others too.

How people spend or think about time is highly subjective: one person may see targets and deadlines as a major source of stress, others may be adrenalin junkies and love the last-minute pressure of a deadline.

CBC can help your client to understand how he thinks about time and whether the way he thinks is helpful to his performance or detracting from it.

Considering personal perspectives of time

The quality of our experience of life lies in the quality of our thoughts within each moment. Each day has 24 hours, but some days pass really fast and others slowly. How time passes is influenced by expectations and emotions. For example, time passes slowly when you are waiting for news of a loved one or are bored and have too little to do. Time passes fast when you are having fun or engrossed in a task you enjoy.

CBC models enable clients to review the way they're approaching time and whether their approach is helping or hindering their achievement of results. They develop constructive ways of thinking about time so as to manage it more effectively.

Self-knowledge is key, so that your client can understand whether he's the sort of person who is:

- ✔ Spontaneous and hates to plan, allowing events to happen in a seren-dipitous fashion: This sort of person lives in the moment to such an extent that he can forget to leave enough time to achieve a task or catch a train.

- ✔ A planner, mapping out the future with specific sequential steps and knowing how to achieve the end result well in advance: In fact he often completes the task before the deadline.

Whatever their preferred styles, people can find new ways of managing time so that they do not just follow their habitual approach. People who enjoy last-minute deadlines are in their element when time-pressured, but may need to motivate themselves to be more proactive to allow time for the unexpected. They can change their thoughts from 'I'll do it later' to 'What's stopping me doing it now?'

People who hate to be under time pressure may lose the ability to think clearly, alarming themselves with thoughts like 'I have just too much to do in too little time.' Developing more constructive thoughts such as 'I can do the best I can in the time available' can help them to remain calm and focused.

Ask you client to plan key tasks at a time of the day when his mind is most active – for example by considering whether he's a morning or evening person, a lark or an owl. Some people love to work deep into the night; others can be much more effective when they first wake.

Problems your client may bring to sessions include:

- ✔ **Low boredom threshold:** 'I'm bored with this task now, so I'll just flit to another job for a few minutes.'

- ✔ **Not delegating:** 'I have to do this job myself because I am not sure that anyone else is as competent as I am. Anyway, they're already so busy.'

- ✔ **Not meeting deadlines:** 'No, I haven't got that task complete yet; I forgot that you needed it for today.'

- ✔ **Not prioritising:** 'I don't know where to begin. . .'

- ✔ **Not saying 'no':** 'Yes, I am sure I can take on that task,' even though he's already struggling under a mountain of work.

- ✔ **Perfectionism:** 'I have to do everything perfectly. I can't be satisfied with less and I don't trust anyone else to do the task as well as I do.'

- ✔ **Procrastination:** 'Let me just see what else I can do before I start that task.'

- ✔ **Stress and overwhelm:** 'I've just got so much to do that I can't think straight, so I don't know what I'm supposed to do.'

Identify the thoughts your client experiences during the situation in question. Then challenge whether these thoughts are:

- ✔ **Rational and logical:** Is there a law that states that because you think this way about the situation, everyone finds it logical and necessary to do so?

- ✔ **The way everyone thinks:** How might other people approach this situation?

- ✔ **Helpful:** Is the way you're thinking helping you to accomplish the task and maintain peak performance?

If your client's thoughts are not all the above, prompt him to develop more constructive and self-supportive thoughts that address his problems in a more helpful way, such as 'I can prioritise and motivate myself to undertake the most important tasks first in a calm and confident manner.' Remind him that he has to focus on these new thoughts and reinforce them frequently so as to build new habits.

Getting organised

Disorganisation can cause confusion and delay. External clutter can clutter the mind, so your client may need to review his approach. General principles include:

- ✔ To-do lists provide structure and a sense of achievement, but they don't work for everyone.

- ✔ Put tasks and dates into his diary, computer, and mobile phone.

✔ Set a reward for effort and achievement.

✔ Ask others to remind him of plans.

✔ Get him to delegate.

✔ List priorities on a variety of levels:

- Most important and most urgent

- Most important but less urgent

- Urgent but not important

- Not urgent or important

Develop an achievable and personalised system that your client feels able to maintain. Many people go on time-management courses but hear only about systems that work for others but not them. Consider the following within this area also:

✔ **Dependencies:** On whom is he dependent for the completion of work? Who is dependent on him for completion of work? How smoothly do these relationships work for the easy flow of information?

✔ **Saying 'no':** Managing demands is a key aspect of time management. People can feel guilty that saying 'no' sounds unhelpful. However, it can be worse to say 'yes' to a task that your client knows he can't complete, and then admit failure two weeks down the line, by which time it can be too late to delegate it to someone else.

✔ **Time-wasters:** Who and what wastes his time? Colleagues can interrupt work, chatting about unimportant gossip. Elicit the thoughts that allow your client to be susceptible to these situations – 'I'd better help John because. . . ' or 'I can't tell his I am busy because it sounds rude.' Develop more assertive language, for example 'I'd love to listen but I am really busy now on a deadline. Can I get back to you?' 'Do Not Disturb' signs can work too!

Saying 'no' is actually negotiating priorities. If your client is already snowed under and his boss asks him to undertake more work, suggest that he lists all the current tasks and projects and assertively discusses priorities. Role-play can be a useful way of practising language and behaviour. You can play the boss or colleague while your client experiments with his negotiation skills: 'I would like to help you. However I already have. . . tasks to do. What would you like me to focus on first?'

Time-management strategies are common sense, but how a person is thinking and feeling is key to whether he keeps up a system or practice. Your client needs to identify the benefit to himself so as to develop both thoughts and behaviours that support the will to action.

Delegating and empowering others

Delegation is key to peak performance. However, you may find that your client finds it difficult to let go and trust others, delegates too much, or gives unclear instructions.

Identify the thoughts and emotions that block successful delegation practices. Perfectionism is one of the most common blocks to delegation. For example, your client may need to consider the long-term benefit of allowing others to discover and make their own mistakes, just as he did.

New managers can find it difficult to let go of the routine tasks and projects to take on a more strategic role of driving the performance of a team forward to achieve results. This change of role takes adjustment, because some managers may not see the strategic aspects of their work as real work and feel uncomfortable not being in the thick of the daily tasks. They may also mind-read or make assumptions that others don't see them working and be anxious that they're not gaining the approval of all their staff.

The problem–emotion–plan or *PEP model* is useful in addressing your client's delegation goals. This model can be used in many different situations because it identifies the emotional reasons behind your client's behaviours as well as developing a plan to solve the problem. This example shows how the model can be applied to time and delegation.

1. **Problem identification:**

   • **Clearly define the problem:** Client: 'I have too much to do and too little time. There are so many tasks that I can't think straight.'

   • **Consider the consequences of continuing to have this problem:** 'I shall get exhausted. I have already made one or two mistakes, and I know that I shall make some more.'

   • **Consider the consequences of solving this problem:** 'I would feel less stressed and able to focus on the most important and strategic aspects of my role.'

   • **Is there any part of you that wants to maintain the problem? If so, why?** 'Well, I suppose if I am honest, I feel important and needed when I am busy. Looking busy makes me look as if I am achieving, even if I am not! And I know that if I do the tasks myself, they will be done really well, even if I have to rush other tasks.'

2. **Exploring the emotion:** Apply the ABCD model to exploring the emotional factors of the problem:

- **A = Activating event** (e.g. a specific incident relating to the main problem detailed in section 1):

    'My boss asked me to arrange for a presentation to be made to demonstrate the annual productivity of our department. I could have delegated it to Mark, but decided that I would do it myself. In the end, I had so many other things to do that I made a mistake in the figures that I calculated, and also didn't have time to check fonts in the presentation so it looked rather a mess.'

- **B = Belief/expectation:** Write down any thoughts that were in your head about the activating event: what were you demanding of yourself, others, or the world? 'Shoulds' and 'musts'.

    'I was thinking "I must do this piece of work because I can prove how efficient I am as manager of the department and put all the points I want to make to prove how much I have done to increase productivity." I was also thinking "I ought to give other people this task, but I must do it myself because I don't trust them to do it as well as I do."'

- **C = Consequence:** Consider the emotion detailed at the beginning of section 2 and define any secondary emotions (for example feeling angry at being frightened).

    'I felt anxious about the presentation, so this drove me to do it myself.'

    'I feel cross with myself about being anxious because I know really that I should have delegated it to Mark as he is perfectly capable of doing it and it would have been a good opportunity to introduce him to senior management.'

- **D = Dispute the belief: Is the way you are thinking about this logical?**

    'No. I could have approached this in many ways.'

    Would everyone in this situation feel the same way?

    'No. Many other managers would have delegated this task or worked in collaboration.'

    Is it helpful for you to continue to hold this belief/expectation?

    'No, I really need to learn to delegate and let go, so that I relieve myself of some of the pressure, plus learn to empower others by allowing them to try new things and make mistakes where necessary. Of course they may actually shine by doing it better than I would have done, and I have to learn to accept that too!'

3. Plan: Develop a practical and achievable plan:

- What is a positive future outcome? To let go and delegate more often.

- How might others manage this situation? They would realise that part of being a manager is to delegate work to the team and mentor team members' progress where necessary.

- Personal management plan: Identify your plan of action:

- Behaviours that will help me to do this: Clear communication to my direct report to delegate the task in future.

- What emotion will help me? Feeling flexible, calm, and trusting.

- How will I feel physically? Motivated and energised so that I inspire my direct report to feel confident of his own abilities.

- What images would be helpful? Remembering the first major project that my boss delegated to me when I was first in this role. Seeing my direct report successfully completing the task.

- What thoughts will help me achieve this outcome? We all have to begin somewhere. If I keep trying to do everything, I shall make some major mistakes or get ill! My direct reports are a capable bunch and they can always ask for help if they need it, so I can learn to believe in them.

- What interpersonal skills would be helpful? Good eye contact, clear message, conveying trust in others.

- What biological interventions/lack of interventions would be helpful (for example less caffeine, more deep-breathing exercises)? I shall make sure I haven't had too much caffeine, because that just makes me even more nervous and hyper, and I would probably convey that nervousness to others.

- Create an action plan to rehearse these skills in order to help you manage the event (for example training and/or daily practice).

- What: I shall evaluate the projects as they come in, and give the first appropriate task to one of my direct reports.

- When: We get new projects in at the beginning of the month, so I shall start next month.

- Why: Because it makes sense and I can then concentrate on developing our strategic vision for next year.

This example shows how this manager's behaviour was being driven by his thoughts and emotions, blocking his ability to delegate to his team members. This problem is not uncommon, and you can help your client to analyse his approach. He needs to make an adjustment transition, but he can soon appreciate that he just cannot undertake all the tasks himself.

Working with Others to Achieve Results

No-one works in isolation. Clear communication is an essential part of achieving peak performance individually and as a team. Good relationships are key but can easily be damaged in the everyday cut and thrust of the workplace. When your client's objective is to raise the bar to personal performance, you can help him to review the thoughts and expectations that play a part in his everyday communication with colleagues and staff.

Considering everyday contact

Performing well in the workplace is a continuous experience. That said, no-one can remain at his peak all the time, nor can he arrive at 'perfect' behaviours or relationships. Hiccups always occur. For example, your client may tell you about one or more of the following situations, all of which can impact on productivity:

- ✔ Arguing with a colleague
- ✔ Having a natural aversion to a colleague or member of staff
- ✔ Intuitively not trusting someone, without knowing why
- ✔ Not expressing his needs honestly
- ✔ Shouting at his direct report
- ✔ Trying to build a relationship with a client but being rebuffed
- ✔ Withholding information for the sake of his own ego and pride

Check how your client thinks about the situation he describes. Does he think 'I'm right and they're wrong' and blame others? Or is he blaming himself for communication problems? Or is he totally confused? What are his own needs? In how many different ways can he experiment with language so as to achieve greater understanding with those with whom he works? What might he find out if he stands in the other person's shoes?

I cover lots of aspects of communication and relationships in Chapters 11 and 17, but I make a few points here about some of the problems that occur in everyday working relationships that can impact effective performance:

- ✔ Backbiting
- ✔ Cliques
- ✔ Competitiveness
- ✔ Jealousy
- ✔ Need for harmony leading to the avoidance of issues

⮞ Obsequiousness

⮞ Truculence

People often do not address problems directly and honestly. Instead, they hold their hurt or anger in until it reaches boiling point. Withholding information from the other person that may, in fact, resolve the problem can poison relationships. This bad feeling frequently has a direct impact on outputs and can sabotage countless projects. Suggest your client keeps a daily record of problems that arise and observes how they impact his feelings. Should he become aware that his emotions are escalating, he can plan proactively to take steps to discuss the issue calmly, before his feelings prevent useful discussion.

Bernard had a problem with his manager, Steve, who delegated tasks to members of Bernard's team directly, without going through Bernard. His coach applied the ABCD model to identify perspectives that may be causing the problem. (Refer to Chapters 1 and 2 for more on this model.)

⮞ **A = Activating event** – Steve was giving work to Bernard's team.

⮞ **B = Belief** – Bernard was thinking 'He should not do this;' 'He ought to come and discuss this with me;' 'They're MY team so he must communicate with me first.'

⮞ **C = Consequence** – Bernard became angry but also hurt and disempowered by Steve's actions. He felt his confidence undermined by this action. His became defensive towards Steve. Bernard resented Steve's behaviour so he stopped communicating information to him. It had become a tit-for-tat situation.

⮞ **D = Disputing the beliefs** – Bernard's coach asked him to consider whether his thoughts and expectations were as follows:

- Just because Bernard would prefer Steve to communicate with him first rather than direct with his team member, was there a written law that said he must do so? Bernard replied that there was no law. However, it had been common practice with his previous boss, and he realised that he had made an assumption that Steve would behave the same way, without clarifying it between them.

- Would everyone feel the same way that Bernard did? Bernard acknowledged that some managers might not be upset by Steve's behaviour. But other managers might be so upset that they'd have discussed the matter with Steve directly by now, which Bernard had not yet done.

- Were Bernard's thoughts and expectations helping him to manage the situation? Bernard considered his thoughts quite reasonable but not helpful. He recognised that his defensive behaviour was

> negatively impacting on his relationship with his boss and result-ing in reduced productivity because he was focusing more on this problem than on his own performance targets. 'My personal response to Steve's behaviour is to be upset by it. This problem is a playground power struggle. Unless I am honest with Steve about this situation, he may not be aware of how his behaviour impacts on me, so I shall discuss the problem with him directly and see what agreement we can come to that is mutually acceptable.'

Steve's response was 'It was just quicker to go direct to your team member rather than wait until you were there. I didn't mean to upset you.' They agreed that whenever Bernard was available, Steve would take the issue to him, but when the task was urgent and Bernard was not available, Steve would go ahead and delegate the task directly to the team member. This solution was an acceptable compromise for both parties.

This type of misunderstanding is common. Some managers avoid issues, think-ing that they have to be totally competent otherwise their staff won't respect them. If your client is trying to be the perfect manager, he can begin to accept that no-one has the capacity to resolve every single problem. A manager who is always strong and perfect is not as approachable as a manager who is a member of the human race.

Being on show

Public speaking, presenting, and making a client pitch or sale can be a regular part of workplace responsibilities. However, many clients fear these events because their performance is judged by others. CBC models can enable them to prepare to perform more effectively on these occasions.

Assess your client's negative thinking patterns and how these patterns impact on his feelings and behaviours, using the NATs and CATs models. See examples of this in Tables 16-4 and 16-5. (See Chapter 6 for more on NATs and CATs.) Identify the link between the thought and the feeling that results from it. Evaluate whether these thoughts and feelings help your client to feel confident in presenting to others.

Table 16-4	NATs and Presentations
Overcoming NATs (Negative Automatic Thoughts)	*Feelings and Behaviours Likely to Be Stimulated by NATs*
I shall screw up.	Doubt, and probably will screw up.
I may look stupid.	Feel physically awkward.
I may forget my words.	Focus too much on remembering words, and not focus on the audience.
What if I can't answer a question?	Fearful, panic – so probably won't remember the facts.

Once your client understands the impact of his thoughts on his feelings, and how his thoughts negatively influence his behaviour, encourage him to develop thoughts to enhance and support his performance. You can do this by asking questions such as 'What thoughts would support you to feel more confident when you present?' or 'How can you think of your audience in a way that boosts your confidence?'

Table 16-5	CATs and Presentations
Developing CATs (Constructive Automatic Thoughts)	*Feelings and Behaviours Likely to Be Stimulated by CATs*
I may not do a perfect presentation but I shall do my best.	Flexible and more relaxed, so likely to be able to make more jokes and be 'with the audience'.
Instead of feeling 'on show', I shall think of the presentation as a two-way conversation and allow the audience to ask questions.	More relaxed – the presentation is a conversation like any other. As long as I have prepared, I should be able to respond, and if I can't answer a question, that is okay. I can always get back to them as I would if this were a normal conversation.
I am there to be seen, but I am also seeing them. They matter as much as I do.	This attitude feels more balanced. When I am fearful, I am focusing my mind and energy on myself and my worries. When I think about them and look at them, I open up my thoughts and my energy.

Thoughts influence the success or failure of a presentation. Perfectionism results in anxiety and is irrational. The perfect presentation does not exist. Nervous energy is inward-focused. Your client may be worrying more about how he may come over, rather than in conveying the message. Constructive thoughts support his performance. The pursuit of excellence is rational and achievable. He can only do his best. This attitude removes nerves and allows him to be focused on his audience rather than on his fears.

Part IV
Applying CBC in Organisations

"One's his trainer, one's his cognitive
behavioral coach."

In this part . . .

This part focuses specifically on workplace issues. I introduce some of the topics that clients are likely to raise in such sessions, exploring issues involving career transitions – such as promotion, redundancy and retirement.

I also cover how to help clients to maintain peak performance under the pressure of targets and workload, and the tricky business of managing other people, including issues such as conflict, influencing, motivation, and building effective and creative teams.

Chapter 17

Exploring Emotions and Communication in the Workplace

*H*uman beings all get emotional from time to time. Emotions drive motivation, ambition, competition, and performance. Emotions such as jealousy, anxiety, and resentment can sabotage teamwork and productivity. Beneath every sharp suit beats a heart and stirs a mind that frets about life and work in one way or another. The office may not look like an emotional place, but human beings have emotions in every moment of their lives – they just may not tune in to them.

Many business managers know that the success or failure of their organisations can be down, in large part, to the emotional state of their employees. Economic fluctuations and changes in the business environment inevitably influence profit, but the way people manage these situations really makes the difference to whether an organisation weathers the storm or not.

As a CB coach, you probably work with both managers and staff to help them understand the role of emotions in business and to develop their ability to manage their own and other people's emotions.

CBC works on the principle that the view a person takes of a situation, rather than the situation itself, causes disturbance. How a person thinks has a direct impact on her feelings. As a CB coach, you're in an excellent position to help your client tap in to the emotional power that exists within her organisation, developing her resilience to buffer against the bad times and leveraging enthusiasm and motivation to drive up performance, productivity, and teamwork.

In this chapter, I introduce strategies that you can share with your client to help her manage the emotions and challenging situations she faces in the workplace.

Tuning In to Emotional Signals

Emotions are survival mechanisms. They warn you that something is not right. They lead you in one direction for your protection and in another for your enjoyment and development. Emotions signal whether people and situations are meeting your needs. Babies scream when they are unhappy, which alerts parents to the fact that they want something, be it food, drink, or comfort. As you grow up, a part of you still wants to scream occasionally, or cry, or even hit someone when you are upset or your needs are not met.

CBC can help people understand that their thoughts and expectations drive their emotions. A CBC programme offers an immediate mechanism for changing how your client feels by changing how she thinks. You can help her understand this process and find out how to recognise her emotions and the thoughts behind them.

Gauging emotions

Your client needs to recognise her emotions. However, people in the workplace are often too busy thinking in a cerebral way about targets, deadlines, and workload to tune in to their emotions.

You can start a discussion about emotions, introducing the *emotions gauge* that I show in Figure 17-1. This lists a variety of emotions to begin to help your client identify the emotions she experiences. It also asks that she records how frequently these emotions occur and what situations trigger which emotions, so that she begins to become more aware of her feelings. Identify trends, for example whether your client spends more time experiencing negative or positive emotions, and help her to understand how her thoughts are impacting her emotional state. The thought 'I'll never manage this situation' will inspire anxiety, whereas the thought 'This is a challenging situation, but I can manage it' will help your client remain calm.

Hijacking emotions

Most adults manage their emotions most of the time, and the emotional and rational minds work in tandem. However, when a sudden event occurs or a set of pressures build up to a point where the individual feels she can't stand it, the rational mind may cease to function properly. People can lose control or respond in automatic mode, failing to consider the consequences of the action they're taking. This is referred to as *emotional hijacking* – when our emotional mind overwhelms our reason.

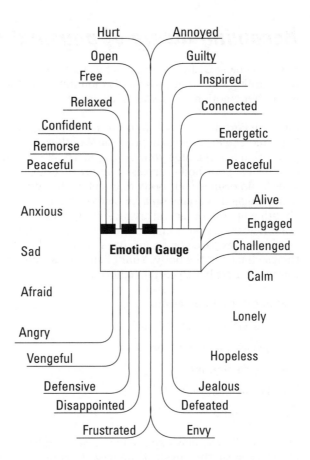

Figure 17-1:
Emotions
gauge.

People often regret their behaviour and also lose credibility with their colleagues as a result of their outbursts, whether it be tears or anger. Once your client understands this process and recognises the thoughts and triggers that might stimulate this response, she can develop the ability to stop for a moment before reacting.

Daniel Goleman, author of *Emotional Intelligence,* explains how the small area of the brain known as the *amygdala* is crucial in helping us react to physical danger, enabling you to respond in thousandths of a second when threatened. You respond quickly because the signals that go from the eye or ear to the thalamus area of the brain go direct to the amygdala rather than through our cerebral cortex, or thinking brain. In moments of physical danger, the survival value of this direct route is great and can save lives. Research shows that signals that route direct to the thalamus are quick but imprecise. This *precognitive emotion* is based on neural pieces of sensory information that have not been analysed in depth – people may therefore react independent of, or prior to, rational thought.

Becoming aware of physical changes

Physical changes always accompany emotions. Your client can tune in to certain warning signs that pressure is mounting, and therefore avoid instances where her emotions overwhelm her reason.

Candace Pert, in her book *Molecules of Emotion*, argues that emotions are a basic molecular, biological process. Whether an event is real or imagined, your brain manipulates your biochemistry. If you imagine yourself relaxing on a beach, your body relaxes. If you're anxious about an imagined situation, your brain primes your body to develop strength or speed. Whether you're being mugged, working on a help desk and listening to an irate customer shouting at you, or feeling anxious about making a presentation, the brain nonetheless responds immediately, releasing adrenalin, noradrenalin, and cortisol to prepare you to survive a physical threat. As this occurs, many things change in the body. Your client can watch out for the physical symptoms that alert her to certain emotions:

- ✔ Short, rapid breathing
- ✔ Butterflies in the stomach
- ✔ Sweaty palms and forehead
- ✔ Goose pimples
- ✔ Tense muscles
- ✔ Dry mouth

Interestingly, you may experience these symptoms during excitement and anger, because the physical changes are similar. Think of a time when you were angry with someone or feeling excited about going out on a new date: the sensations are alike. Your client can develop thinking processes that help her leverage this. A young manager promoted to a new job focused on the thought 'I am feeling excited by this opportunity,' instead of 'I am feeling nervous about this new job,' and found it helped her communicate with more authority during her first week at work.

Seeing how thoughts drive feelings

Tuning in to emotions requires your client to become more conscious of the physiological signals. She also needs to tune in to the thoughts and demands that stimulate emotion, as behind emotion the mind is at work. Examples of thoughts and the emotions those thoughts can trigger include:

- ✔ 'I am not getting what I need.' (frustration, anger)
- ✔ 'I feel threatened because I fear I shall be overlooked for promotion.' (anxiety, fear)

✔ 'That person isn't doing what I want them to do.' (resentment, anger)

✔ 'I feel happy so I shall choose this activity again.' (happiness, contentment)

✔ 'I just can't wait for my wedding.' (excitement, anticipation)

✔ 'I should have called my mother today.' (guilt, shame)

✔ 'How could my boyfriend have forgotten my birthday?' (disappointment, hurt)

✔ 'I made such a mess of my presentation yesterday.' (embarrassment, shame)

✔ 'John has just bought a fantastic new car.' (envy, jealousy)

✔ 'My life just doesn't seem to be going well.' (sadness, melancholy)

Your role as a CB coach is to work with your client to tune in to and identify the emotions, physical changes, thoughts, and expectations involved in the situations she faces. You can ask questions to help your client analyse her thoughts and then better manage her emotions. Ask your client whether her thoughts are:

✔ **Rational and logical:** Is there a law or logic to say that this is the way to think about the situation?

✔ **The approach everyone would take in this situation:** How might someone else think and manage this situation?

✔ **Helping her manage her emotions and the situation:** What thoughts and behaviours would help you manage your emotions in this situation?

✔ **Likely to trigger behaviour and action she may regret:** How is your current thinking impacting your behaviour? How else might you think in future to ensure a result with which you are satisfied?

Where you can see that her views are unhelpful, help your client identify what thoughts and approaches can be more supportive to her emotional equilibrium. Ask her to identify an emotion that would be more helpful to her in future, and work with her to consider what thoughts would enable her to experience this emotion.

Logging emotions

Emotions – whether comfortable or uncomfortable, useful or inhibiting, peaceful or violent – should still be felt, honoured, and acknowledged. All emotions play a useful part in your client's life, signalling what does and what doesn't work. However, many adults are uncomfortable when they experience powerful feelings. Some consider that doing so isn't 'professional' or grown-up. For this reason, people often try to ignore them. Keeping an *emotions log* in which your client records events and accompanying emotions can help her become attuned to what she feels – and why. I give an example in Table 17-1.

Table 17-1		Emotions Log	
Event	*Physical Signals*	*Emotion*	*Underlying Reason, Thought, or Demand*
Colleagues talking loudly when I am trying to concentrate on writing a report	Tense jaw and muscles, frown, raised heartbeat	Anger	'I need silence to write well. They ought to shut up.'
Hoping a client pitch goes smoothly	Feeling jumpy, unable to sleep or concentrate, butterflies	Anxious excitement	'Everything must go well or it will be awful.'

In addition to the primary emotion that people experience, there may also be an underlying *secondary emotion* that is a judgement or belief relating to the primary emotion; for example:

✔ Feeling angry at themselves for feeling sad

✔ Feeling frustrated with themselves for not being able to express their hurt

✔ Feeling depressed that they couldn't manage their anger

These secondary emotions tend to be rather judgemental. When your client understands some of these processes and the fact that everyone experiences emotion, it can be easier for her to accept herself as an emotional being. She can also become aware that she has options to manage and leverage the power of her feelings in a constructive and helpful way.

Developing Emotional Intelligence

Emotional intelligence, or EQ, is about managing and leveraging emotions within everyday situations. As thoughts drive feelings, CBC provides strategies to enable your client to become both emotionally aware and emotionally intelligent. By changing her thoughts, she discovers how to manage her feelings. Emotional intelligence falls into two main categories:

✔ **Personal competence – self-awareness and self-management:**

• Understand feelings.

• Know where they come from.

• Acknowledge emotions and know how to manage them.

• Know how to motivate yourself and others.

✔ **Social competence – social awareness and relationship management:**

- Recognise and manage the emotions of other people, and develop empathy.

- Express feelings appropriately and develop good relationships.

Emotional intelligence is now recognised as a differentiator for success in the business world. When recruiting staff, organisations see many candidates with the same sets of qualifications and capabilities. Being technically competent is one thing. What management want in today's complex world is the added value that emotional intelligence brings with it – someone who can work in teams, talk to customers, emanate positive energy, inspire, and motivate themselves and others.

Exploring the impact of emotions in business

Some managers consider that emotional intelligence is a soft skill with no relevance in the business world. They underestimate the real business consequences of poor emotional intelligence, which can be seen in most organisations. The events of the 2008 credit crunch demonstrated how the power of emotions can drive both hubris and fear with devastating effects. These consequences can include:

✔ Sabotage of projects and teamwork

✔ Conflict, leading to a block on progress

✔ Empire-building and lack of knowledge- or information-sharing, leading to delays and duplication

✔ Demotivation and low morale, leading to low productivity and delays

✔ Loss of customer relationships

✔ Deals and mergers breaking down as a result of ego or conflict

---

EQ is a leadership skill

Warren Bennis wrote: 'Emotional intelligence is much more powerful than IQ in determining who emerges as a leader. IQ is a threshold competence. You need it, but it doesn't make you a star. Emotional intelligence does.'

All these consequences equate to loss of time and money. You therefore want to enable your client to manage emotions in herself and others. The ABC model, which I describe in Chapter 2, can be a useful model in helping your client respond appropriately to the challenges she faces.

Emma arrived at a training course red in the face and flustered because she had been cut up on the motorway and forced to move into the wrong lane of traffic, and was late as a result. She had been unable to calm her anger after the incident. Her coach applied two processes to help her manage this situation better in future: the ABC model and the *0–10 pressure gauge,* which is a way of measuring the level of pressure she is feeling and helps her to gain perspective. Here is Emma's ABC model:

- ✔ **A = Activating event:** Being forced by an aggressive driver to move into the inner lane of the motorway. This event meant that Emma missed her turning.

- ✔ **B = Belief or expectation:** Emma realised that she had lost her cool because she was experiencing two thoughts. The first thought – 'He should not have driven like that: his driving is unacceptable and I can't stand it' – made her angry. The next – 'I'm going to be late for the training course now and that's awful because I can't stand being late' – made her anxious.

- ✔ **C = Consequential emotion and behaviour:** Anger at the driver; anxiety about being late. Her behaviour was that she drove rather too fast and entered the training room in a flustered and anxious state, apologising profusely for being late. Her physiology also reflected her anxious state, because her face was red and she had a stress rash on her neck.

In discussion with her coach, Emma understood that her thinking had driven her emotional responses. She saw also that another person may just have shrugged their shoulders and been quite calm about being late.

In order to help her dispute the rationality and helpfulness of her thinking, her coach then used the *0–10 pressure gauge*. Emma was asked to stipulate what level of stress she had reached during the incident on the motorway on a scale of 0–10, with 0 being zero stress and 10 being high stress. She responded that she was at least 9. 'X' marks the spot she chose.

0————————————————————X——10

The coach explained to Emma that she'd find it helpful to check her perspective when she had high stress levels. He explained that he was going to ask her a series of questions to help her assess her perspective on the situation. The questions are designed to push a client out of her comfort zone to imagine worse scenarios and decide how important the event really is within the context of her whole life. Make up your own series of questions depending on the situation of your client. The questions the coach asked Emma were:

- ✔ If you came home this evening and discovered that your child had been taken to hospital, where does that place your stress level on the 0–10 pressure gauge? Does this perspective change your rating for the current situation? *Yes.*

- ✔ If you discovered that a loved one had a serious illness, where does that place your stress level on the gauge? Does this perspective change your rating for the current situation? *Yes.*

- ✔ If you found that you had been given redundancy or fired, where does that place your stress level around the incident? *Lower.*

- ✔ How important will this incident be in three months' time? *Not important at all.*

When you work with your client in this way, your aim is to enable her to take a bird's eye view of her life. This view helps her to understand that she may be upsetting herself unnecessarily over a small incident.

At the end of 0–10 pressure gauge exercise, Emma decided that the incident only deserved a 3.

0————X———————————————10

From this point, the coach asked Emma to dispute the 'B' of the ABC model and consider how helpful it was to her to have those thoughts and expectations around the situation of being cut up on the motorway. Emma realised that her thoughts were driving her to feel both anxious and angry – and to drive too fast. She also realised that a business consequence could have arisen from this situation: had she been on her way to a meeting with one of her customers, she would not have given a good impression entering the meeting room flustered, red in the face, and so deeply apologetic about her tardiness.

Emma decided that, the next time, she would try to stay calm by focusing on the following thoughts:

- ✔ I'd prefer it if this person had driven considerately, but I can shrug my shoulders and manage it if they don't.

- ✔ I'd prefer to be on time all the time, but I accept that, on occasion when things are beyond my control, I may be late.

- ✔ I can keep calm and arrive at the meeting in a confident professional manner.

The next morning, she reported that her journey had gone well and that despite being five minutes late due to a traffic jam, she had kept her calm and driven carefully.

Thinking constructively

When your client is aware of how her thoughts drive her emotions, she feels more in control. She realises, sometimes for the first time, that she does have a choice about the way she feels. Through CBC, she starts to develop new ways of thinking to maintain emotional balance and to enable her to access an emotion that will help her to manage a situation more effectively. Examples include:

- ✔ **Becoming anxious during a merger or restructure:** The underlying thought may be: 'I may be made redundant.' Alternative: 'I can't guess what changes will happen, so I won't worry about it yet.'

- ✔ **Becoming cross when her idea isn't acknowledged during a meeting:** The underlying thought may be: 'They should listen to me.' Alternative: 'I'd prefer it if they had adopted my idea, but I can continue to share my solutions.'

- ✔ **Becoming resentful when her boss doesn't say thank you:** The underlying thought may be: 'She should thank me for my efforts.' Alternative: 'I'd rather she thanked me, but I know I did a good job anyway.'

By helping your client to apply models such as the ABC model and pressure gauge, she begins to manage situations more effectively in future.

Handling healthy and unhealthy emotions

CBC distinguishes between healthy and unhealthy emotions. Healthy emotions are natural and appropriate. 'Twisted' thinking triggers unhealthy emotions and in some way infers a threat to the individual's sense of personal security.

Unhealthy emotions include anger, anxiety, depression, guilt, hurt, morbid jealousy, and shame. Coaches see such emotions as unhealthy because they're the result of twisted thinking such as:

- ✔ **All-or-nothing thinking:** 'This can never work.'

- ✔ **Catastrophising:** 'I can't stand it!' 'It is awful!'

- ✔ **Discounting the positives:** 'Nothing is going right here.'

- ✔ **Emotional reasoning:** 'I *feel* stupid, so I must *be* stupid.'

✔ **Fortune-telling:** 'I know my suitcase will get lost in transit.'

✔ **Labelling:** 'I made this mistake so I am a complete failure.'

✔ **Mind-reading:** 'I'm sure my partner is unfaithful.'

✔ **Personalisation or blame:** 'How could I have done that?' 'How could you have done that?'

Healthy emotions include annoyance, concern, disappointment, non-morbid jealousy, regret, remorse, and sadness. These emotions are healthy because they're based on objectivity rather than supposition or twisted thinking. They're also healthy because the emotion is regarded as natural within the context of that situation.

Emotional intelligence is not about squashing feelings. Instead, EQ involves the following process:

1. **Acknowledging the emotion:** For example: 'I feel anxious.'

2. **Understanding the belief that is stimulating the emotion:**

   • Is this anxiety about something rational or imagined?

   • Is this anxiety appropriate or inappropriate?

   • Is this anxiety helping me to manage the situation?

   • If not, what is a more appropriate and helpful belief to hold about the situation?

3. **Developing a more rational and appropriate way of managing the situation:** 'I feel anxious, but I can put this situation in perspective and find a way to think about it that can help me manage it.'

Feeling sad if you're bereaved, mourning the end of a broken relationship, and being disappointed if someone lets you down are appropriate emotions. Less appropriate is holding guilt, shame, or morbid jealousy about a situation from which you can move on and develop. Work with your client to focus on more healthy ways of responding to situations in future.

Uncovering the Consequences of Stress in the Workplace

You're bound to have a few stressed clients pass through your coaching rooms from time to time. Stress in the workplace continues to be a problem. Despite many initiatives to support staff managing stress, a Health and Safety Commission report in December 2007 stated that the number of people seeking medical advice for work-related stress had risen from 110,000 in 2005 to

530,000 in 2007. A huge 58 per cent of all absenteeism is due to stress-related illness. The Department of Health estimates that the cost of stress-related absence and its impact on productivity takes 5–10 per cent off the bottom line of each UK business. So stress prevention makes business sense.

Many changes have occurred in the world of commerce over the last 15 years that have increased the pressures on individuals. These include:

- ✔ Global trends have created a greater sense of insecurity in the workplace.

- ✔ Competition is greater, both on an individual and an organisational level.

- ✔ Mergers, acquisitions, and an obsession with restructuring can result in redundancy, having to reapply for your job, or having to adjust to change.

- ✔ Firms focus on targets, measurement, and shareholder value more than they did in the past.

- ✔ The pace of change has increased, and a huge increase in information and communication due to technological developments has occurred.

- ✔ Families fragmenting and global economies becoming increasingly interdependent has led to social and economic change.

Some managers argue that stress is an essential ingredient of good performance. The adrenalin kick of motivation and a search for excellence are certainly useful factors in productivity. However, stress occurs at the point when perceived pressure on an individual exceeds her ability to cope, and this pressure actually limits clarity of thought and decision-making capability. People make very different decisions when they're calm and confident to when they're stressed and anxious – they also communicate very differently.

In Figure 17-2, I demonstrate the journey from lack of arousal, up through motivation, to peak performance. This has been adapted from Dr Peter Nixon's Human Function Curve, demonstrating that people have a tipping point over the top of the curve when the feeling tips from motivation (on the top left area) to one of 'It's all just too much and I can't cope,' when they experience a sense of being overwhelmed and of exhaustion (as the curve dips to the right). This tipping point is the point that managers and individuals need to avoid if they're to bring out the best in themselves and their staff. They also need to be aware of legal requirements so as to avoid expensive litigation.

One in six people report their jobs to be very or extremely stressful (CIPD, 2008). When working with a stressed client, identify the following:

- ✔ What stress means to them
- ✔ Factors and situations that cause them stress
- ✔ Signs and symptoms of stress
- ✔ Strategies to manage situations more effectively

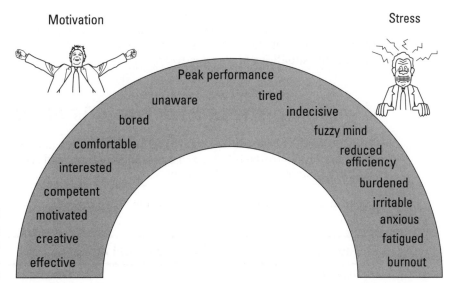

Motivation   Stress

Peak performance
unaware   tired
bored   indecisive
comfortable   fuzzy mind
interested   reduced
                                              efficiency
competent   burdened
motivated   irritable
                                                   anxious
creative   fatigued
effective   burnout

Figure 17-2:
The stress
curve.

I show some of the common causes of stress in the workplace in Table 17-2.

Table 17-2	Common Causes of Stress in the Workplace
Personal	*Relationships*
Too much or too little work	Bad relationship with boss, colleagues, and/or subordinates
Time pressures and deadlines	Personality conflicts
Bad physical environment	Thwarted ambition
Role ambiguity	Bullying or harassment
Over- or under-promotion	Inability to express needs
Fear of redundancy and lack of security	Low team or organisational morale
Lack of skills	Divided loyalties
Lack of self-awareness and self-management	Family commitments and lack of work–life balance
Inability to cope with change	Delegation difficulties
Perfectionism	Ambiguity around boundaries

Ask your client to make three lists headed 'Personal', 'Work', and 'General stress' and list the stressors she experiences in each category. Then ask her to give each item a mark on the scale of 0–10, 10 being high stress, 0 being low. Work with her to assess how each item is impacting her life, her health, and her performance. She is the best judge of those areas that may need addressing, whether due to high levels of stress or due to boredom, perhaps because she feels her skills are under-utilised. Help her to problem-solve those areas she wants to change and to develop thoughts and actions to manage the situations more effectively.

Managing stress with the 3As model

The CBC model of the 3As is useful here. I introduce this in Chapter 13. Ask your client to go through her list of stressful situations and record what she can alter or avoid, or needs to accept.

I give an example in Table 17-3 to show how this process can work.

Table 17-3	The 3As Model In Action	
Personal	*Work*	*General*
e.g. financial difficulties (8/10)	e.g. conflict with boss (9/10)	e.g. train delays (9/10)
Alter: Pay off credit card bills monthly to avoid interest.	Alter: Manage by being assertive.	Alter: Write to transport company and accept that a delay is probable.
DIY (6/10)	Likely merger with US competitor (7/10)	Economic downturn (5/10)
Avoid: Until the summer!	Accept: There's nothing I can do about it.	Accept: There's nothing I can do about it other than be careful.

Empower your client to realise that she can take action to problem-solve the situations that cause her stress. This realisation provides a sense of control which, in itself, reduces pressure.

Identifying symptoms of stress

As with any emotion, stress changes the body's chemistry. In Figure 17-3, I demonstrate how, when sensory input reaches the brain and indicates a threat, the body primes itself for strength or speed: the fight or flight response.

The problem with workplace stress is that the stress is often long-term and psychological rather than physical. Therefore, the fact that the body responds to stress by preparing you for physical strength is not that useful.

Stress makes you strong but does not enhance the brain's ability to process the type of complex thinking that is required in the workplace. As Dr David Beales, a specialist in this field, commented recently: 'There is not enough oxygen in the brain to solve a problem or make a good decision.' This problem occurs because the blood has been diverted from the thinking brain to the emotional brain, which diverts energy to the muscles to provide the fight or flight response.

During stress, breathing becomes deregulated, leading to what is known as over-breathing or hyperventilation, which can cause dizziness because of abnormally low levels of carbon dioxide in the blood. This is relevant should your client become stressed in situations such as making a sales call or presentation, because it impacts voice delivery as well as thinking. Advise your client to become aware of the impact of stress on mental activity. Instead of being good for business, stress is likely to be detrimental.

Long-term stress depletes the immune system and can lead to sickness. Use Figure 17-4 to demonstrate symptoms. Each person has her own vulnerable spots. Where one person gets back or neck ache, another gets colds and flu, another digestive problems, another skin rashes. Help your client to identify the first symptoms they personally experience so that they discover how to watch out for them and take early action to prevent things getting worse.

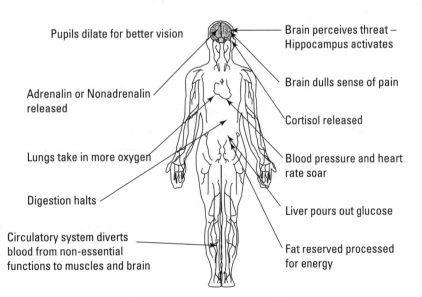

Pupils dilate for better vision

Brain perceives threat –
Hippocampus activates

Adrenalin or Nonadrenalin released

Brain dulls sense of pain

Cortisol released

Lungs take in more oxygen

Blood pressure and heart rate soar

Digestion halts

Liver pours out glucose

Figure 17-3:
Physical stress response.

Circulatory system diverts blood from non-essential functions to muscles and brain

Fat reserved processed for energy

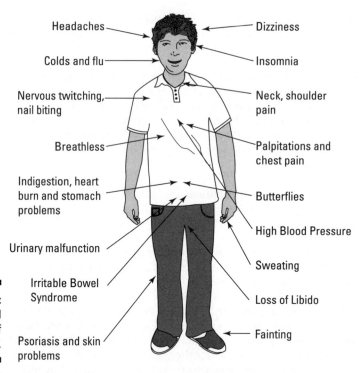

Figure 17-4:
Physical
symptoms of
stress.

Headaches —
Colds and flu —
Nervous twitching,
nail biting —
Breathless —
Indigestion, heart
burn and stomach
problems —
Urinary malfunction —
Irritable Bowel
Syndrome —
Psoriasis and skin
problems —

Dizziness
Insomnia
Neck, shoulder
pain
Palpitations and
chest pain
Butterflies
High Blood Pressure
Sweating
Loss of Libido
Fainting

When action is not taken to resolve issues, there can be long-term health consequences such as:

- ✔ Coronary heart disease
- ✔ High blood pressure
- ✔ Blood clotting as plaques form in blood vessels
- ✔ High levels of glucose leading to diabetes
- ✔ Reduced mental ability causing memory loss

Educate your client about the three stages of behaviour change to watch out for in themselves and those around them:

1. Early behavioural symptoms of stress:

   • Speeding up – no time for conversation, constantly fidgeting

   • Loss of sense of humour

   • Not eating properly

   • Making mistakes, missing deadlines

   • Increased alcohol consumption

2. Behavioural symptoms as stress builds up:
   - Memory loss, poor concentration
   - Anxious, demoralised
   - Lack of confidence, low self-esteem
   - Over-working, long hours
   - Insomnia, waking early
   - Impatient and intolerant

3. Danger symptoms of stress:
   - Constant fatigue, loss of energy
   - Difficulty making decisions
   - Tearful, unable to cope
   - Burnout and clinical depression

Both physical and behavioural changes indicate that a person may be stressed. The best approach is prevention, so the more information that both managers and individuals can have about stress the better. This information enables them to take action before the situation deteriorates.

Understanding strategies to manage stress

Stress and challenge are always going to be a feature of most people's lives. Your key is to provide understanding and strategies to develop personal resilience in your client. Your client has five key ways to manage stress:

- **Changing thoughts:** Transform thoughts such as 'I can't manage this situation, everything is awful, and I can't stand it' to 'I can manage and will take action step by step.' (Refer to Chapters 1, 2, and 6 for more information on developing constructive thoughts.)

- **Exercise:** Physical exercise reduces the chemical impact of stress. This exercise could be walking, running, dancing, swimming, or playing tennis, but not necessarily a strongly competitive sport such as squash. A good walk can do wonders for the mind and body. (Refer to Chapter 13 for more information on developing health.)

- **Lifestyle:** Behavioural actions such as good diet, exercise, sufficient daylight, and developing assertive communication skills in order to manage difficult situations all help. (Refer to Chapter 13 for more information on this.)

- **Meditation:** Learning to experience an altered state of mind through meditation can enhance the immune system and lower blood pressure. (See Chapter 21 for more information on imagery and relaxation exercises.)

✔ **Physiology:** Breathing slowly into the diaphragm, counting in for the count of 7 and out for the count of 11 can be beneficial. Ask your client to try relaxing the body, limb by limb from head to toe, thinking 'I am relaxing my forehead, I am relaxing my neck, I am relaxing my shoulders. . .' down through the whole body progressively. (Refer to Chapters 13 and 21 for more information.)

Investigating the Impact of Emotions on Communication

One of the most noticeable and common consequences of a raised emotional state is its impact on relationships. An article in the *Sunday Times* magazine in July 2006 stated that 45 per cent of people regularly lose their tempers at work. As Aristotle wrote in *The Nicomachean Ethics:* 'Anyone can become angry – that is easy. But to be angry with the right person, to the right degree, at the right time, for the right purpose, and in the right way – this is not easy.'

People communicate very differently depending on their emotional states. Sometimes being angry or hurt is totally appropriate. At other times, people don't manage their emotions, and communication breaks down with instances of:

✔ Blame or bullying

✔ Tears used as manipulation

✔ Sulking, victim, or martyr behaviour

✔ Making blanket personal statements such as 'You're impossible'

If your client mentions that her emotions negatively impact on her relationships, work with her to unpack the experiences. What was she expecting of herself and the other person? What emotions did she experience? How did she behave? How else could she have managed the situation to produce a better outcome? Could her own response have fuelled problems? Awareness in itself often changes behaviour and empowers a person to take responsibility for her part in resolving a problem.

Building bridges across differences

One of the common emotional issues in the workplace is that people do not agree with one another. Mutual respect and the acceptance that each person has a right to her own opinion is vital for easing emotional tension in relationships. In fact, one person can often solve the problem that another can't solve, because she has a different perspective. A few tips follow to share with your client to build bridges across differences of opinion. You can also refer to the section on assertiveness in Chapter 11.

Do:

✔ Remember that while you prefer that other people agree with you, they have a right to their own opinions.

✔ Stick to your purpose and goal, but be willing to be flexible. What are you trying to achieve? What is your part and what is theirs?

✔ Use 'I' statements so as to take responsibility for your own opinions and views.

✔ Try to acknowledge one aspect of the other person's point of view, even if you don't agree with it all.

✔ Focus on the behaviour and its emotional impact rather than condemning or judging the whole person. For example, say 'When you interrupt me in front of my client, I feel you are being rude, and I would prefer you to wait until I have finished before you add your own comments' rather than 'You're rude.'

✔ Try to give objective positive feedback as well as express differences. The feedback sandwich of one positive, one negative, one positive, can maintain the relationship and still leave people with a strong message.

✔ Differentiate between needs and wants. Is what you're requesting really essential or is it a 'nice to have'?

✔ Ask questions so that the other person has to think about the problem and come up with her own solutions.

✔ Maintain eye contact and ensure that your body posture and physiology is relaxed, open, and encouraging collaboration rather than division.

Don't:

✔ Tell – persuade the other person of your opinion and show them the benefit for themselves in accepting your views and suggestions.

✔ Say 'you must', 'you have to', 'you ought to', or 'you should'; say, 'could you', 'would you', or 'I would like you to'.

✔ Express opinions as facts. Take responsibility for your own views, so instead of saying 'The targets are perfectly realistic and achievable,' say 'In my view, the targets are perfectly realistic and achievable.'

✔ Generalise and just focus on the negatives and the problems. Focus on the solutions and potential actions you can both take to resolve the problem.

✔ Mind-read and pretend you know what the other person is thinking or feeling. For example: 'You just think I am incompetent, don't you?' If necessary, ask or alternatively say: 'I get the impression you may consider me incompetent.'

✔ Use the word 'can't' when it could be replaced with the word 'won't'. For example 'I can't raise that issue with the boss' could more accurately mean 'I won't raise that issue with the boss.'

✔ Personalise or label – 'You're impossible, you never listen.'

Many people are fearful of difference of opinion, but debate is natural and can shift perspectives and stimulate more creative solutions. However, when people are feeling insecure, they can feel threatened and become either aggressive or defensive. The secret is how the message is conveyed – 93 per cent of communication is in the voice tone and body language; only 7 per cent is the content of what is being said.

Suggest that you and your client carry out role-play scenarios where she practises expressing her opinions in a tone that is cooperative and collaborative. Encourage her to seek a mutually acceptable solution where both parties feel satisfied.

Managing conflict

When agreement cannot be reached, there can be conflict. Conflict is a part of life. It can be a creative debate or an aggressive exchange of entrenched views. Some people love conflict, and others avoid it at all costs. The outcome depends on how each person is thinking and whether she is able to manage her emotions.

Where agreement is required, both parties need to remain objective and manage their emotions. If your client has a conflict situation, you can help her to plan how she wants to manage herself. Before any workplace meeting where she may face a conflict situation, ask her to identify:

✔ Her desired outcome

✔ Her intention to work towards a resolution that is mutually acceptable

✔ Her strategy for the discussion and negotiation

✔ A mutually convenient time and a neutral place that is neither party's own territory

✔ A third party, if required, to facilitate or mediate the process

Your client can take responsibility for her own emotional state before entering any situation where she may experience conflict. CBC helps her to be prepared to apply her emotional intelligence so as to manage her own and the other person's emotions in a constructive way. Share tips for planning how she can manage the meeting itself:

- ✔ Check that your thoughts are supportive of a calm state of mind.

- ✔ Don't personalise: separate the individuals from the conflict.

- ✔ Express your desired outcome and needs.

- ✔ Look at and listen to the other person; don't interrupt or finish sentences. Allow the other person to express her opinions and goals.

- ✔ Brainstorm solutions.

- ✔ Check understanding – clarify or paraphrase, for example 'So what I understand you to have said is. . . ' or 'Would you mind repeating or clarifying that statement because I am not sure I understood you.'

- ✔ Stick to the point: take one issue at a time, and check that what you're saying is relevant.

- ✔ Avoid blaming or making comments for the sake of your own ego or to hurt someone deliberately.

- ✔ Be prepared to negotiate.

- ✔ Recognise when you may need the help of a third party.

Managing anger

Some people are more emotionally volatile than others. When a work role is very stressful, clients may need specific support in managing anger. CBC strategies provide useful tools to help your client manage her emotions. Help her become aware of the factors that spark impatience and anger. These include:

- ✔ **Frustration:** When other people carry out tasks in the 'wrong' way or too slowly

- ✔ **Perceived inefficiency:** When other people don't do tasks that your client wants them to do

- ✔ **Stress:** Leads people to be on a short fuse and become irritable and impatient

- ✔ **Unfairness or a sense of injustice:** When others make decisions or take actions that do not meet your client's personal standards or demands

If your client tends to get angry or lose emotional control, you can, in the calm of the coaching session, explore how her thoughts fuel her anger. For example, she's probably adopting negative or pessimistic thinking, or being judgemental or perfectionist, and in some way feeling threatened. You can help her analyse whether the views she's taking are rational and helpful to her in managing the situation. You can then help her adopt anger-management techniques such as:

- ✔ Plan supportive thoughts before she enters the room

- ✔ Identify what physical triggers can make her aware of mounting anger

- ✔ If necessary, ask to take time out for a break and say 'Shall we cool it and remind ourselves of our goal here.'

- ✔ Count to 10 before speaking.

- ✔ Breathing and emotions are linked, so take a breath in, hold it for the count of three, and slowly breathe out focusing on the statement 'I can remain calm.'

- ✔ Keep checking that her viewpoint is in perspective: are her thoughts rational and accurate or is she tending to personalise issues?

- ✔ Sit in the other people's shoes: what are their needs and concerns?

- ✔ If the other person gets angry, ask a question that breaks her angry state – for example, about a different aspect of the issue.

- ✔ Remember that where she sees anger, she also sees pain. Show compassion towards the underlying hurt, because this can remove the volatility of the anger.

Planning emotions

People can choose emotions by focusing their minds on what they feel like within the desired emotional state that helps them to manage a situation. The mental, emotional, and physical state is created by messages from the brain, and the memory works to recreate the experience when asked to do so.

Suggest that your client identifies what feeling may help her to achieve the desired result in the meeting. Encourage her to enter the room feeling optimistic about a solution, so that she starts the meeting on a positive note and adopts the appropriate body language to match this emotion.

Managing negative, unhealthy, and unhelpful emotions can transform conflict into understanding and agreement and, as a CB coach, you can play a part in facilitating this.

Going into neutral

Alan asked Tony, a colleague in another office, to prepare data for him, to be supplied by the end of the month. The end of the month came and went and no data appeared. Alan felt annoyed and let down, so sent an email to Tony: 'Where is the data I requested for the end of the month?' There was no response, so Alan sent another email: 'I need that data! Please get this to me by Friday.' When there was no response, Alan called Tony and shouted at him down the phone, 'Hi, it's Alan. I need that data Tony. Make sure it is with me by Monday at the latest,' and put the phone down, not giving Tony any time to respond. There was still no data on Monday. Alan's boss had observed this situation and suggested that Alan review his tactics. 'Tell me, Alan, how would you feel if you received emails and a phone call like this?' Alan had never considered how his words may impact on Tony, nor had he considered what other deadlines and pressures Tony may have on at the moment. He had been too much in his own head and his own needs. Alan's boss suggested that he go 'into neutral', visualising himself packaging up his emotions and putting them aside while he had a polite conversation with Tony to see what the problem was with regard to the delivery of the data. He also suggested manners and consideration such as phrases like 'How are things going with you? I understand you may have other pressures at the moment? Is there a specific problem with the data? Do you need more information from me? Is there anything I can do to help? What action are you able to take on this now? By what date can I expect to receive it?' Alan reported to his boss that he discovered that two of Tony's team had been away on extended sick leave and that there had been a major technical fault with the systems that he had to work on. Tony also confessed to being angry at the way Alan had spoken to him, and that this had sent him into a stubborn and uncooperative frame of mind. Alan and Tony worked through the problem, and Tony delivered the data three days later.

Chapter 18

Coaching Teams

. . . .

. . . .

As a CB coach, you may coach an entire team now and again. Team-working is a part of working practice within every organisation. Of course, your client may have a home team too, potentially consisting of partner, children, and anyone who helps him at home. The ability to work together for a common purpose produces results. In today's world, teams do not necessarily work in the same building. A team's members may work all over the world and work virtually across geographical, cultural, and language divides.

In an ideal world, the team gains from the unique thinking and expertise of each individual. This gain is great in theory but doesn't always work as easily in practice. Human nature is such that people frequently rub one another up the wrong way and fall out – and this falling out can sabotage the efforts of the whole group.

Team coaching involves moving the group towards agreed objectives, helping people to understand who they are and how each individual contributes to the whole. You can take a team through most of the exercises in this book. The CBC approach identifies how the individual thoughts of each person within the group impact not only on that person's feelings and behaviours but those of the whole group.

In this chapter, I introduce processes and models to help you plan and deliver a coaching programme for a team. For the sake of clarity, I have shaped this information around a team coaching session for a group of up to 20 people who know one another reasonably well.

Coaching teams is very rewarding. You're often able to facilitate subtle changes to the way people think about themselves and those with whom they work that make a real difference to understanding, empathy, and collaboration. You can find many other exercises to draw on throughout this book which apply as well in teams as for individuals. These include *thinking errors,* as described in Chapter 2, *bridging the difference* from Chapter 15, *possibility thinking* as described in Chapter 10 and *assertive communication* from Chapter 11.

Planning CBC for a Team

How you design a coaching programme depends on the team's objectives, how large the team is, how great the team members' issues, and how much time they're able to give you. You need to agree objectives and decide whether the manager is a part of the team activities or not. Whether he is depends upon the specific circumstances of the group and whether the manager's presence may hinder the sharing of individual experience.

I generally find that a staged process is more effective than a one-off 'away day', because the team may find it too easy to spend one day working on issues but then go back to their respective desks and work in exactly the same way that they did before, forgetting all that they practised in the session.

I recommend that you first run a session of one to two days. Adding an overnight stay allows people to relax socially in the evening, which develops communication on different levels to the norm. Follow up this initial session with two review sessions. These can be anything from a two-hour top-up session to another one or two days to flush out further issues and actions for change. You need to gauge precisely what is required, based on the group's needs and objectives.

For greatest benefit, make sure that the coaching workshop is off site – away from the group's usual place of work. The location changes the energy and also prevents the inevitable drift back to the desk, the emails, and the phone calls that come in. Where possible, choose a pleasant environment where people can relax and enjoy a new vista, because a new view changes their thinking and approach. Try to use a room with natural daylight, because daylight raises and maintains concentration and energy. Allow for a working day that encompasses breaks and a space for a meal. Again, this space develops more off-the-record conversation, and individuals share problems and issues, personal stories, and jokes in a way they don't have time for during the normal working day.

Designing coaching sessions

A team can be any group of individuals from two to several hundred, who cooperate together for a common purpose, project, or goal. Before you design the CBC sessions, you need to work out the style and nature of the team and understand its main function. Most teams benefit from diversity of approach, but any good team needs the following:

- Behaviours and actions that drive towards common goals rather than sabotage or pull away from them. The team benefits from alignment of focus and supportive ways of behaving together that enhance the whole team's performance.

- Joint problem-solving activities which involve honest discussion to raise and identify problems so that the whole group can generate solutions towards team objectives.

- Open communication to address challenges relating to the task and also relating to any personality or personal issues. Effective teams avoid 'group think', and each person is willing to constructively confront policies or approaches that they perceive will not work.

- Shared knowledge and updating of events, making time to ensure that each person is kept abreast of latest developments, rather than making assumptions that other team members will somehow know of events.

- Shared vision, to ensure that each member of the team knows exactly what the goal is that he is working towards, so that people do not pull against one another or work at cross purposes.

- Shared responsibility for the final outcomes, each team member taking personal accountability for his part in the achievement of team goals.

- Understanding of roles and responsibilities, so that each team member understands his own contribution and how his role impacts the roles and responsibilities of others.

The above is all very well in principle. In reality, people in the workplace are very busy and sometimes work on opposite sides of the globe, so keeping up with team communication can be difficult. Equally, individual performance may be focused on specific operational targets, and team-building activities may not be rewarded. Some of the problems that occur in teams are:

- The team is a virtual team made up of people scattered across the globe who don't find it easy to communicate.

- Each individual wants to be *the* success story or leader within the group so as to come out of it with the greatest accolade – and possibly the greatest bonus!

✔ Teams are supposed to work together as a flat structure, and yet the structure of the organisation in terms of grades, promotions, and bonuses is set up to drive competitiveness between individuals.

✔ Teams make many assumptions about what people do or don't know about the project or goal.

✔ People have irrational expectations that other people should, ought to, or must behave the way they want them to, and can't accept it if they don't.

✔ Cliques develop who work well together but exclude or alienate other members of the team.

✔ The manager has favourites who are privy to information and have the most prestigious aspects of a project delegated to them.

None of these problems is disastrous, but any or several of them can interrupt the cooperation of the group to succeed in the achievement of its goals.

CBC enables the team members to stop and reflect on their behaviours and whether they are supporting priority activities. It provides the opportunity to review *how* the team members work together alongside *what* they are doing to achieve targets.

When coaching a team, you can help the group:

✔ Reflect on any existing or potential issues they may have in working together

✔ Agree objectives and ensure that they do share a common vision

✔ Understand diverse approaches, talents, and strengths, and leverage these

✔ Check assumptions and expectations to ensure that they're rational and helpful

✔ Develop strategies for open communication that bridge different styles, including guidelines for managing conflict

✔ Develop creative problem-solving practices

✔ Ensure that daily routines of working practice support peak performance

✔ Encourage analysis and critical thinking, but discourage negativity

✔ Focus on the positives so as to raise morale, motivation, and action towards agreed goals

Your role as a CB coach is to take the group through a process in which the team members make decisions for themselves about how they may think and behave differently in future. You can introduce the team members to CBC theories and models so that they develop the ability to apply the methods, including:

✔ Understanding the impact that thoughts have on feelings and behaviours

✔ Checking assumptions or mind-reading that has not been clarified

✔ Evaluating whether expectations of one another are reasonable

✔ Developing constructive and affirmative thoughts to support the achievement of shared goals

As in individual coaching, your role as a CB coach is to help the team reach solutions by posing questions rather than advising on what to do. The questioning techniques included in Chapter 1 can easily be adapted for teams.

Checking clarity of purpose

Managers can be so pressurised and focused on operational targets that they assume that team members understand the aims and purpose that the group is working towards. The CB coach checks that each person does, in fact, have a clear idea of what the team is trying to achieve, over what period of time. It works well to allow a short period of individual reflection on each of the questions below, followed by each person sharing his experiences in small groups around a flipchart. You would then draw together the group's input in a plenary session to ensure that the whole team ends up with a clear understanding of:

✔ Who are we?

✔ Where are we going?

✔ How are we going to get there?

✔ What part can I play to reach this goal?

Team members can find it surprisingly difficult to question group behaviours that have built up over a period of time. People who have worked together for several years sometimes do not fully understand what a colleague does, or with whom he has to liaise and share knowledge. Rather than confront the issue, people can say 'yes' at a meeting but not fully understand what is expected of them or not buy in to the task. The CBC team session enables people to raise these questions and find ways of addressing any underlying problems that exist within the team.

The only way to ensure that everyone is working from the same song sheet is to ask them individually for their own versions of a team target. For example, during a recent merging of departments, some of the diverse views of the change project were:

- ✔ I have to complete these spreadsheets.

- ✔ I have to produce a Gantt chart of what will be achieved over a period of time.

- ✔ We are going to provide a better service to our clients.

- ✔ We will be a more streamlined department, working more efficiently.

- ✔ I have to create new software solutions to merge the two departments' systems.

- ✔ I am assuming they mean that I have to liaise with the team in Germany, but I am not quite sure why, when, or how.

- ✔ Oh, here we go again with another change. I'm just going to do what I have always done until someone tells me precisely what else I am expected to do.

- ✔ I don't understand what they want – why can't they talk in plain language instead of jargon?

You can see that the way each individual is thinking about a project can help or hinder success. Team coaching can help to clarify assumptions and raise and confirm facts and expectations. You would help the group to understand the part each individual plays in achieving the final result.

You can allow each team member time to write down his own version of what he assumes is required. The group can then share their individual versions on a whiteboard, mind map (a graphic way of organising ideas and information, described in Chapter 5), or flipchart, and you can draw out the themes that may relate to functions or actions, so that mutual understanding evolves.

Thoughts are invisible, and thoughts are where misunderstandings between team members may occur, with one person imagining that others must know how he feels, or assuming that he has shared a solution or a piece of information when in fact he hasn't (or the other person wasn't listening). A visual record of the goals and objectives on a screen, flipchart, or whiteboard provides a consensual view that all can see and share. This view provides the opportunity (and the responsibility) to express any concerns, queries, or ideas about the outcomes.

Leveraging Diverse Approaches

A team comprises many different people, with different skills, talents, and experiences. The team is a talent bank that can be invested in to produce value, or it can be a wasted asset. Each member of the team can benefit from using time to identify how to value the diversity that exists in the group and develop strategies to leverage this resource for the good of everyone.

Identifying styles and strengths

Any team consists of individuals, and each person is unique. Team members will differ in how they think about work, how they manage their emotions, and their styles of communication and behaviour. Problems often occur in groups when one or more team members are of a different type. I list some individual behavioural styles below, with an example of how each behaviour may differ from those of other members of the team:

- ✔ **Analytical:** Working with detail, facts, and figures and wanting to examine everything with precision before taking actions. Others may be more creative, talking in themes and concepts, less interested in data or statistics and more interested in the big picture.

- ✔ **Extrovert and talkative:** Working out thoughts and ideas 'out there' in the conversation or discussion that arises. Others may be introvert, developing their thoughts and ideas through inner reflection, evaluating their contributions carefully before opening their mouths and sharing them.

- ✔ **People-oriented:** Focusing on feelings and mood, on how people work together, whether they're communicating well both within the team and with other teams and customers. Others may be more interested in setting up practical or technical systems, procedures, and processes to drive forward results.

You have several psychometric *profiling methods* at your disposal to evaluate individual personality and behavioural traits. A profile provides information that helps team members understand why some people get on easily whereas others are in conflict and confusion. Generally, you carry out an assessment on each individual within the team, followed by a group session where the team members share the findings and decide how best to apply the readings to enhance communication and performance. Some examples of profiling methods include the following:

✔ **Belbin:** This method identifies team roles, such as whether someone is a completer-finisher, plant, resource-investigator, monitor-evaluator, shaper, co-ordinator, team worker, implementer, or specialist.

✔ **DiSC:** This method assesses *dominance* (the desire to take power and control of one's environment, win, excel, conquer, affect one's own future); *influence* (the desire to cause others to act to further your own aspirations, be liked and accepted, project a good personal image); *stability* (the desire to maintain things as they are, be secure, work slowly, be reasonable and sincere, question, and gather information); *compliance* (the desire to have an ordered society, clear rules and criteria, and a system developed through perfect logic and analysis).

✔ **Herrmann Brain Dominance Instrument® (HBDI):** This assesses thinking preference in four quadrants based on the specialised brain (earlier known as Left-brain/right-brain.). The quadrants are: A, Blue, (Rational/ Analytical); B Green, (Organisers/Safekeepers); C, Red, (Empathisers/ Feeling-oriented); D, Yellow, (Synergisers/Experimental).

Thinking preference influences how people process information, the priorities and satisfaction they have for certain factors of their work, their decision making and how they communicate. Refer to Chapter 15 for more on HBDI.

✔ **Myers–Briggs Type Indicator (MBTI):** This method measures psychological preferences in how a person perceives the world and makes decisions, identifying whether he is extrovert or introvert, gathers information through sensing or intuition, makes decisions through thinking or feeling, and plans or runs his lifestyle through judging or perceiving.

You can easily encompass these models into CBC team coaching. The profiles provide an immediate stimulus for discussion and make sure that you emphasise that there is no 'right' or 'wrong' way to be: each way is different and unique. Whether people totally agree with their profiles – and you're not saying that the profiles are the 'truth', only a suggested insight – people generally gain understanding both of themselves and their colleagues. I find that in providing a theoretical model that explains difference, people gain a real 'aha!' moment as to why they're not finding it easy to communicate or understand one another. There can also often be a great deal of laughter, with comments such as 'Oh, *that's* why we never understand one another!' Each individual develops the ability to shape his information in a way that is meaningful to the style of the other person, rather than only communicating from his own perspective.

Teams can discover how to value difference and recognise that no one person ever has all the answers or sees all the perspectives: that is why we need each other. In my experience, team relationships become deeper through team coaching.

Self-knowledge and understanding of others sets the ground for people to leverage diverse strengths and talents for the good of the whole group. Instead of a team saying to someone 'different' 'This is the way we do things around here so you'd better do the same,' they can begin to say 'Well, this is how we have done things in the past – how might you approach this issue?' This attitude allows for greater creativity and lateral approaches. Work with the group members to identify how their individual thoughts are influencing their relationships. Are they being judgemental about someone who is different to them? What thoughts and behaviours can help them to devise a better way of working together in future?

Understanding the role of the manager or team leader

The team manager can find out how to bring out the best in each individual so as to enhance the performance of the whole group. His own personal style and preference inevitably influences which team members he feels more comfortable with. However, he also needs to concentrate on those with whom he feels least comfortable, because these people can provide the diversity of approach that can benefit the group.

One aspect of organisational life that I have observed is that many structures and systems are based primarily on rational, analytical, and procedural methodologies, or what is termed as a 'left brain' approach. Often, this approach is most highly regarded by management. In today's world of service and knowledge-based industries, the 'right-brain' approach of innovation, vision, and customer focus are essential if organisations are to spot the next trend or customer need and retain their competitive edge. You can help the team leader to value both perspectives so as to gain a more holistic approach. Refer to Chapter 15 for more information.

Help the team leader to involve all team members in discussions, and watch out for the extroverts doing all the talking. It can be hard to engage the quieter members of the team, but their ideas and solutions can bring different perspectives. Introverts often don't make their ideas heard in organisations because they're uncomfortable sharing their thoughts in a large group, though may do so in smaller groups. The team manager may be missing out on these views.

Conference calls and large meetings may be daunting for introvert thinkers, who may be uncomfortable sharing information in a large group or until they've a 'perfect' solution. An introvert can be encouraged to understand that even if the others are noisier, their own ideas may well be as relevant.

They may find it easier to share discussion in small groups or with the manager before the meeting, rather than be expected to speak up in a large group.

The *meetings model* provides structure to enable people to develop thoughts and behaviours that help them break through natural reserve or overcome their fear of failure. CBC can help the group identify actions to ease these issues. You can use the model to plan a meeting, individually or as a group. The model poses the following questions:

- What is your ideal outcome?
- What are the benefits to you and others of this outcome?
- In order to be at your most able to support that outcome, how do you need to feel emotionally?
- When you generally have that emotional feeling, how does your body language change?
- How can you visualise the meeting going well?
- What key things do you want to say?
- How can you make sure that you really listen to what other people have got to say and understand their points of view?
- How can you make your point in a way and using language that others 'hear' and acknowledge, rather than in your own language and with your own priorities?
- How can you make sure that you talk to them adult-to-adult (cooperative, equal, problem-solving), not parent (high status talking down), nor child (low status talking up)? Refer to Chapter 11 for more information.
- How can you visualise the other person in adult-to-adult images – for example, whatever his physical presence, you and he are looking at one another eye to eye?
- How can you make sure that you feel you've as much right to equal power and self-expression within a relationship as any other person has?
- What thought or thoughts can help you to maintain all the above during the meeting?
- What clothes can you wear to help you feel confident?
- What physical environment or meeting place supports your goals?
- What action do you need to take to be prepared?

Through team coaching, the team leader can gain insight into how he can help different people communicate, share, and even to disagree with others. Without diverse approaches, the team can never 'catch' or perceive the full picture that they need to take into account when working through problems and challenges. Conflict of opinion can lead to more creative debate. You may well be working individually with the team leader to plan the team session. The manager or team leader can:

✔ Explain that difference does not mean argument

✔ Explain that each person is entitled to his own thoughts and opinions

✔ Explain that each different opinion adds to the richness of the picture and information that the team needs to take into account in order to solve problems and manage projects

✔ Explain that another person's opinion does not threaten a person's security or position, but is just that – an opinion

✔ Ensure that people do not present opinions as facts

✔ Keep people focused on the common objectives of the group

✔ Maintain the balance to ensure that critical thinking is valued but is also set in the context of optimism

✔ Explain that ideas, information, and opinions do not constitute labelling. Team members should avoid personal comments such as 'You're stupid if you don't get this opinion,' and instead say 'Do I need to explain this more clearly?'; and 'You're always negative and difficult' rather 'When you do. . . (specific incident) I find it difficult.'

The CB coach facilitates this process by helping managers and team members to identify their own needs and share them with others, so as to develop new ways of working that ensure the smooth running of the whole group.

Appreciating expectations and accountability

Each person within a team is accountable to the whole team for the success of a project. Each member needs to be empowered and clear about his own strengths and unique contribution, so that he doesn't helplessly look to other people to solve his problems for him.

When a person is unclear about his role or is in conflict with someone with a different approach, it can sabotage team efforts, for example if he withholds vital information or drags his heels in not completing a piece of work. This sabotage can directly impact results.

You can ask each team member to share with the group his understanding of:

- ✔ His strengths and expertise, and how they can apply them
- ✔ His role and specific responsibilities
- ✔ The people with whom he needs to liaise and cooperate

Sharing individual perspectives ensures that all team members know each other's roles and responsibilities. People can also comment and ask questions to clarify any concerns, and offer suggestions to enable the group to work more effectively together in future.

The following is a feedback exercise you can apply, allowing each person to share:

- ✔ This is what I enjoy and find rewarding about working with you. . .
- ✔ This is what I am expecting of you. . . : is this how you're thinking of it?
- ✔ This is what I find difficult about working with you. . .
- ✔ This is what I would like you to do differently if you're able. . .
- ✔ This is what I think we can do to work more effectively together in future. . .

The focus of this exercise is the future, not the past. Make sure the exercise is not a session where people moan or criticise others for the sake of it. You need to manage the group to be constructive and maintain a focus on solutions for enhancing team working.

When people are fundamentally different in style, and criticism and judgement have become a part of their relationship – for example: 'He should do it this way because that's the way I need him to do it' – try asking CBC questions such as:

- ✔ Just because you'd rather this person behaved this way, how is it logical that he must?
- ✔ What might he need or want you to do differently?
- ✔ What part is your own thinking, emotion, and behaviour playing in upsetting this relationship?

Check that the team members' expectations of one another are reasonable. Encourage thoughts such as 'I would prefer it if. . . behaved in this way, but I can accept that he does things differently, and can manage the situation anyway.'

Focus on individual thoughts and solutions that support open communication and a mutual effort to work together towards common goals.

Encouraging teamwork, not competition

Team members often need to put ego second and common good first. This attitude is not always easy to achieve. The competitive spirit has often been instilled in people from schooldays and can be healthy. You can help individuals to understand that they have options about how they think and approach situations. Rather than operating from a habitual knee-jerk response, they can identify situations where they're being helpful and rational by being competitive, and other situations where they may choose to put their competitive feelings aside and focus on cooperation instead. Instead of thinking 'I must win and be the one who stands out as the most successful person in the group,' they can start to think 'Sometimes I can push myself to stand out, but at other times group success is more important and my success can be derived from the benefit of the whole.'

Although all teams need a leader, teams depend on individuals pulling together, not seeking to stand out. This pulling together can be difficult when promotion and reward procedures may recognise those in the limelight.

When team members are competitive and lose sight of the common goal, they may fall back into power struggles. Such struggles can lead to anger, resentment, manipulation, jealousy, hurt, or generally stroppy behaviour.

Competition can happen within teams and between teams. For example, frequent problems and resentments often exist between back-office and front-office staff in business, the public sector, the health service, and the police force. People may lose the ability to focus on common ground, and instead take their polarised stances. Through CBC, you can reconnect the people in a team to:

✔ **Common aims and purpose:** The underlying function of the group and the specific goals that the team is in business to achieve.

✔ **Common ground:** This includes concerns, stresses, environment, and expectations.

> ✔ **Inter-dependencies:** For example, traders cannot function without the administrative function, managers without doctors, doctors without nurses, entrepreneurs without financiers, and so on.
>
> ✔ **Key thoughts, emotions and behaviours:** In particular, ones that bring their efforts together in one consolidated effort rather than as individuals or groups pulling in separate directions.

Some members of the team may be happy to take a step back, and may feel better working quietly or alone. These may be technical thinkers or experts in their fields, who the team calls upon for specific information, but who may not have to play an integrated team part all the time. Emphasise that the success of the whole reflects the success of each individual and vice versa. Teams always have leaders and followers: teams are a place where leaders evolve and emerge. However, a leader needs the group as much as the group needs the leader. Discuss how the team can build strategies to create the environment that supports each person's individual approach.

Aligning Action for Common Goals

Common focus of action is key to successful teams. This focus is not always easy to achieve because individuals are busy with individual responsibilities and deadlines. People may make assumptions that another team member knows what he is supposed to do, or duplicate a task that has already been completed. Clear communication is therefore essential for aligning action.

Pulling together through challenges

Teams often face challenges: targets, deadlines, complex problems or projects, and personality issues. Team members have to pull together even when they may not feel enthusiastic about doing so, rising above the difficulties.

With specific projects and goals, you can suggest that the group applies the ABCDE model in order to agree the type of thoughts and emotions that aid success. (Refer to Chapter 2 for more on this model.) You can write the model up on a whiteboard and collect individual thoughts around the situation being discussed.

A team was demotivated about not winning a client. We worked through the ABCDE exercise, as I show in Table 18-1.

Table 18-1		Team ABCDE Exercise		
A: Activating Event	*B: Belief or Expectation*	*C: Emotion and Behaviour*	*D: Disputing how Helpful or Rational B is*	*E: Exchanging Thoughts*
e.g. client pitch	*They'll never buy it.*	Fear, anxiety impacting the 'feel' of the presentation, including words used, body language, and voice tone	'Never' is a big word – what would make them buy it?	*We can do a good job.*
	We're not perfectly prepared.		Is there such a thing as perfect?	*We have as good a chance as any other team to win this job.*
	We haven't got all the answers.		Would anyone ever have all the answers?	*We are excellent; no-one is perfect.*
			How else can we approach this?	*We can go in there feeling positive.*

Through CBC, you can help the group devise strategies for managing challenges when they arise by:

1. **Setting goals.** What would success look like?

2. **Identifying likely issues, blocks, and problems,** and planning strategies to address them if they arise.

3. **Agreeing actions and behaviours** that move the group towards a successful result.

4. **Identifying thoughts** that support constructive team behaviours.

Each team member has a responsibility for the impact he has on other people in the team, particularly during difficult times when everyone is under pressure.

Try asking individuals to write down words that others may use to describe them personally during a stressful period. Suggest that they're honest with themselves about these words. You may or may not choose to ask them to share the words they've listed so as to clarify whether other people are, in fact, thinking about them in this way. Point out that unless they have specific evidence, the words may be without basis other than mind-reading and assumption.

Now suggest that team members write down a set of words that they would like other people to apply to them, and ask them whether they need to make any changes in their behaviour in order to receive those comments. For example, a person may write down that he wants to be seen as cooperative and less confrontational during challenging times. You need to prompt him to consider what action he has to take to become more cooperative.

This model can be a useful one to use to enable the group members to agree how they can manage difficult periods in future. In Table 18-2, I show the process that the team can work through in order to identify behaviours they want to drop and those new behaviours they want to adopt.

Table 18-2	Changing Team Behaviours		
Challenge	*Old Behaviour*	*New Behaviour*	*Constructive Thoughts to Support New Behaviour*
Complex project with deadline	Long hours, becoming irritable, sick absence, taking anger out on partner when getting home	Rotating cover, ensuring that colleagues eat properly. Not staying late out of habit. Asking for help instead of being a martyr.	'We can cooperate during challenging projects instead of each blaming the other for our stress.'

Demonstrate to the group that the words they choose to use with one another during challenging times have an emotional impact on the person receiving them. They need to consider language carefully in order to maintain good team relationships. Examples include:

✔ 'You haven't put enough detail into that presentation' may make someone feel a failure. Instead, the person could have said 'Have you thought about including. . . next time you present?'

✔ 'Why don't you share client information with me. You're a lousy communicator' labels the other person a bad communicator. This comment could have been phrased: 'It would be helpful to have the latest information on our client before the meeting next time. Can we set up a system for sharing and updating?'

You're not suggesting that individuals should not raise the issues. Nor are you recommending that everyone has to be 'nice' to one another all the time. Business results still need to be achieved. Instead, you're aiming to help the group members to find a more constructive and collaborative way of working together to achieve good results.

A *team charter* provides a record of desired behaviours, rights, and responsibilities. Identify behaviours that support the smooth running of teamwork. Then ask the group to decide which of those behaviours they think are 'rights'. Finally, ask them to identify what they consider, in the light of these rights, are their personal responsibilities for action. I show an example in Table 18-3.

Table 18-3	Team Charter	
Desired Behaviours	*Rights*	*Responsibilities*
e.g. open communication	Updating others with relevant information and events	Sally: I shall send an updating email once a week with the latest information on what I have personally been doing.
		Ed: I shall share info from Germany with the team.

Using a team charter, you can capture the thoughts that drive the behaviours that the team identifies. In this way, each team member has articulated and shared with others the actions he considers he is responsible for.

Using the power of optimism

A balance towards optimism aids success. Most groups have a few negative thinkers or pessimists. Workplaces always have those who congregate in corners or around the coffee machine to moan about the latest initiative or 'the management'. There may equally be a few 'Pollyanna' thinkers, who see everything as wonderful and are irrationally positive.

The psychologist Dr Martin Seligman, Chairman of the University of Pennsylvania Positive Psychology Center, has researched optimism extensively. His research demonstrates that people can grow to be optimistic. Optimism within a team increases:

✔ Health

✔ Innovation

✔ Longevity

✔ Morale and motivation

✔ Sales

✔ Success of entrepreneurial effort

Through team coaching, people can begin to engage with the power of optimism without losing the faculty to evaluate information in an analytical or critical way.

Pessimism can lower morale and may well not be accurate. The devil's advocate who challenges every new idea or solution can be helped to understand how that feels for others on an emotional level. He may think it perfectly rational on a cerebral level, but not have understood how constant negative challenge can demotivate people and sometimes even stop them sharing ideas.

The over-optimistic 'Pollyanna' thinker can become aware of how he needs to be sensitive to the realities of life. For example, problems do exist in business and can't be ignored. However, they can be addressed and managed.

Asking a question can be more effective than 'telling'. It makes the person think more carefully and identify a rational balance that is optimistic but realistic. I show a few examples in Table 18-4.

Table 18-4	Challenging Pessimism to Develop Optimism
Statement: When Someone Says...	*Question*
'Everything is going perfectly.'	'What are some of the challenges that the team is facing at the moment?'
'No-one supports me.'	'Who exactly does support you?'
'Everything's screwed up.'	'What specifically has gone well?'
'The client will never buy it.'	'What would make them buy it?'

Optimism encompasses hope and energises people to action. Believing that something can be successful is more likely to make it successful. Suggest that the team members record optimistic statements that motivate them to mutually beneficial action.

Part V
The Part of Tens

"Well, the first thing we have to do is get you
motivated for work again, Mr. Clampkiss."

In this part . . .

If it's a For Dummies book, it's got a Part of Tens, and this is no exception. In this part I give lots of quick reference hints and tips, including ten ways to help people develop a positive focus, and ten imagery exercises to develop confidence.

I also provide gentle reminders to you, as the coach, to remember that both you and your client are human and fallible. We all screw up occasionally, so I include tips about self-acceptance and continuous development.

Chapter 19

Ten Ways to Develop a Positive Focus

*H*ow we think shapes how we feel. The focus of our thoughts is therefore the key to emotional equilibrium. I believe that the quality of our life depends far more on the quality of our thoughts than on the events we experience. Thinking about our thinking and switching the nature and focus of our thoughts can enhance our quality of lives.

Everyone has ups and downs, but even in the worst times we can maintain control of how we respond to those events and find a way to manage our feelings. If we focus on how awful an experience is, we may incapacitate ourselves and undermine our ability to cope, often with the result that we feel more miserable than the event deserves. A thought such as 'This experience is difficult, but I have the capacity to manage it in the best way I can' is likely to be more helpful than 'I can't stand it.'

CBC provides your client with thinking systems to address the many and varied situations she experiences in life and in the workplace. In this chapter, I give you a few quick tips to share with your client about how to maintain a positive focus of attention, not in an unrealistic way but in a way that is balanced and in perspective.

Avoid Living in an Imagined Future

Many fears exist in our imagination rather than in reality – but those fears spoil the moment. This thinking pattern is known as *fortune-telling*: we imagine the worst without evidence that the worst is happening.

Examples of worries that create anxiety include fear of flying, worrying that someone is late home, imagining that economic downturn inevitably means recession, and worrying about poverty or homelessness when you still have a roof over your head, a job, and money in the bank.

If the worst happens, your client can take action. In the meantime, she can do whatever she can to avoid negative events. Beyond that, your client can relax and appreciate what she still has. Enjoy the moment, or it can be wasted.

Be Specific – Don't Generalise

Show your client how to check facts around generalisations such as 'always', 'nothing', 'no-one', 'never', 'always', 'everyone', and 'everything'.

Consider the following phrases:

- ✔ My boss *always* focuses on what I have done wrong.
- ✔ *Nothing* ever goes my way.
- ✔ *Everyone* says that movie is brilliant.

Now replace the phrases above with the following:

- ✔ Has there ever been a time when your boss focused on something you did right?
- ✔ Can you think of an example of what has gone your way?
- ✔ How many people have you actually spoken to who have seen the movie?

Generalisations seldom reflect reality, and people often use them for dramatic effect. Help your client to get into the habit of listening out for these words both in her own thoughts and also in the language of others.

Change Your Thinking, Change Your Life

How we think influences how we feel. How we feel determines whether we enjoy life or not. Going through life thinking about what isn't working, who doesn't like or approve of you, and what is wrong about your body, your partner, your financial situation, or your job, makes life a pretty miserable experience. Focusing on what is working and what you can value in yourself, others, and the situations you face leads to greater happiness and quality of life.

Suggest that your client keeps a journal for a week, recording all she values and appreciates. At the following session, discuss whether keeping a diary has made a difference to her level of happiness during that period of time. The diary can become a daily practice that enables her to achieve greater quality of life.

Don't Catastrophise

Don't over-dramatise. Life happens. Things go wrong. But make sure that your client knows how to differentiate between the serious problems and the everyday blips and challenges. Some questions your client can apply:

- ✔ How important will this issue be in 12 months' time?
- ✔ What makes this problem so awful?
- ✔ Am I making a drama out of this situation to get attention?
- ✔ What's the worst that can happen here?
- ✔ What resources do I have to manage this situation?
- ✔ Who can help me?
- ✔ What thoughts help me feel confident about managing this situation?

Build up your client's confidence that she has the personal resilience to manage the situation. Focus on the thoughts and actions that help to manage it.

Also define which of your client's problems are within her control and which are not: no-one should sweat over things she can't change!

Focus on Your Strengths and Achievements

To focus on the positive, we have to *notice* the positive. Make sure that you open your client's eyes to the good things that exist around her and that she has created through her lifetime. Some examples to share with your client include:

- ✔ Consider your work role and make a list of all the skills and competencies that you contribute to that role.
- ✔ Don't delete the positives. Instead, focus your attention on them. Success builds success.

✓ Look around your home and observe purchases you've made that reflect your choice and taste – books, CDs, paintings, posters, furniture, plants, flowers, electronic equipment, clothes, and photos. Appreciate the quality they bring to your life and congratulate yourself on your choices.

✓ Notice the small actions you achieve every day – you can include putting laundry in the washing machine, responding to an email, and making a sales call as positive actions.

✓ Relish the special moments you experience, whether in love, in nature, on your travels, through meditation – any place or situation where you feel a sense of connection to life.

✓ Remember your achievements and successes such as work projects, exams, discovering how to play an instrument, or getting a job.

✓ Think about your family, friends, colleagues, and the people you attract into your life. Recall what they see in you, compliments they make, and your contribution to the relationships.

Get Evidence – Don't Assume

Assumptions lead people astray. Rather than assume that someone thinks negatively about us, we need to check for evidence. People damage many relationships because they imagine that someone else is thinking ill of them, and this imagining can lead to defensive or aggressive behaviour which is based on supposition rather than reality.

We mustn't assume that somebody knows what we want her to do. We need to check with her or just tell her. Mind-reading is not an accurate skill: the man who assumes that his partner *knows* what he wants for his birthday may be disappointed. Likewise, the manager who assumes that her direct report *knows* what she requires may fuel a potential misunderstanding.

Your client needs to have the courage to ask for evidence and facts and deal with realities. Otherwise, she may be worrying herself needlessly. If a problem does exist then at least she can address it rather than working around erroneous thinking.

Keep Things in Perspective

Avoid all-or-nothing thinking. Many people have the habit of seeing things as perfect or as disastrous, infeasible, or impossible. This kind of thinking is seldom accurate. Support your client's ability to be rational and logical in the way she thinks about a situation by developing evaluating questions such as:

- ✔ Just because something didn't work once, does it mean that it won't in future?
- ✔ Am I only seeing the negatives in this situation?
- ✔ Are there shades of grey here?
- ✔ Which aspects of this situation can help me to achieve my goals?

Enable your client to gain a balanced perspective that supports her ability to move towards her objectives.

Stop Letting Emotions Lead to Conclusions

Emotional mood leads people to inappropriate actions. You can help your client to ensure that her feelings do not cloud her judgement of a situation. For example, someone may be feeling extremely happy and loving one day and make the assumption that her new boyfriend is feeling the same, and shower him with an inappropriate amount of affection. Someone who is feeling gloomy may make the judgement that no-one else in her team feels energised enough to make the sales call to a new client. Someone who is feeling guilty searches for a reason and remembers some small lapse of consideration towards her father, which she blows up to be a worse omission than it really is.

Feelings aren't facts. Your client can find out how to observe her emotions and be more objective in her responses: 'Just because I am feeling this way, does it actually mean that the situation is. . . ?'

Think Flexibly

Through CBC, people develop flexibility of mind, observe their thoughts, and check whether they can think in different ways about situations. Useful questions to stimulate flexibility of perspective include:

- ✔ How might someone else see this situation?
- ✔ In how many different ways can you approach this?

Listen for words such as 'must', 'ought to', 'should', 'need to', and 'got to', and challenge the basic demands that your client makes of herself, others, and the situations she faces. Statements such as 'I must format this presentation in this template' and 'I ought to agree to do this task even though the task is not my responsibility' can be challenged by:

✔ 'Who says?'

✔ 'What would happen if you didn't?'

✔ 'Where is it written that you must?'

✔ 'How else can you approach this problem?'

Often, habit shapes our behaviour. Your client can start to question the demands that she makes of herself and to question her demands on others. This questioning can liberate your client and lead to the development of new ways of thinking about and approaching situations. Ultimately, your client realises that her own rules are not everyone's rules – that often no written rules exist to say that someone *must* do a task in a particular way.

Try Not to Label

One failure does not make someone a 'failure'; one inconsiderate action does not make someone 'inconsiderate'. Develop your client's ability to focus on specific behaviours, actions, and events and not give a person a label that is universal. For example: 'I felt it was inconsiderate when you didn't help me with that heavy case' (one event) rather than 'You're so inconsiderate' (a label).

Labels such as 'good' or 'bad' are seldom accurate, because people are unlikely to be consistently good or bad all the time. Labels such as 'selfish', 'unkind', or 'arrogant' are frequently subjective generalisations, so encourage your client to recognise that she also needs to take other perspectives into account.

In fact, people label countries, organisations, governments, the National Health Service, the police, or a particular race, culture, religion, or class on information that is often based on little more than one article they happened to read in the paper, or one person's opinion, rather than the whole story.

Chapter 20

Ten Ways to Accept You're Human

*F*inding the balance between valuing your unique personality and yet not imagining you are special is difficult. Being happy in your skin can take a lifetime. Accepting your humanity and human fallibility is an integral part of CBC theory. No human being is perfect – but equally no human being is completely imperfect. By valuing both his strengths and his weaknesses, your client can accept himself as a human being. In this chapter, I provide tips on helping your client accept himself and the fact he's human.

Comparing Yourself with Others Isn't Worth the Effort

Each person has special talents and strengths and unique experiences of life. Some achieve greatness, others steadiness, others power, others financial security, others spiritual contentment, others reward through helping people. As Epictetus wrote in around 100 AD: 'Seek not that the things which happen should happen as you wish; but wish the things which happen to be as they are, and you will have a tranquil flow of life.'

Yet the green eyes of jealousy and envy can lead people to compare themselves with others and feel 'less than': 'Why can't I have that house, car, figure, outfit, wife, money, job, opportunity, happy family. . . ?' Such thoughts usually lead your client to feel miserable. He loses sight of the advantages and benefits he has and focuses only on what others have. This attitude can result in a feeling of loss, a chip on the shoulder, defensiveness, bitterness, or resentment.

Your client can begin to recognise when comparison is useful and when comparison is meaningless. Measurement of performance, productivity, and targets has become a part of life in the workplace, and can serve a purpose when well administered. But generally, human beings and human lives are too complex to compare in any really measurable way. One person may have greater wealth than another, but measuring happiness or contentment is notoriously difficult because every person experiences both joy and pain during a lifetime. An apparently idyllic life from the outside can sometimes mask a tragedy. For example, a family living in a luxury home, with plenty of money, and beautiful loving children may be experiencing a tragedy on the inside: bereavement, sickness, addiction, and depression can affect anyone. You only have to look at the struggles of certain celebrities to realise that the perfect life does not exist. Fame and fortune do not necessarily equate to happiness.

Success and happiness are subjective. CBC techniques help people to appreciate what they value, and pursue the goals they personally find meaningful.

Everybody's Unique

No human being alive is precisely like your client – and there will never be a human quite like him again. His DNA and genes, the thoughts and feelings he experiences second by second, and the environment in which he grew up and spends his time are totally unique.

Show your client how to use this uniqueness of perspective to contribute to life, his workplace, and his family and friends. Many people find this attitude difficult. They self-censor, thinking 'Other people must have had this idea before' or 'They may think this idea is stupid.' Yet he may well find that others won't have had exactly that thought, because no-one else has the same brain or has had the same experiences.

Not all of us do 'great' or 'famous' things, but all of us can stamp our mark on the world in some way, through friendships, through family, through work, through kind words or deeds, through the emotional energy we create. Help your client to identify the factors about himself that he considers to be unique and plan how he can share these with others.

He may make excuses why he can't make his mark – perhaps status of birth, or a specific problem. However, many people overcome adversity to stamp their unique potential on the world during their lifetimes – look at an event like the Paralympics. So help your client to value whatever he can offer and be prepared to take whatever action is necessary to leave his personal legacy.

Everyone Needs Help Occasionally

We all need help and support. This need is part of being human.

Many people imagine that being independent and not asking for help shows strength. But showing vulnerability and calling on others acknowledges the fact that no human being knows it all or possesses all skills. Help your client to understand that the more emotionally mature person usually accepts that other people bring perspectives and strengths that he does not have.

CBC does not produce robots who never feel down or upset. Enable your client to accept that he needs a shoulder to cry on occasionally and friends to help him solve problems. Suggest that your client builds up a network of people on whom to call for emotional support, for practical help, for business advice, for networking socially or professionally, and for wise counsel and advice.

Life Always Has Its Challenges

However much CBC we undertake, however well developed we are personally and professionally, life has a habit of tipping us off our pedestals occasionally. We may achieve greater emotional equilibrium through applying the CBC models and then an adverse event pushes us right back where we started. Such setbacks can be difficult for your client, so help him to prepare for the ups and downs of life.

All kinds of events can suddenly interrupt your client's calm: something someone says, falling in love, being hurt by his partner, a threat to his security at work, or an economic or political event. In a moment, your client forgets the skills he has developed and he shouts at someone, bursts into tears, or reverts to old thoughts and behaviours. Encourage your client not to chastise himself for falling off his perch and being human.

Help your client develop an emergency toolkit to call upon in difficult times – identifying an affirmative statement, developing new ways of thinking or approaching the situation, taking a deep breath, or practising asking for time out.

Your client can become his own coach, staying mindful through the challenge so that he can analyse and rationalise his response and identify a constructive approach. Gradually your client develops greater resilience to challenges and knows that he can pull a CBC technique out of his toolkit.

CBC makes life easier to manage – but never a total cinch.

Nobody's Body's Perfect

Few human beings accept their bodies uncritically. Part of the human condition seems to be finding fault with your own appearance. Your client can gain a rational and balanced perspective of his body by starting at a position of self-acceptance and a will to enhance what's good rather than change what's bad.

Knowing what I do now and applying CBC I realise that I could have appreciated my body more, earlier in my life. Now, in my 50s, I could find it easy to see faults and wonder who that person is in the mirror. But the person is the me that I am, and in ten years' time one thing is certain – that body will be older – so I have discovered how to appreciate how it is today.

Ask you client to focus on the good parts of his body. What can he value? What works? For example, consider the autonomic systems of heart, digestion, breathing, thinking, and sensing. He needs to appreciate as much as possible, even if his body is a little fatter or thinner than he prefers. That body is an essential part of what is giving him life: a vessel. Accepting his physical presence provides a springboard to gain even greater fitness and health.

Not Everyone's Watching You

Some people personalise events and life. They claim 'I can't possibly go jogging, because I'd look stupid.' Or they say: 'I can't walk into a bar by myself, because people may look at me.'

But everyone is *not* thinking about, talking about, or watching your client. He is not the centre of everyone else's universe: other people are more likely to be busy thinking about something completely different – usually themselves!

Encourage your client to accept that he *can* go jogging or walk into a bar, because he probably won't be noticed. Your client is just another member of the human race. Recognising your normality can be liberating and enable people to do things they previously had been fearful about.

The Perfect Human Being Doesn't Exist

Has anyone ever met a perfect human being? Perfect in every way? Or a totally imperfect human being, with absolutely no good points whatsoever?

Everyone has good points and bad points – and so does your client. Explain to your client why measuring up against some impossible, irrational, non-existent standard isn't a great idea. Encourage him to focus instead on his good points and to make a list of areas that he wants to change or develop.

Some people are defensive and unable to admit their weaknesses, and focus only on their strengths. Others see only their weaknesses. Through CBC, your client can begin to accept that he is unique but imperfect – just like everyone else. He can still seek to develop his potential throughout his life-time, benefiting from mistakes and arriving at a more realistic self-image of himself and others.

Encourage your client to pursue excellence, not perfection.

We're All Fallible

We all make mistakes sometimes. Most people occasionally tell little white lies, feel jealous, gossip behind someone's back, forget a birthday, betray a school friend, say or do something they later regret, forget to make an important call, or let down a colleague. These omissions are all part of being human.

No-one goes through life without making mistakes, occasionally hurting someone or disappointing themselves and others. But some people give themselves an unbelievably hard time when they do something stupid, some-thing human. You can help your client to accept that making mistakes is a natural part of life. Every human being is fallible, and messing up occasion-ally is inevitable.

Being honest about when we have screwed up, or apologising for harsh words that we have said to someone or erroneous assumptions that we have acted upon with adverse affects, is a stronger and more rational way of being. 'I'd prefer it if I hadn't done that, but I can benefit from the experience and think about how I can do things differently next time' can be a more useful approach.

You Never Achieve Complete Approval

No person on earth wins the approval of all the people all the time. But each one of us receives pleasure and acknowledgement from certain individuals at some point.

If your client strives for 100 per cent approval, he is likely to be exhausted and disappointed after a while. Some people find it very difficult not to receive the approval and recognition of every person they meet or come across, even though this expectation is irrational. This attitude can lead people to say things they don't really believe in order to gain approval. They may even take action that discomforts them in order to remain within a peer group. You can see this situation happening in the workplace and in any community where you have a ringleader or cliques of people. This type of person can find themselves in the wrong group or wrong role in his attempt to fit in.

Everyone has to make unpopular decisions:

- ✔ Parents to discipline children
- ✔ Partners to disagree with a spouse
- ✔ Bosses to chastise a direct report who is out of line

Through CBC, you can help your client define what he believes in and to develop resilience to not always receiving 100 per cent approval for his opinions or actions. Doing what we consider to be right (without being abusive or intolerant of others) is the best any one of us can do, even if not everyone agrees.

You Need to Belong – Just Like Everyone Else

Humans are social and tribal. We survive through building communities. The need to belong can stimulate unhelpful behaviours such as email addiction and incessant partying driven by a fear of being alone. Your client can find out how to identify healthy behaviours and unhealthy behaviours.

People gain a sense of belonging in many healthy ways. We feel 'connected' to the human race through our family, friends, local community, culture, religion, nation, and continent. We may catch the eye of a stranger in the street who smiles out of the blue, or share a joke on a commuter train. Help your client to build up a sense of himself as someone connected to others, and specifically with the people he cares about.

Chapter 21

Ten Imagery Exercises to Develop Confidence

*V*isualisation or imagery exercises are an extremely powerful support to the practice of CBC. Research demonstrates that as a person imagines herself carrying out a task, her brain activates in exactly the areas that it would if she were actually doing the task. Even the muscles tense appropriately to reflect the activity.

As a person imagines feeling confident, her nervous system and the physiology of her body respond. Athletes use this mental rehearsal technique to imagine themselves successfully winning a competition, actors mentally rehearse their roles, and business people picture themselves dealing with difficult situations at work.

Simply by imagining lying on a beach, we can relax our bodies and muscles and reduce our stress levels and blood pressure. This imagining can boost our immune system, because stress slows down the healing process of the body. Imagery is powerful stuff!

In this chapter, I include imagery exercises that may be relevant to your client's situation. You can tailor these exercises more specifically to your client's needs by using names and places that apply to her life. Use my suggestions as a basis, but adapt them as you think appropriate. Always share the imagery process with your client before beginning, so she knows what to expect and relaxes and flows with the experience. And always be sensitive to your client's history and health issues in order not to introduce difficult topics without her permission.

Before working with imagery exercises with your client, you may have applied a model such as the ABC model to develop thinking strategies. (Refer to Chapter 2 for more on the ABC model.) The imagery process can support these strategies.

As a general rule, start any imagery exercise by asking your client to sit straight in a chair with both feet on the floor. Suggest that she closes her eyes – she does not have to, but closed eyes facilitate the switching out of the external world. Ask your client to take a deep breath in, hold it for the count of three, and then slowly release. Ask your client to do this breathing three times – imagining that she breathes in peace and tranquillity on her in-breath and breathes out anxiety and tension on each out-breath – relaxing her neck and shoulders as she does so. After three breaths, suggest that she breathes normally and easily, focusing on the easy flow of breath in and out of her nostrils. Then take her through the specific imagery exercise relevant to her situation.

Most imagery exercises can be completed in five to ten minutes. Gradually bring your client back to full awareness by drawing her attention to her senses, so that she is fully alert by the time she leaves the session. She needs to be fully conscious to manage her journey home. Focus her attention on feeling re-energised, for example gradually re-energising her feet and legs, her back, shoulders, and arms, and finally her neck and mind as she opens her eyes. Suggest a stretch to stimulate the supply of blood and oxygen to her body and brain so that she is fully awake.

After the exercise, spend time discussing the experience with your client so as to build on supportive thoughts and images for the successful achievement of her goals.

Beginning to Trust

Some clients have difficulty trusting others, leading to dependency, defensiveness, control, and an inability to delegate to others, for example:

- A parent who wants her partner to help with the children but criticises him for not doing it 'her' way
- A manager who overworks because she does everything herself rather than trust her direct reports to develop the ability to do a good job themselves

Imagery can help your client to realise how much her life depends on trusting others, and others trusting her. This interdependency is how the world works, how organisations or a community function.

When your client is relaxed, suggest that she begins to think about all the people she has had to trust through her lifetime – her parents, grandparents, uncles, aunts, friends, teachers.

If you're aware that your client has been abused or suffered a traumatic event, be sure to work *very sensitively* around the people you mention. However, ultimately, your client can understand that one person being untrustworthy does not make all people untrustworthy, and that one event need not cast a shadow over all events or people.

Ask your client to think of her everyday life and how many people she needs to trust: family, friends, colleagues, a nanny. Scan her life so as to help her become aware of the unknown people in whom she trusts her life: taxi drivers, pilots, house-builders, roofers, electricians, and mechanics who build the cars, trains, and planes she's travelled in. How she relies on their good work to tighten the right bolts and weld essential parts together. Help her to acknowledge, if possible, that her life cannot function without this trust. Ask her also to consider people who have had to trust in her.

Lead her into the situations she currently faces and ask her to build images of letting go of control and trusting others, step by step, to carry out some of the tasks that she currently doesn't allow them to do or for which she watches over them like a hawk. Suggest that she imagines herself feeling relaxed and confident as she trusts others to carry out tasks. Prompt her to remember some of the mistakes she personally made so as to allow others to find out for themselves and recognise that her own way is not necessarily the 'right' and only way. Suggest that she builds images of how her life may improve if she finds out how to trust, not irresponsibly but in a more rational and balanced way. Ask you client to capture one image that reminds her of how she can start to trust herself and others.

Being Visible and Seen

People can sometimes feel invisible. Your client may shrink at social events, or feel shy and inadequate in meetings. This behaviour is often because she deletes the conversations and moments where she has been seen and focuses only on the negative or fearful experiences. Imagery practice can help her to feel 'seen' in a positive light.

Ask your client to recall some of the people she's met in her lifetime, all the times she has been seen and visible. Prompt her to remember facts and visual images of scenes from childhood. Perhaps she remembers teenage pranks or childhood mischief with friends, so that she relaxes and sees herself as both visible and human. Prompt her to think of public events – perhaps where she won a prize, gave a talk, or sang a song.

Elicit some of the good things that other people have said about her, the moments when she was in the spotlight and very much visible, for example a sports event, passing an exam, an 18th birthday party, getting married, getting a job or a promotion. Focus on the mental, emotional, and physical sensation of being seen, looking people in the eye and having them look in her eyes. She would not be talking to an invisible person! Suggest that she practise the feeling of being seen in a positive light, where other people observe the best in her. She can practise this feeling before meetings, social events, or presentations.

Imagining Your Way to Success

This exercise can be helpful for people who are having difficulty identifying or describing goals.

When your client is relaxed and ready, explain that you plan to ask her to imagine that she wakes up in her 'ideal life'. She can imagine having anything she wants, so she needs to consider what she wants to change. Does she wake up in her own home or has she moved house? Does she work in the same place?

Prompt her to build images of what may change in different areas of her life and work. What is she doing on that ideal day? With whom is she working and how does she feel about her work? Suggest that she considers her relationships and builds images of how these relationships look if they are working really well. Ask her to think about herself and consider whether she notices anything different about the way she personally looks or feels.

By knowing your client's environment and context, you can make more specific suggestions and lead her through any particular aspects of her life or work that may be relevant. When you feel that she's had time to consider these aspects, suggest that she opens her eyes. Discuss the experience. Work with her to identify specific goals and identify what thoughts, behaviours, and actions can bring these goals to fruition.

Losing Bad Habits with Aversion Imagery

Some clients want to change their regular habits to develop healthier lifestyles. Imagery can be a useful tool, for example to help your client to develop an aversion to those things to which she was previously attracted. For example, if your client wants to give up smoking or stop eating chocolate, try suggesting that she builds images of herself going to the cupboard and finding that the packets of cigarettes or chocolates look mouldy and disgusting. When she takes a puff or a bite, the taste is revolting. Your client needs to build powerful negative images so as to give her brain a strong message that she wants to drop these behaviours.

Managing Sickness

There may be times when your client has to manage a period of sickness or a long-term illness. Imagery cannot heal your client, but it can reduce her stress and therefore aid recovery and the healing process. Extensive research shows that the power of the mind can help stabilise illness and enable your client to enjoy life more fully despite a problem. Imagery exercises can also help her to focus on present reality rather than the fears of 'what if' the illness gets worse (which it may or may not).

Suggest that your client builds up a picture of her body and focuses on all that she knows to be healthy and functioning well. Focus on parts of the body you know to be unaffected, for example that her heart still beats, the blood and oxygen still circulates, the lungs still function, and so on. Ask her to feel appreciation for this miracle that is her body in all its complexity. Whatever her sickness, remind her of all the aspects of her physiology that work, including her mind. Help her to focus on the positives.

When it comes to the sick area of your client's body, ask her to imagine how her body's natural processes and antibodies work hard to fight the sickness. Suggest that she build images of her body functioning well to keep her as healthy as possible.

Many people catastrophise and imagine the worst when they're sick. Suggest that your client works with the facts, with the sickness as it stands today. Just because she reads of another person's negative experience, for example, on the Internet, does not mean that this same negative thing is waiting for her. She has her own unique body, so prompt her to build images of that body working hard to heal her in whatever way it can.

Discuss with your client how this exercise feels, and check that her thinking is as much in perspective as possible. Focusing on the positive supports the healthy functioning of the immune system, whereas stress and anxiety reduce it. Suggest that she practises this exercise at least once a day to help her focus on practicalities rather than allowing her mind to obsess on fears.

Motivating Yourself

Imagery visualisation can work to motivate people towards changing behaviours. For example, if your client wants to develop the habit of going to the gym, you can help her to build positive images about how great she feels as she gets ready, as she works out, and as she finishes her session. Reinforce the positive images and messages around the behaviours she wants to adopt.

Planning to Manage Situations

This exercise is what I call the 'picture library', because the imagery depends on the situation that the person is facing. In her memory bank, your client has experienced all emotional states – joy, happiness, sadness, anxiety, enthusiasm, confidence, and so on. The memory holds the precise sensory experience that occurs when she is in those states. Therefore by focusing on her feeling of confidence, she can remember what it feels like to be confident. It doesn't matter if the memory of confidence occurred many years ago, or in a situation that is different to the one she currently faces: the physical and emotional sensations of confidence are the same whatever the situation.

The picture library is in her head. She can take out the memories most helpful to the situation she needs to face. For example, if she wants to give a client pitch, she may choose to remember what she feels like when she is upbeat and confident; if she has a date, she may choose to remember what she feels like when she's attractive and sexy. If she is to give a presentation, she may choose to remember what she feels like when she is confident and articulate. If she needs to create a new software program, she may choose to remember what she feels like when she is focused, concentrating on detail. The variety is enormous.

Ask your client to identify and plan how she wants *to feel* in the situation. For example, if the situation is a presentation, she may want to feel confident. Then ask her to relax and close her eyes and remember what she feels like when she is confident:

- ✔ When did she feel confident before?
- ✔ What changes does she notice physically when she feels confident?
- ✔ What changes does she notice emotionally and mentally?
- ✔ What thoughts help her feel confident?
- ✔ What images help her feel confident?

Ensure that she relives the experience in her mind, as if it were now. Then take her forward through time, like the fast-forward on a video or DVD, building self-supportive images leading up to the event so that she feels confident and ready, seeing things unfold in the way she chooses. Ask her to include the other people involved, behaving in the way that she wants them to. Suggest that she sees herself maintaining her own ability to manage the situation even if things don't go precisely as she chooses. Identify a self-supportive thought to caption the images. Adapt this caption to the relevant situation.

Putting Life in Perspective

This imagery exercise can be good for clients who have a tendency to be pessimistic, to catastrophise, or to have a 'poor me' attitude. The exercise is designed to broaden your client's thinking and put her problems in perspective.

Suggest that your client closes her eyes and starts to think about the problem she has described to you. Ask her to rate the problem on a scale of 0–10 (0 being not much of a problem and 10 being a big problem). Describe the facets of the problem to her as she has previously described them to you.

Explain that you're about to take her on a mental journey across the world. You're not diminishing the reality of her problem but trying to help her gain a bird's-eye view by imagining people in different parts of the world who also have problems, but of a different kind. Start near her home, asking her to imagine people in different situations, considering her own problem in the context of those of other people. Begin to mentally 'fly' her across the world, to Europe, Eastern Europe, Russia, Asia, India, the Middle East, through Africa, and any other areas you feel relevant. Decide which countries you choose to visit and in what order. Ask her to consider some of the problems that people experience elsewhere and notice whether the rating of her own problem changes. Be careful not to be judgemental or suggestive that it should: your client needs to judge her perspective herself.

Eventually ask her to open her eyes, discuss what she experienced, and whether it has impacted on the way she looks at her own situation.

Relaxing the Mind to Relax the Body

Stressed or anxious people tend to hold a great deal of tension in their bodies, particularly around the neck and shoulders. This imagery exercise takes your client through a process of progressive relaxation to help her release pressure stored physically in her body. As stress reduces the effectiveness of the immune system and impairs clarity of thought, this exercise can help your client to relax and refresh her mind. This exercise can also be applied to 'thought-stopping', which helps your client to switch off her negative thinking habits. Refer to Chapters 6 and 9 for more information.

When she is ready, focus her attention on her forehead and suggest that she relaxes any tension she has in that area. Suggest that she imagines softening the area around her eyes and visualises the tension being released with her out-breath. Take her progressively through the body, breathing in peace and tranquillity and breathing out tension, as you draw her focus down from the forehead and eyes, softening the jaw, softening the neck and shoulders, and imagining the tension leaving her body on each out-breath. Take the focus down through her arms, relaxing tension in her wrists and hands, and down her back, relaxing and opening her chest and lung area, breathing in relaxation, breathing out tension. Take her focus down through her legs, relaxing tension around the ankles and feet.

After leading your client through her body to her feet, suggest that she stays relaxed for a few minutes, allowing her breath to flow easily in and out and letting her body relax. Ask her to picture an image to help her remember and access this calm state in future, such as a place she's visited, an imagined place, or a symbol or image of herself. The image needs to be her own, not one that you suggested. The image becomes a trigger image that she can focus on to help her relax in future.

When appropriate, suggest that your client becomes more aware by focusing her attention on her feet and ankles, imagining that with both the in-breath and out-breath she becomes more alert, feeling relaxed and refreshed. Draw her focus up through her legs and back, through her lungs, shoulders, and neck, suggesting that she become more aware of feeling alert, relaxed, and refreshed as she goes up through her body. As she reaches her jaw, eyes, forehead, and brain, she can open her eyes, feeling relaxed, refreshed, and able to continue her day.

Using Morning Mindfulness Imagery

Mindfulness is a state of mind where your client discovers how to be mentally present in the moment, paying attention to herself and her situation in a purposeful and non-judgemental way. She becomes a tranquil observer of herself, her emotions, and her behaviours. She is in the 'now', not worrying about anything else. She may wake up in a nervous state, hurrying out of bed and starting the day in a way that is rushed and stressed. This brief imagery exercise is designed to help your client centre herself and feel balanced as she starts her day. She can reconnect to this feeling by focusing her mind on the image she created to remind her of being 'mindful' throughout the day.

Ideally, your client does this exercise in a peaceful place, but she can practise it surrounded by children or family, in a meeting, or making the dinner. The exercise is a state of mind–body awareness.

Ask your client to take her attention from her 'thinking' to her heart area, to the core of her being, the solar plexus. This experience is a sensory one, an awareness of her 'presence' in the world, of how she is feeling physically and emotionally at that moment in time. Explain that she can observe these feelings without judging herself as good or bad. Ask her to take a deep breath and imagine a feeling of balance spreading through her whole body so she feels peaceful, alive, and alert. This focus can take her 'beyond' thought.

Suggest that she builds pictures of the day ahead, seeing herself mentally present and balanced in the various situations and events planned.

This practice need only take a minute or two once your client has built up the ability to build images. The more she practises this method, the easier it becomes, reconnecting with the mental awareness of being mindful of herself within each situation, whether on the bus, in a meeting, or at home.

Appendix

· ·

*T*his appendix contains a umber of useful resources for the aspiring CB Coach, including lists of useful contacts and the cream of the many CBC books that are out there. First of all, though, I present an ABCDE log for you to use with your clients. You can read more about how to use the log in Chapter 2.

A. Situation:	B. Belief, Expectation or Thought	C. Consequence	D. Dispute your thinking	E. Exchange Thought: What would be a more helpful thought if you face this situation again?
		Emotion	Was it rational?	
		Behaviour	Would others think this way?	
			Was it helping you achieve your goal?	

Useful Contacts

In this part of the appendix you find a selection of useful websites for anyone interested in developing their CB coaching techniques. There simply isn't room here to list every book, article, or organisation involved in CBC. If you're keen to find out even more, your best move is to search the Internet.

If you want to get in touch, you can contact me at **Positiveworks Ltd:** www.positiveworks.com; Tel: +44 (0)207 736 1417. My company provides personal and professional development through coaching, training, facilitation and mediation.

Albert Ellis Institute, www.rebt.org ; Tel: 212 535 0822. World-renowned psychotherapy institute committed to advancing emotional well-being.

Association for Coaching: www.associationforcoaching.com; E-mail: enquiries@associationforcoaching.com; membership association for professional coaches and organisations involved in coaching or related training.

British Association for Behavioural and Cognitive Psychotherapies (BABCP): www.babcp.com; Tel: +44 (0) 161 797 4484; Can provide details of accredited therapists.

British Association for Counselling and Psychotherapy (BACP): www.bacp.co.uk; Tel: +44 (0) 1455 883300; See their website for a list of practitioners in your area.

The Centre for Stress Management: www.managingstress.com; Tel: +44 (0) 20 8228 1185. An international training centre and stress consultancy. Carries out stress management and prevention programmes, stress audiets and research, stress counselling, coaching, and training.

Chartered Institute of Personnel and Development: ww.cipd.co.uk ; Tel: +44 (0) 20 8612 6202; professional body for those involved in the management and development of people.

Dr David Beales: www.mindfulphysiology.co.uk; Tel: +44 (0) 1285 760286; coaching behavioural physiology in health care.

David D Burns: www.feelinggood.com; author of *The Feeling Good Handbook*.

Gladeana McMahon: www.gladeanamcmahon.com; Tel: +44 (0) 20 8852 4854; UK Co-Founder of Cognitive-Behavioural Coaching, Vice-President Association for Coaching, Director, Professional Coaching Standards, Cedar Talent Management and Co-Director, Centre for Coaching.

Health Circles Ltd: www.healthcircles.co.uk; Tel: +44 (0) 1628 666 069. Programmes and coaching to improve health and quality of life by creating healthy minds and bodies.

Herrmann International: www.HerrmannInternational.com; Tel: +1 828 625 9153. Creator and provider of the HBDI (Herrmann Brain Dominance Instrument). Provides information on validated thinking styles analysis: what it is, how it can be used, completing a personal profile, and information on training courses.

International Stress Management Association: www.isma.org.uk ; Tel: +44 (0) 1179 697284; professional body and membership association promoting the prevention and reduction of human stress and best practice in the field of stress management.

Nick Edgerton: www.nedgerton.plus.com; Tel: +44 (0) 20 8318 5735; Chartered Psychologist providing training and consultancy.

Professor Stephen Palmer: www.centreforcoaching.com; Tel: +44 (0) 208 228 1185; Director of the Centre for Coaching, London:, a leading provider of coaching and psychological coaching training. Director of the Coaching Psychology Unit, City University: www.city.ac.uk/psychology.

The Lazarus Institute: www.thelazarusinstitute.com; Tel: (609) 683 9122; providing the highest quality, non-medical, mental health service offering an integrated, holistic, multimodal approach.

Books

Age Matters, Employing, Motivating and Managing Older Employees: Helen Whitten and Keren Smedley (Ashgate Publishing)

Counselling for Stress Problems: Stephen Palmer and Windy Dryden (Sage Publications)

Confidence Works – Learn to be Your Own Life Coach: Gladeana McMahon (Sheldon Press)

Emotional Intelligence: Daniel Goleman (Bantam)

The Feeling Good Handbook: David Burns, MD (Plume)

Future Directions, Practical Ways to Develop Emotional Intelligence and Confidence in Young People: Helen Whitten and Diane Carrington (Network Educational)

Handbook of Positive Psychology: edited by C.R.Snyder and Shane J. Lopez (Oxford University Press)

Learned Optimism: Martin Seligman (Vintage)

Life Coaching: A Cognitive Behavioural Approach: Michael Neenan and Windy Dryden (Routledge)

Handbook of Coaching Psychology: A Guide for Practitioners: Stephen Palmer and Alison Whybrow. (Routledge)

Motivation For Dummies: Gillian Burn (Wiley)

No More Anger – Be your own Anger Management Coach: Gladeana McMahon (Karnac Books)

Overcoming Low Self-Esteem, A self-help guide using Cognitive Behavioural Techniques: Melanie Fennell (Robinson Publishing)

Performance Coaching For Dummies: Gladeana McMahon and Averil Leimon (Wiley)

Index

FOR DUMMIES®

Do Anything. Just Add Dummies

UK editions

BUSINESS

978-0-470-51806-9

978-0-470-99245-6

978-0-470-75626-3

FINANCE

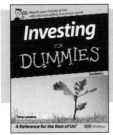

978-0-470-99280-7

978-0-470-99811-3

978-0-470-69515-9

PROPERTY

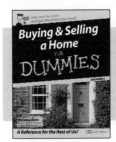

978-0-470-99448-1

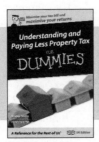

978-0-470-75872-4

978-0-7645-7054-4

Backgammon For Dummies
978-0-470-77085-6

Body Language For Dummies
978-0-470-51291-3

British Sign Language
For Dummies
978-0-470-69477-0

Business NLP For Dummies
978-0-470-69757-3

Children's Health For Dummies
978-0-470-02735-6

Cognitive Behavioural Coaching
For Dummies
978-0-470-71379-2

Counselling Skills For Dummies
978-0-470-51190-9

Digital Marketing For Dummies
978-0-470-05793-3

eBay.co.uk For Dummies,
2nd Edition
978-0-470-51807-6

English Grammar For Dummies
978-0-470-05752-0

Fertility & Infertility For Dummies
978-0-470-05750-6

Genealogy Online For Dummies
978-0-7645-7061-2

Golf For Dummies
978-0-470-01811-8

Green Living For Dummies
978-0-470-06038-4

Hypnotherapy For Dummies
978-0-470-01930-6

Available wherever books are sold. For more information or to order direct go to
www.wiley.com or call +44 (0) 1243 843291

13902_p1

FOR DUMMIES®

A world of resources to help you grow

UK editions

SELF-HELP

978-0-470-01838-5

978-0-7645-7028-5

978-0-470-75876-2

HEALTH

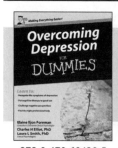

978-0-470-69430-5

978-0-470-51737-6

978-0-470-71401-0

HISTORY

978-0-470-99468-9

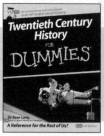

978-0-470-51015-5

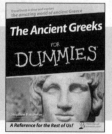

978-0-470-98787-2

Inventing For Dummies
978-0-470-51996-7

Job Hunting and Career Change
All-In-One For Dummies
978-0-470-51611-9

Motivation For Dummies
978-0-470-76035-2

Origami Kit For Dummies
978-0-470-75857-1

Personal Development All-In-One
For Dummies
978-0-470-51501-3

PRINCE2 For Dummies
978-0-470-51919-6

Psychometric Tests For Dummies
978-0-470-75366-8

Raising Happy Children For
Dummies
978-0-470-05978-4

Starting and Running a Business
All-in-One For Dummies
978-0-470-51648-5

Sudoku for Dummies
978-0-470-01892-7

The British Citizenship Test
For Dummies, 2nd Edition
978-0-470-72339-5

Time Management For Dummies
978-0-470-77765-7

Wills, Probate, & Inheritance Tax
For Dummies, 2nd Edition
978-0-470-75629-4

Winning on Betfair For Dummies,
2nd Edition
978-0-470-72336-4

13802_p2

FOR DUMMIES®

The easy way to get more done and have more fun

LANGUAGES

978-0-7645-5194-9

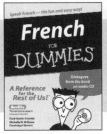

978-0-7645-5193-2

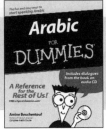

978-0-471-77270-5

MUSIC

978-0-7645-9904-0

978-0-470-03275-6
UK Edition

978-0-7645-5105-5

SCIENCE & MATHS

978-0-7645-5326-4

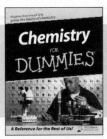

978-0-7645-5430-8

978-0-7645-5325-7

Art For Dummies
978-0-7645-5104-8

Baby & Toddler Sleep Solutions For Dummies
978-0-470-11794-1

Bass Guitar For Dummies
978-0-7645-2487-5

Brain Games For Dummies
978-0-470-37378-1

Christianity For Dummies
978-0-7645-4482-8

Filmmaking For Dummies, 2nd Edition
978-0-470-38694-1

Forensics For Dummies
978-0-7645-5580-0

German For Dummies
978-0-7645-5195-6

Hobby Farming For Dummies
978-0-470-28172-7

Jewelry Making & Beading For Dummies
978-0-7645-2571-1

Knitting for Dummies, 2nd Edition
978-0-470-28747-7

Music Composition For Dummies
978-0-470-22421-2

Physics For Dummies
978-0-7645-5433-9

Sex For Dummies, 3rd Edition
978-0-470-04523-7

Solar Power Your Home For Dummies
978-0-470-17569-9

Tennis For Dummies
978-0-7645-5087-4

The Koran For Dummies
978-0-7645-5581-7

U.S. History For Dummies
978-0-7645-5249-6

Wine For Dummies, 4th Edition
978-0-470-04579-4

Available wherever books are sold. For more information or to order direct go to www.wiley.com or call +44 (0) 1243 843291

13902_p3

FOR DUMMIES®

Helping you expand your horizons and achieve your potential

COMPUTER BASICS

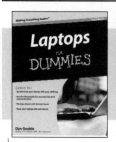
978-0-470-27759-1

978-0-470-13728-4

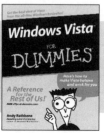
978-0-471-75421-3

DIGITAL LIFESTYLE

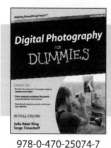
978-0-470-25074-7

978-0-470-39062-7

978-0-470-17469-2

WEB & DESIGN

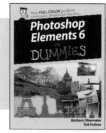
978-0-470-19238-2

978-0-470-32725-8

978-0-470-34502-3

Access 2007 For Dummies
978-0-470-04612-8

Adobe Creative Suite 3 Design Premium
All-in-One Desk Reference For Dummies
978-0-470-11724-8

AutoCAD 2009 For Dummies
978-0-470-22977-4

C++ For Dummies, 5th Edition
978-0-7645-6852-7

Computers For Seniors For Dummies
978-0-470-24055-7

Excel 2007 All-In-One Desk Reference F
or Dummies
978-0-470-03738-6

Flash CS3 For Dummies
978-0-470-12100-9

Mac OS X Leopard For Dummies
978-0-470-05433-8

Macs For Dummies, 10th Edition
978-0-470-27817-8

Networking All-in-One Desk Reference
For Dummies, 3rd Edition
978-0-470-17915-4

Office 2007 All-in-One Desk Reference
For Dummies
978-0-471-78279-7

Search Engine Optimization For
Dummies, 2nd Edition
978-0-471-97998-2

Second Life For Dummies
978-0-470-18025-9

The Internet For Dummies, 11th Edition
978-0-470-12174-0

Visual Studio 2008 All-In-One Desk
Reference For Dummies
978-0-470-19108-8

Web Analytics For Dummies
978-0-470-09824-0

Windows XP For Dummies, 2nd Edition
978-0-7645-7326-2

13902_p4